Freemasonry and the Vatican

A&B Publishers Group
Brooklyn, New York
112389

WORKS BY THE SAME AUTHOR

1928 *Les Forces Secrètes de la Révolution*
1931 *Refusé par la Presse*
1932 *La Franc-Maçonnerie, Puissance Occulte*
Les Juifs Maîtres du Monde
1934 *Tempête sur le Monde*
La Franc-Maçonnerie d'après ses documents secrets
1936 *Le Portugal Renaît*
La Société des Nations, Super-Etat Maçonnique
La Mysterieuse Internationale Juive
La Guerre Occulte (in collaboration with E. Malynski)
1937 *Histoire Secrète de la Révolution Espagnole*
1939 *Le Plan Communiste d'Insurrection Armée*
1941 *La Franc-Maçonnerie contre la France*
1942 *L'Enigme Communiste*
Israel Destructeur d'Empires
1943 *Les Forces Occultes dans le Monde Moderne*
1961 *Espions Sovietiques dans le Monde*

TRANSLATED INTO ENGLISH

1929 *The Secret Powers Behind Revolution*
1967 *Judaism and the Vatican*

Freemasonry and the Vatican

COVER CONCEPT: *ACT COMMUNICATIONS*
COVER DESIGN: *A & B PUBLISHERS GROUP*
COVER ILLUSTRATION: *INDUSTRIAL FONTS & GRAPHIX*

Library of Congress Cataloging-In-Publication Data

Poncins, Leon de
[Freemasonry & the Vatican]
Freemasonry and the Vatican: a struggle for recognition/by Leon de Poncins
p. cm.
Originally published:Freemasonry & the Vatican. London: Britons Pub., 1968
Includes bibliographical references and index
ISBN 1-881316-91-2 (pbk.: alk paper)
1. Freemasonry—Religious aspects—Catholic Church. I Title

HS495. P6 2000
366'. 1—dc21 00-044189

A&B PUBLISHERS GROUP
1000 Atlantic Avenue
Brooklyn, New York,
11238

00 01 02 03 04 9 8 7 6 5 4 3 2

Manufactured and Printed in the United States

CONTENTS

ILLUSTRATION

"To the crowd me must say: we worship a God, but it is the God one adores without superstition. To you, Sovereign Grand Inspectors General, we say this, that you may repeat it to the brethren of the 32nd, 31st and 30th degrees: all of us initiates of the high degrees should maintain the Masonic religion in the purity of the Luciferian doctrine. If Lucifer were not God, would Adonay, the God of the Christians, whose deeds prove his cruelty, perfidy and hatred of man, his barbarism and repulsion for science, would Adonay and his priests calumniate him? Yes, Lucifer is God, and unfortunately Adonay is also God . . . religious philosophy in its purity and truth consists in the belief in Lucifer, the equal of Adonay."

Albert Pike, quoted in A. C. de la Rive: *La Femme et l'Enfant dans la Franc-Maçonnerie Universelle*, p. 588

"The duty of the Knight Rose-Croix is to combat the bastard Gnosticism inherent in Catholicism, which blinds the eyes of faith, turns hope into a pedestal, and charity into egoism . . . the secret teaching of the supreme leaders of Freemasonry may be summed up in these words: to establish the rights of Man, the privation of which constitutes a usurpation against which all means of action are permissible."

La Massoneria, Florence, 1945

"Behind the activity and intrigues of those in the foreground a gigantic struggle is taking place. It is the struggle between angels and devils for the salvation or ruin of mankind. The leader of the infernal spirits is Satan. At the head of the heavenly hosts is the Queen of the Angels, with Saint Michael as her standard-bearer. He who has said no to God has entered the lists against her who has said yes. This is the true sense of the present world happenings and the only philosophy of history that can explain the last causes."

Cardinal Suenens: *Théologie de l'Apostolat*, 1951
pp. 212-214

"Holy Michael the Archangel, defend us in the day of battle; be our safeguard against the wickedness and snares of the devil. May God rebuke him, we humbly pray: and do thou, Prince of the Heavenly Host, by the power of God thrust down into Hell Satan and all wicked spirits who wander through the world for the ruin of souls."

Prayer ordered to be recited after Mass
by Pope Leo XIII, and now discontinued

I

THE CAMPAIGN IN FAVOUR OF FREEMASONRY

THERE is at present in Catholic circles a constant, subtle and determined campaign in favour of Freemasonry. It is directed by the progressive brigade, currently enjoying so great an influence in France, and is assisted by pressures (whether open or secret) on the part of a considerable number of the clergy—pressures also exerted by the Catholic Press, and even by prelates among the French bishops and cardinals.

Its avowed object is to obtain from the Vatican, and from the Council while it was in session, the revision or, better still, the annulment of the various condemnations pronounced by the Popes upon Freemasonry since 1738. More specifically, its aim is to bring pressure upon the Roman Curia to obtain such an annulment.

The campaign relies for its success upon certain books, cleverly drawn up in such a way as to present Freemasonry in a favourable light, and it commands sources of information and means of propaganda far more extensive than those available to people who defend the traditional position, for newspapers, books, magazines, the radio and public platforms are all open to receive its voice. Furthermore, it receives the tacit support of the Order itself.

To find the first signs of this new tendency, we must go back as far as the twenties. An aged German Jesuit, Father Gruber, an expert on Masonic matters, made contact with three highly-placed Masons, Ossian Lang of New York, and Dr. Kurt Reichl and E. Lehnhof of Vienna, in order to study the possibilities, first of a truce, then of a permanent *modus vivendi,* which would put an end to the furious war which has raged between the Catholic Church and Freemasonry since 1738. These contacts were exceedingly discreet, not to say secret, and they remained virtually unknown to the public at large.

The first public expression of this new attitude took place in 1937. In that year a Mason of high degree—the 33rd—who was also a man of a most independent mind and a writer of quality, Albert Lantoine, published a book which aroused bitter controversy in various quarters. This was his *Lettre au Souverain Pontife,* and the following passages, which have been taken from this work, contain the gist of his thesis. In his preface to Lantoine's book, the celebrated Freemason Oswald Wirth clearly sets out the basic problem:

"For two centuries the Church and Freemasonry have been at war. On both sides tempers have risen, and troops are mobilised for action, unwilling to suspend hostilities. And yet the leaders do not trouble to hide the fact that it's an absurd conflict proceeding from an unhappy misunderstanding. One can hardly order a sudden about-turn to armies on the field of battle, but is a 'cease-fire' impossible? Could the Pope see his way to giving such a signal? That is the question Albert Lantoine is asking."

(A. Lantoine: *Lettre au Souverain Pontife*, p. ii)

Albert Lantoine in no way shirks the opposition existing between the Church and Freemasonry.

"*We are freethinkers—you are believers. Let us not dwell too long on this formidable difference between us. . . .*

(A. Lantoine, ibid., p. 53)

". . . This gulf cannot be bridged and never will be. On our side and on yours it has given rise to various hostile acts. The question is: in the face of our common danger today, should we not perhaps silence such expressions of our differences?"

(A. Lantoine, ibid., p. 18)

Lantoine recognises the various premonitions and portents of a world and civilisation that are going to die.

"They multiply upon the rotting corpse of modern society just as Juvenal saw them swarming on the decomposing body of imperial Rome. (A. Lantoine, ibid., p. 23)

". . . In these sad times in which we live, must those religions which still survive persist in fighting one another with taunts, lies and excommunications? Freemasonry seeks to exalt Man; the Church to exalt God. Must they be rivals? Not at all. In spite of all, they come together. The thinker who will not compromise on what his duty commands, the believer who stands by the demands of his religion: these two are linked—in spirit—over and above the differences between their principles."

(A. Lantoine, ibid., p. 44)

Lantoine, in short, is proposing a truce, and he then launches into a long passage of special pleading, in which he seeks to show that Freemasonry was not, in the beginning, either revolutionary or anti-religious, but that, on the contrary, it was provoked by the Church and turned into her mortal enemy by the Church's unjust condemnations. As this is the theme which is being taken up again and developed by progressive thinkers today, we will only refer to it in passing.

"The Church's hostility has contributed in large measure to that anti-religious character for which the Masonic Order is known—and which it actually has, at least in Catholic countries. . . .

(A. Lantoine, ibid., p. 81)

". . . Your bulls of excommunication, notwithstanding all the natural and supernatural motives which may have inspired them, were a serious political blunder. . . . (A. Lantoine, ibid., p. 69)

". . . It is your Church—the Roman Church—which has foolishly pushed the Freemasons into the opposing camp. They themselves had no desire to be found there, and I will even say, no matter what wrath I may call down from both sides, that they did not deserve to be sent there. Nevertheless—since honour so demanded!—there they have remained.

"They are there now.

"And yet there have come upon us those times of horror foretold in the Scriptures, when the barbarians shall spread over the whole earth like the Fourth Horseman of the Apocalypse. In the face of this upsurge of Instinct, victorious at last over our twin apostolate; in the face of this brute onslaught of those purely materialist appetites which will deal death to all our dreams—should we remain at odds with one another?

"Perhaps.

"Perhaps we should . . . in the very depths of our souls. For your God cannot pardon the Rebellious Angel, and that Angel will never submit or renounce his dominion.

"But should we remain enemies?

"No!" (A. Lantoine, ibid., pp. 91-92)

According to Lantoine, it is part of the onward march of history since the Renaissance that the Catholic Church must fall apart and dissolve. Since this process cannot be reversed, a secular religion must take its place—that is, Freemasonry.

"When she sowed the fateful seed of Equality in the minds of the helots, Christianity sounded the death-knell of all Aristocracies. So it was that she undermined the foundations of Graeco-Latin civilisation, just as the French Revolution, inspired by the same mad charity, pierced the armour of Gallo-Roman society.

" 'Paganism and the Old Régime stood for the Rights of an Elite. Christianity and the Revolution stand for the Rights of Mobs.' In these noble words the philosopher Izoulet notes the degradation—in the exact sense of the word—which your humanitarianism has inflicted on humanity. . . .

"The City of the future foretold in the Gospels has become the City of today. Lenin has fulfilled the hope sown by the Son of Man.

"Let us be fair to Catholicism. She never foresaw such an interpretation of her doctrine. Exalting the humble to abase the proud, ending for good and all that doctrine by which the Inequality of Man seemed an order consecrated by God, she never cherished any insane ambition to destroy social hierarchy, without which no human group—whether family, tribe or nation could subsist. . . .

"The Church believed that those outcasts whom she had emancipated would still, for ever, bow themselves to her discipline—a discipline no longer based on the inequality of men but on the just inequality of functions—a discipline on which was erected that magnificent civilisation of the Middle Ages, still so little known and so unfairly denigrated. But from the day when they first broke away from that discipline, the slaves, whose fetters she had been the first to break, have become slaves totally unfettered. . . .

"They all dream of raising themselves to equality with their masters. They prefer equality in slavery to inequality with independence." (A. Lantoine, ibid., pp. 120-123)

Lantoine concludes that there is an élite on both sides; to save that élite, Catholicism and Freemasonry must work together.

"In a world given over to appetite, any élite is naturally denounced. Its high rank would offend the law of universal mediocrity.

"All the same, this élite remains, among you, among us. Thus, instead of continuing to fight among themselves, ideologies both intellectual and spiritual must coalesce to save Beauty. What does it matter that their opinions differ? In the present hour of distress, both must step down from their mutually exclusive sectarianism, for the presumption shown by rationalism seeking to explain everything is equal to that of religion which will not admit that it is fallible. . . . (A. Lantoine, ibid., p. 137)

"In this modern world given over to appetite, Freemasonry and the religions remain spiritual forces. Rid them of their trappings and there remains the undeniable loveliness of their principles. I know they will never agree. The Church has set supernatural limits to truth which we shall for ever repudiate. But even if there is no bridge to link those virtues peculiar to each of us, we can, each along our own path, aspire towards our ideals without hatred. . . .

"Religion, which seeks to purify, and Freemasonry, which seeks to cultivate men's minds, are equally opposed in their respective spheres to unbridled appetite.

(A. Lantoine, ibid., pp. 160-163)

"There is a higher sphere where knowledge and Faith, though they cannot meet, can at least tolerate one another. To those seeking the one, to those who possess the other, they give the same delights and the same anguish. There is as much purity and grandeur in the words of the philosophers as in the Word of the Redeemer.

"*So much the better, I say. Possessing critical and inquisitive minds, we are the servants of Satan. You, the guardians of truth, are the servants of God. These two complement one another. Each needs the other.*"

(A. Lantoine, ibid., pp. 168-169)

I do not know whether this sentence was intended by Lantoine to be taken literally, or whether he meant: "In your eyes we are always the servants of Satan." But during a conversation we once had on this matter, which, moreover, was conducted with perfect courtesy, Lantoine said to me: "I was wrong, I didn't use quite the correct term. I should have said servants of Lucifer." I merely reproduce his remark here for what it is worth.

Lantoine was a historian and a thinker of great merit. He was a sincere Freemason, of charming personal character, and he kept apart from all contact with politics. He concealed nothing, and openly declared that he was an atheist. He was severely critical of certain aspects of the Catholic Church but he did not spare Masonry either. He had obviously lost the faith he originally held in democracy and rationalism.

His offer of a truce was frank and honest. It has often happened in history that an armistice has been signed with an enemy; it was for the Church to enquire into the merits and expediency of such a proposal. Moreover, it was not particularly welcomed on the Masonic side. Let us quote what Michel Dumesnil de Gramont, Grand Master of the Grand Lodge of France, wrote in his book, *La Maçonnerie et l'Eglise Catholique* (pp. 9-12), bearing in mind that the Grand Lodge of France (Scottish Rite), the obedience to which Lantoine belonged.

is the spiritual branch of Freemasonry, according to modern progressives:

"An opponent of Masonry, in severe but courteous terms, wrote a few years ago that Catholic civilisation did not understand liberty in the same way as did Masonic civilisation, adding that 'as no reconciliation is possible between two such opposite principles, one or other of them will have to disappear.'

"Commenting on such a clear and forcible conclusion, the author of the booklet published in September 1934 under the auspices of the Grand Lodge of France, recognised that any reconciliation was in fact unthinkable.

"As far as Albert Lantoine is concerned, it would not be inappropriate to speak of his conversion.

"In fact, not so long ago, Albert Lantoine professed to be not only anti-clerical, but anti-Christian.

"Today, while still priding himself on the purity of his Masonic attitudes, Albert Lantoine no longer thinks it an honour to our Order that it should have been condemned by the Church. Catholicism now appeals to him as a protector of the noblest spiritual ideals, and even, as Antonio Coen thought, as the champion of freedom of thought.

"We are not clear how this new attitude can be reconciled with the accusations of perverted morals constantly brought against Christianity by the author of *Hiram couronné d'épines* (1926). No matter: Albert Lantoine is well within his rights in attempting this difficult compromise.

"But he goes further. Following the example of those repentant sinners who, towards the end of their days, return to devout habits and drag their entourage along with them, Lantoine would like French Masonry to accompany him in his pilgrimage towards Rome, and the watchword he offers our Order is a remark of Clavell's suggesting that Freemasonry is a complement to Christianity.

"His *Lettre au Souverain Pontife*, in which this theory is developed, is bound to cause a profound sensation in the bosom of the Grand Lodge of France.

"Many Masons of the Grand Lodge have been worried by Albert Lantoine's suggestions and have wondered whether those whose responsibility is to administer the Lodge have not perhaps been tempted to adopt them themselves.

"It is these anxieties which we have tried to answer. . . .

"We are told, and with truth, that there are prominent ecclesiastics who would agree with Lantoine's point of view and be willing to implement such a truce as he suggests. We hesitate to cast doubts, but we know that other very different attitudes are to be heard within the Church.

"The Church, considering herself as entrusted with a divine mission, will never treat on equal terms with any earthly organisation and will always demand total submission.

"Perhaps Masonry would obtain the truce desired by Lantoine and his friends if it consented to address to the Holy See a letter similar to that through which Action Française was relieved of the interdict promulgated by the Congregation of the Index.

"We cannot think that there are many Masons in the Grand Lodge of France who would set their names to such a petition, and by so doing sign a spiritual death warrant for our Order."

The fearful conflict of 1939-45 interrupted all attempts to negotiate, but they were resumed more eagerly than ever as soon as the war was over.

The campaign which Father Gruber had secretly begun from the Catholic side was resumed in France, this time openly, by another Jesuit, Father Bertheloot. Between 1945 and 1948 the latter published a series of articles and books, all most carefully drawn up with a view to preparing for a rapprochement between the Church and Freemasonry. These books, moreover, were supported by serious documentation. Among others, he wrote:

Les Franc-Maçons devant l'histoire;
La Franc-Maçonnerie et l'Eglise Catholique—motifs de condamnation;
La Franc-Maçonnerie et l'Eglise Catholique—perspectives de pacification.

The campaign for closer relations between Freemasonry and the Church remained quiescent while Pius XII was Pope; obviously the flame was smouldering beneath the ashes, but the progressives, who by this time enjoyed considerable influence within the Church, realised that they had little chance of success during the Pope's lifetime.

With the accession of Pope John XXIII, and the growth of the new conceptions of ecumenism which followed this event, something like an explosion took place. A sudden flowering of works devoted to Freemasonry blossomed forth from a variety of authors. Historians, philosophers, journalists, politicians and lecturers, all worked, each in their own sphere, in favour of a reconciliation between the Catholic Church and Freemasonry. One received a distinct impression that this was the outcome of an international campaign.

carefully orchestrated, as it were, and whose nerve-centre lay in France.

The Second World War had wrought profound changes in life and created new conditions of existence throughout the entire world. Among these were:

(1) The existence, which was an unprecedented event in history, of a considerable body of progressive clergy at Rome, where they rapidly achieved widespread and growing influence;

(2) The election of a Pope—John XXIII—who was believed by the progressives to favour their cause;

(3) The increasingly formidable danger of Communism, which had by then become the second great power in the world, about equal to the United States, and the threat of the extension of its influence in Asia, Africa and South America;

(4) The simultaneous and progressive socialisation of the laws, institutions and economies of political régimes outside the Soviet Union;

(5) The renewal of a religious spirit, or at least of a vague religiosity, which affected even Freemasonry itself;

(6) The meeting of the Ecumenical Council, which was empowered to discuss such problems and to take decisions on them—a Council which was attended by a strong contingent of progressive bishops who were in open conflict with the Roman Curia, which they regarded as consisting of a body of hardened reactionaries.

Taking advantage of these new conditions, the campaign for closer relations with Freemasonry was taken up again with increased strength and with considerable material forces at its disposal. This time it was not a question of abstract discussion; the progressives had an immediate and precise objective in sight—to obtain from the Vatican a reappraisal of the Church's traditional attitude towards Freemasonry and the cancellation of the condemnations pronounced against it. There was, as we have said, a profusion of writers devoted to the task of defending Freemasonry and its interests. Let us mention here, among others:

Maurice Colinon: *L'Eglise en face de la Franc-Maçonnerie* (Ecclesia);
Roger Priouret: *La Franc-Maçonnerie sous les lys* (Grasset);
Serge Hutin: *Les Francs-Maçons* (Seuil);
Roger Peyrefitte: *Les Fils de la Lumière* (Flammarion);
Guy Vinatrel: *Communisme et Franc-Maçonnerie* (Presses continentales);
Yves Marsaudon: *L'Oecuménisme vu par un Franc-Maçon de tradition* (Vitiano);
J. Corneloup: *Universalisme et Franc-Maçonnerie* (Vitiano).

We should also mention the Hourdin press group, which produces a collection of Catholic progressive publications, newspapers and magazines, such as *Informations Catholiques Internationales*, *Témoignage Chrétien*, and others.

Nevertheless, amid this avalanche of propagandists, three names emerge as especially important: Father Riquet, S.J.; the Catholic writer, Alec Mellor; and the Freemason, Marius Lepage, Worshipful Master of the Lodge at Volnay.

Father Riquet has attracted notice since the war as a result of his vigorous campaigns in favour of Jewish and Masonic circles. He has various direct contacts with these groups, and he gave a lecture at the Volnay de Laval Lodge at the invitation of its Worshipful Master, Marius Lepage, who is at the forefront of the campaign on the Masonic side.

The writer, Alec Mellor, a lawyer by profession, is the quasi-official mouthpiece for the progressive party in these matters. He works closely with Father Riquet and Brother Lepage. We do not in any way seek to belittle the worth or ability of these three persons, but we do dispute their evidence, their arguments and their conclusions.

Alec Mellor pleads his case in two important books, *Nos Frères Séparés*, which has recently been published in England as *Our Separated Brethren*, and *La Franc-Maçonnerie à l'Heure du Choix*, published in 1961 and 1963 respectively.

These two books must be read by the modern student of the problem of Freemasonry for two most important reasons:

Firstly, because Mellor expounds in them in the most complete detail the progressive arguments in favour of Freemasonry;

And secondly, because they are published by Mame of Tours in France, an old and respected Catholic publishing house, and they carry the imprimatur of their diocese. As regards the imprimatur, it is true to say that, in the eyes of the Catholic Church, this only certifies that the book contains nothing contrary to Catholic doctrine in matters of faith or morals: it does not in any way signify or imply agreement on the part of the Church with the opinions expressed therein. Nevertheless, in the eyes of many unthinking members of the public, the imprimaturs on Mellor's books signify that they carry the official approval of the Catholic hierarchy, and that they have a peculiar importance for that reason.

We shall take these two books as the basis for our study of the relationship between the Church and Freemasonry, and in answering the case as presented by their author, we shall take our stand on Masonic documents whose authenticity is beyond question.

It would be hard to find anywhere in the world a problem more complex and mysterious than Freemasonry; there is scarcely any question more hotly disputed or subject to such conflicting accounts; no other problem so resists lucid analysis. Yet it is a matter of vital importance, for it is closely linked with the whole great drama of subversion in the modern world.

Thus we shall endeavour to set out the essence of the problem, and let us begin by summarising briefly the spirit and purport of Mellor's arguments.

Mellor has nothing but haughty disdain for Catholics who warn their co-religionists against Freemasonry, and whom he describes as "integralists".

> "By antimasonry is implied here a certain kind of intellectual clumsiness and laziness which tends systematically to explain everything, particularly the misfortunes of a country, in terms of Freemasonry. It is a fixation, an obsession, coupled with a pseudo-literary form of expression. Commercial considerations may enter into it, but much more often what is revealed is a mentality of fear, hatred and persecution. It is a psychosis. Freemasonry is merely its theme. It differs only in its complexion from other psychoses, two of which, at least, are well known in psychiatry: the anti-Jesuit and the anti-Semite.
>
> "Antimasonry in this sense must be carefully distinguished:
>
> (1) from motivated, reasoned disapproval—whether we consider it justified or not is another matter.
>
> (2) from spiritual condemnations (exemplified by the pontifical bulls, but one might also quote some statements of Protestant views). (A. Mellor: *Our Separated Brethren—the Freemasons*, 1964, p. 243)

> "Medieval literature contains not a single line hostile to operative Masons. Their secrets were never suspect, which, as we have seen, is certainly the best proof that there was nothing to suspect.
>
> "Once the Masonic secret had changed its character and taken on a new significance, antimasonry loomed up.
>
> "The oldest antimasonic suspicions come three-quarters of a century before the first Pontifical condemnation, dating back to a period even before the foundation of Grand Lodge. They come before the rise of speculative Masonry, and are found as long ago as the period of transition. It might be said that the antimasonic spirit was on the watch, so to speak, waiting for the first affirmation of the famous secret. Its first two manifestations were of Protestant inspiration; the popes of the period doubtless knew nothing about the matter. . . ." (A. Mellor, ibid., p. 244)

In both camps are to be found those who will not be reconciled.

"On the Catholic side, they are represented by those who refuse to change their habits of thought and by the sort of intellectuals rightly or wrongly known as integralists.

"The latter are sometimes very competent theologians. In the depth of their being they no doubt feel an anxiety which will not let them rest. Any idea which is in the least degree new, in their eyes smacks of heresy, irenism, or syncretism. The hierarchy are traitors. The Pope himself is not immune from their criticisms.

"Moreover, this kind of man has a moral sense peculiar to himself, accompanied by spying on others and the most indelicate kind of investigation. To unearth the guilty, the integralist is not above nosing in dustbins, picking the locks of drawers, or using methods appropriate to professional spies in order to obtain photocopies of manuscripts, including rough drafts representing only the first stages in a man's thinking. Their minds are neither contemplative nor constructive, for, as a famous saying has it, there are doubtless no problems for them. All that interests them is to bar the way.

"Such are the irreconcilables. Many of them represent only themselves, that is to say, nothingness. . . ."

(A. Mellor: *La Franc-Maçonnerie à l'Heure du Choix*, pp. 451-452)

Thus Mellor, as we see from the above, severely castigates Catholics who are not progressives.

When speaking of Masons or Jews, on the other hand, his heart overflows with brotherly love and Christian charity; the Freemasons are generous, broad-minded and enlightened men reacting with dignity and tolerance against the hateful attacks launched upon them by professional mud-slingers, known as integralists. His bias is so palpable and so extreme that it is enough to make one laugh or close the book. We would hasten to recognise, however, that most of the Masonic authors quoted by Mellor are much more cautious and objective than he is in judging their political or religious opponents. I myself have had the pleasure of interviews with highly-placed English and French Masons, such as Albert Lantoine, and the conversation never descended from the level of objective discussion to that of systematic abuse.

Reading Mellor's books leaves one with the impression that he is the mouthpiece of certain Masonic circles which are allied to progressive Catholics against anyone who stands for tradition, whether in religion or politics.

According to his own statements, Mellor is on terms of close friendship with a large number of prominent Freemasons from whom, exclusive of any other source, he has received his documentary evidence. The list he gives us in his second book, *La Franc-Maçonnerie à l'Heure du Choix*, is imposing:

> "May I be permitted to express my thanks at this point to several Masons, in the order in which their respective obediences will be studied in this book.
>
> "In English-speaking Freemasonry, J. W. Stubbs, Grand Secretary of the United Grand Lodge of England; A. R. Hewitt, Librarian and Curator of Grand Lodge; and my learned friend, Harry Carr, Secretary of that home of learning, the Lodge Quatuor Coronati No. 2076.
>
> "In German Freemasonry, Theodore Vogel, former Grand Master of the Grand Lodge of Germany; Richard Muller-Borner, the present Grand-Master; and Baron Ferdinand von Cles, former Grand Orator of the Grand Lodge.
>
> "In Dutch Freemasonry, C. M. R. Davidson, former Grand Master of the Grand Orient of the Netherlands.
>
> "In Scandinavian Freemasonry, A. Nyvang, Grand Secretary of the Grand Lodge of Denmark, and Lee Davidsen, Grand Secretary of the Grand Lodge of Norway.
>
> "Ernest Van Hecke, Grand Master of the National Grand Lodge of France; A. L. Dérosière, Deputy Grand Master; Jean Baylot, former Préfet de Police and Grand Orator of the Grand Lodge, and several of their fraternity, especially Marius Lepage, who is linked to me by personal friendship.
>
> "J. Corneloup of the 33rd Degree, former Grand Commander of the Grand College of Rites.
>
> "G. Vinatrel and Léon Fobain, Worshipful Master of the old and respected Lodge 'La Bonne Foi' of St. Germain en Laye, of the Grand Orient of France, and also several others of the same fraternity.
>
> "In the Scottish Rite, Charles Riandey, Sovereign Grand Commander of the Supreme Council of the Ancient and Accepted Scottish Rite; Professor Stanislas Bonnet of the 33rd Degree; Sir Donald Makgill, Grand Secretary General of the Supreme Council of the Royal Arch of England, and Major J. D. Reed of the 33rd Degree; the Grand Master, Richard Dupuy, and G. Chadirat and G. Hazan, former Grand Masters of the Grand Lodge of France; Alexis Zousmann, President of the Condorcet-Brossolette Circle; my old and well-beloved friend and fellow-student, Roger Normand, Worshipful Master of the Lodge of the Scottish Hospitallers; and L. Portoukalian, Head of the Secretariat of the Grand Lodge of France.

"Giordano Gamberini, Grand Master of the Grand Lodge of Italy.

"Without mentioning all those who, because of the foolishness of their fellow-men, have received my promise not to reveal their names."

(A. Mellor, ibid., pp. 10-11)

It will be noticed that the above list of acknowledgements says nothing of the notorious cleavage between "regular" and "irregular" Masons—between the rationalist, agnostic and revolutionary Grand Orient, on the one hand, and the spiritualist and non-political Grand Lodge, on the other.

Mellor's evidence is one-sided and comes exclusively from Masonic sources. He quite simply ignores both non-Masonic authors and those Masonic writers whose opinions do not agree with his own.

And yet, since the eighteenth century, there has been a long line of anti-Masonic writers of various nationalities, of whom France has produced more than any other country. Many of them are thoroughly reputable historians and thinkers, who have furnished a considerable body of evidence and whose labours cannot be brushed aside or ignored if one wishes to make a serious study of the question. Yet, with a few extremely rare exceptions, scarcely one of them is mentioned in Mellor's books, as if they had never existed and never written a line on the subject. It would be impossible to give a complete list of them here, and we shall only mention a few of the well-known names among many others.

In France, there are the works of the Abbé Barruel, Gustave Bord, Augustin Cochin, and Bernard Fay, who all specialised in the French Revolution of 1789; Gougenot des Mousseaux, Crétineau-Joly, the Abbé E. Barbier, N. Deschamps, and Claudio Jannet, who wrote in the second half of the nineteenth century; and Monseigneur Delassus and Monseigneur Jouin who made a special study of the part played by Freemasonry in the struggle against religion and in the campaign of world-wide subversion.

Monseigneur Jouin, parish priest of St. Augustin in Paris, deserves special mention here, for he created and directed up to his death a few years before the Second World War, a centre of international studies devoted to Freemasonry, Judaism and revolutionary subversion in the world, and edited a regular magazine, *Revue Internationale des Sociétés Secrètes*. It was probably the only organisation of this kind to have existed in the world, and Monseigneur Jouin was personally commended for his courageous work in exposing the sectarian enemies of religion by Pope Benedict XV in 1919. Monseigneur Jouin was naturally the pet aversion of liberal and subversive elements. The only accusation which can be brought against him is that he was a man of great kindness; sometimes he was a little too kind in welcoming collaborators who were below the standards required for his magazine. Mellor speaks of the *Revue Internationale* with contemptuous and amused condescension. But not all Freemasons would agree with him. Serge Hutin, for example, says in his book *Les Franc-Maçons*, "The collection (the R.I.S.S.) is moreover extremely useful to the historian, for it contains evidence unobtainable elsewhere on the rituals and activities of the lodges, especially of those given over to esoteric and occult sciences. Very cleverly, the editors always start from authentic sources; it is their interpretation which is oriented."

Other French writers include Copin-Albancelli and J. Marquès-Rivière, both former Masons, who have given invaluable testimony on the life and activity inside the lodges; Charles Maurras, A. G. Michel, Henri Coston and R. Valéry-Radot, who have concentrated on Freemasonry's political rôle in France and throughout the world; and P. Loyer and F. Colmet Daage, who were both remarkable lecturers on Freemasonry; not to mention many others.

In England there are the works of Professor Robison, a contemporary of the Abbé Barruel; Nesta Webster, a modern historian of revolutionary subversion, and the only woman to have acquired an international reputation in this sphere; Mgr. Dillon and Walton Hannah; and the Rev. Penney Hunt, a Nonconformist Minister whose studies and revelations ended in an official ban on Freemasonry within the Methodist Church.

In Germany there are Eckert, Dr. Wichtl, and the Baron von Stotzingen.

In Ireland there are Father Cahill, S.J., and Father Denis Fahey, both authors of great importance, who have devoted several large volumes to the study of Freemasonry and world subversion.

In Spain there are the Abbé Tusquets, J. Boor and Mauricio Carl, who devoted himself to a study of subversion throughout the world.

In Poland there is Count Malynski, who published over thirty volumes on this subject alone.

In Italy, there are Senator L. Federzoni and Father Caprile, S.J. The latter writes in the review, *Civilta Cattolica*, and is a theologian who has devoted himself to the study of Freemasonry in Italy for years, but since the nomination of Father Arrupe as Superior-General of the Jesuits, and as a result of the new attitude produced by the Vatican Council, the Jesuit review, *Civilta Cattolica*, no longer publishes articles on Freemasonry, and Father Caprile has been ordered to cease all activity in this sphere.

In Rumania there is Professor A. C. Cuza.

In the United States there are Arthur Preuss, Father H. Thurston and Father Michael Kenny.

There is no question, therefore, that Mellor's evidence is one-sided, since it supports only the point of view of Masonic authors or their progressive allies. However, we are now going to reply to his arguments chapter by chapter, since, as far as we are aware, apart from a few brief articles in specialist reviews, this has not yet been undertaken by anyone.

2

THE PONTIFICAL CONDEMNATIONS

MELLOR attributes the greatest importance to the pontifical condemnations of Freemasonry, and on this point we can entirely agree with him.

The essential fact which stands out in the whole history of Freemasonry, he says, is its condemnation by the Church. Elsewhere he speaks of the immense event that was the first condemnation by Clement XII in 1738, a condemnation many times renewed afterwards.

> "*The prophetic date of 1738 marks the beginning of the conflict in which Freemasonry and the Church were thereafter on opposite sides—surely one of the greatest and gravest conflicts in human history*. It was also clear that from that moment Masonry began to subdivide, progressively losing its purely English character. The local Grand Lodges became more and more independent, an ingratitude of which the mother Grand Lodge of England was to complain from time to time."
>
> (A. Mellor: *La Franc-Maçonnerie à l'Heure du Choix*, p. 48)

These condemnations entail unavoidable excommunication, an embarrassing point for a Catholic writer who fervently proclaims his faith and his respect for hierarchical authority. That, however, is no obstacle to Mellor:

> "But has not a terrible word just slipped from the pen? *Exclusion*! And what about the excommunicated?
>
> "Respect for the 'Power of the Keys' dictates this question to our consciences, certainly; there is one simple answer, however: they too are our brothers.
>
> "Then let us open our arms to them like brothers."
>
> (A. Mellor. *Our Separated Brethren*, p. 15)

The crucial question before us is whether the papal condemnations are final, for if they are, the whole campaign being conducted today for their annulment by liberal-minded priests and laymen is absolutely without foundation.

Clement XII and Leo XIII proclaim that they are final.

With certain oratorical precautions, Mellor and others claim that they are not.

Clement XII ended his famous bull in 1738 with the following solemn condemnation:

> "Therefore, bearing in mind the great harm which is often caused by such societies or conventicles not only to the peace of the temporal state but also to the well-being of souls, and realizing that they are thus in discord with both civil and canonical sanctions. . . .
>
> ". . . in fact, to prevent the hearts of the simple being perverted, and the innocent secretly wounded by their arrows, and to block that broad road which could be opened to the uncorrected commission of sin, and for other just and reasonable motives known to Us; We therefore, having taken counsel of some of Our Venerable Brothers among the Cardinals of the Holy Roman Church, and also of Our own accord and with certain knowledge and mature deliberation, with the plenitude of the Apostolic power do *hereby determine and have decreed that these same societies, companies, assemblies, meetings, congregations or conventicles of Liberi Muratori or Francs Massons, or whatever name they may go by, are to be condemned and prohibited, and by Our present Constitution, valid for ever, We do condemn and prohibit them.*"
>
> (Clement XII: *In Eminenti*, quoted in A. Mellor: *Our Separated Brethren*, pp. 159-160)

In his great Encyclical, *Humanum Genus*, Leo XIII is equally formal and explicit.

> "Since we are aware that our best and firmest hope of remedy lies in the strength of that divine religion which the Freemasons hate in proportion to their fear of it, we hold it therefore to be of supreme importance to utilize all its wonderful salutary power against the common enemy. Accordingly, whatever Our Predecessors, the Roman Pontiffs, have decreed in view of opposing the designs and machinations of Freemasonry, whatever they have enacted to keep men from becoming affiliated to such associations or to withdraw from them, if they had had the misfortune to be already members, all and each of these measures we ratify and confirm by our Apostolic Authority. Full of confidence in the goodwill of Christians, *we beg and beseech each one of them, for the sake of his eternal salvation, to consider it a sacred obligation*

of conscience never in the least to deviate from what the Apostolic See has enjoined in this matter.

"First of all, tear away the mask from Freemasonry and let it be seen as it really is. . . ." (pp. 19-20)

What is Mellor's answer to this?

"Since certain Catholics—without reprimand from the hierarchy —and certain Masons have closed some of the gap between them, one question inevitably arises: will they eventually close it completely? It is the logical corollary of these new tendencies.

"So why avoid it?

"It is, for all that, a very serious question, and it is therefore important to set the problem out with the utmost clarity, without deceit or ambiguity:

"Is the condemnation of Freemasonry, first by Clement XII in 1738 and some fifteen times more thereafter, irrevocable?

"If not, then on what bases could there be reconciliation?

"That is the final problem.

"Canon 1,399 prohibits Masonic books outright.

"These arrangements were the subject of a reminder from the Holy Office on 20th April, 1949, in response to a letter from the Bishop of Trent; and on 19th March, 1950, in the *Osservatore Romano*, Father Cordovani, Master of the Sacred Palaces, again stressed that they were still in force.

(A. Mellor: *Our Separated Brethren*, p. 287)

"They are the juridicial translation of the encyclicals, none of which has fallen into abeyance, including the first, of Clement XII.

"But what one Pope has done, could not another undo? It is necessary here to distinguish most carefully between questions of dogma or morality on the one hand, and factual situations capable of changing on the other hand. The latter come under juridicial rule, which, by definition, can be altered. What are we to understand by Clement XII's proclamation that his bull is *perpetuo valitura*, valid in perpetuity? These two words call for an explanation. They signify that the bull is not a temporary law, limited to the duration of his reign; they could not imply that Freemasonry will never change. That would be ascribing an unduly prophetic sense to them. We must deduce:

"(a) that the Freemasonry which Clement XII wished to condemn is that of 1738, in so far as it is perpetuated, and

"(b) that he did not mean to commit his successors until the end of time, even if modifications of fact changed the whole nature of the problem. And that could not be ruled out.

"These modifications have not yet appeared; indeed, Freemasonry as Leo XIII condemned it proved considerably more deserving of condemnation than any which Clement XII had known. Yet, if the historical facts had been different, these modifications might have taken place.

"Henceforth we can see in what sense condemnation of Freemasonry is irrevocable, which is sufficient for us to understand in what sense it is not irrevocable.

"What will be decided if the Freemasonry of the future should develop in the opposite direction to that which it has taken in the past?

"Quite clearly it is only on this supreme condition that the final step could be taken.

"The theoretical solution is obvious. It is not because of its name that Freemasonry has been condemned, and if in the future a quite different society existed under the same name it is conceivable that it would no longer merit condemnation—at least, not for the same reasons. The old condemnations would not, for all that, be withdrawn. The Pope would simply check that they no longer affected the institution which had preserved the name of Freemasonry, or which had assumed it. . . . (A. Mellor, ibid., p. 288)

"Let us not avoid realities: for the majority of 'Latin' Masons today reconciliation with the Church would not even be desirable. 'Attitudes have hardened', would be the reply from many of them, some through open hostility, others through pessimism.

"But it is the Masonic élite whom we have in mind, those free thinkers in the undistorted sense of the term, those decent men who regard reconciliation as highly desirable, not for the Church to which they do not claim allegiance, but for Masonry, whose deeply sincere members they are.

"It is with spirits such as these, akin to our own, that the dialogue can be started. (A. Mellor, ibid., p. 292)

"If one ignores certain individual excesses (and even some collective excesses which came to nought), Masonry as such has never declared open war on the Church. Its statements of principle are far less denials of dogma than the mutilated 'credos' of confessions separated from Rome. So there is no reason to place it in the first category (as censured by the Church as a declared Enemy). (A. Mellor, ibid., p. 293)

"There is no need to trace the history of all the breaking up which, for some years, has made cracks everywhere in the Masonic structure, the most considerable of which was the break between the Grand Lodge of France and the Grand Orient. One certainty alone concerns us: the institution is still evolving. The old forms are worn out. A new spirit is appearing which tends to break with habits of thought proper to the end of the nineteenth century. The time seems ripe to make a clean sweep of everything which has managed to harm the Masonic ideal. A kind of young Freemasonry is feeling its way. This explosion of generosity will not be short-lived; it deserves to be followed with the most sympathetic attention. . . . (A. Mellor, ibid., p. 297)

"This might be the main outline of a general reconciliation, only sketched in, and not forgetting the extreme prudence which, from the practical angle, must accompany any attempt to put views of this kind into effect. Most Catholics and Freemasons alike will consider it utopian. Some—less lazy—will think that difficulty is not synonymous with impossibility. Some Catholics, it is to be hoped, will even go so far as to admit that in the modern world the Christian's place is everywhere, that it is his absence which creates anti-Christian hostility, and that our separated brethren will return if we hold out our hand to them.

(A. Mellor, ibid., pp. 299-300)

"Contrary to the fable, according to which Freemasonry is a monolithic structure, there is not and probably never will be a more disjointed institution. . . .

"In this era of ecumenism, with the trend towards universal concepts, this force seems to be too deeply rooted in our civilisation to fail to be recognised, and consequently neither the Communist world nor the Church can ignore it. The former, as we have said, is a monstrous transposition of scholastic metaphysics into the political sphere.

"It is no longer a question of discovering whether Freemasonry has or has not been condemned, but of discovering whether any identity exists between Freemasonry as it was when it was condemned and the Freemasonry of today or tomorrow. What was not condemned was the name 'Freemasonry'.

"For the Catholic, this problem presents no obstacle. His conclusion will be, if he has any historical sense, that a 'dialogue' should be held between the Church and the Order. . . ."

(A. Mellor: *La Franc-Maçonnerie à l'Heure du choix*, p. 478)

As one can see, Mellor works up to the point very laboriously, but it is when at last he does openly confront the problem that the juggling commences. For indeed he has to show that the Vatican has been wrong for nearly two hundred and fifty years, in that it has falsely condemned Freemasonry, and this he has to do without rising up against the Vatican's authority, and without setting it in opposition to himself. An exercise in walking a veritable intellectual tight-rope.

This is how Mellor proceeds.

All the papal condemnations are reduced to the first, Clement XII's in 1738, and this in turn is reduced to the sole motive—the Masonic secret.

> "The bull of Clement XII", he says, was a "doctrinal document of far-reaching effect, containing the seeds of all other condemnations of Freemasonry."
>
> (A. Mellor: *Our Separated Brethren*, p. 165)

Indeed, Clement XII's condemnation is almost the only one with which he is concerned in his two books, as if the subsequent history of secular strife between the Church and Freemasonry can be traced solely to the Bull of 1738.

Yet, according to Mellor, the motives for the condemnation are not clearly described in Clement's bull. In other words, they are inconsistent, and cannot be taken seriously.

> "On the Masonic question many tons of printed paper have been published. August Wolfstieg's *Bibliographie der freimaurerischen Literatur* comprises more than 50,000 titles alone. For all that we are still waiting for the answer to one question, the one from which everything issues: why was Freemasonry condemned by the Church in the first place? (A. Mellor, ibid., p. 15)

> "Paradoxical, mysterious, inexplicable in a word (barring a secret motive); so the bull of Clement XII still seems."
>
> (A. Mellor, ibid., p. 84)

However Mellor recognises—for his books are full of contradictions—that Clement XII was an excessively tolerant pope and that the condemnation was the fruit of long study in consultation with the Cardinals.

> "There were no popes more gentle, more accommodating, so to speak, than Clement XII and Benedict XIV. We shall see that the latter, through love of peace, took benevolence to the point of sending a projected encyclical to the French Minister before publishing it officially. They were men of the eighteenth century, as far removed as possible from the theocrats of the Middle Ages and even from certain modern Popes. It is probable that, faced

with the same problem, a Pope like Pius XI would have reacted much more energetically, and one can imagine what would have been the reactions of an Innocent IV or a Boniface VIII.

"The same observation can be made for those Cardinals, more patrons of the arts than theologians, who were involved in the condemnation: Corsini, Ottoboni, Zondedari, Giorgio Spinola. It is sufficient to look at their portraits to feel carried away into a different world of easy religion, sacred art, Italian diplomacy. They seem to be smiling still. (A. Mellor, ibid., p. 150)

"The spirit reigning in Papal Rome in the eighteenth century was at the opposite pole from the Inquisitorial spirit, and it took all the provocation which the affirmation of the Masonic secret seemed to possess to awaken in such tolerant Churchmen a spiritual anxiety which would far sooner lie dormant. If Freemasonry, stepping out of Time, had been able to choose its judges from the long history of the Church, it could never have found any more open to indulgence, and even laxity. (A. Mellor, ibid., p. 151)

"These then are the characters: highly placed prelates of their time, with all the non-ecclesiastical quality, in the modern sense, which that could imply; and there is no hiding the fact. These men belong to history just as they are. None of them appears as a theologian. Clement XII himself has left no reputation as a scholar. They were Italian lords, sumptuous, benevolent, lax—lax in their religious vigilance—and it is precisely these aspects which prevent their belonging to the race of Inquisitors. . . .

(A. Mellor, ibid., p. 154)

"The only common denominator for all the Masonic tendencies was the secret, but in requiring secrecy Freemasonry was not denying any dogma, was not even emitting a single thought. There was, even so, a hint there, a presumption of heresy, to which was added a second one: the large number of heretics—namely Protestants—who belonged to the society. Without being theologically heretical, it was therefore, vehemently suspected of heresy none the less, which in canonical terms permitted excommunication. . . . (A. Mellor, ibid., p. 155)

"Consequently there need be no surprise if the gestation of the bull took nearly a year. Never was the famous saying better confirmed, that the Church is never pressed since Eternity is on her side. . . .

"A text finally emerged. How many times was it re-read to the Pope and redrafted, in view of its inevitable vagueness? . . .

> "Probably when Clement XII, that old man at death's door, a living ruin of a man, put his signature at the bottom of the document which his eyes could not see but which was destined to have repercussions down through the centuries, it was yet he alone, perhaps, who appreciated the importance of that moment, who understood the reasons for the act to which his signature gave birth." (A. Mellor: *Our Separated Brethren*, p. 156)

What is one to make of all this? The condemnation of 1738 was not the result of a decision which had been taken lightly, far from it. Powerful motives, then, must have impelled it. What are they? And what has the bull itself to say in this connection?

One must remember that it was hardly customary at that time to justify pontifical decisions in detail. Popes were regarded as serious men who knew what they were talking about and who did not lightly take such grave decisions, in a word, men whom one could trust in matters which concerned the affairs of the Church.

The bull expressly mentions the secrecy with which Freemasonry surrounds itself as a reason for its condemnation, and then adds:

> "Bearing in mind the great harm which is often caused by such societies or conventicles not only to the peace of the temporal state but also to the well-being of souls, and realizing that they are thus in discord with both civil and canonical sanctions. . . .
>
> ". . . in fact, to prevent the hearts of the simple being perverted, and the innocent secretly wounded by their arrows, and to block that broad road which could be opened to the uncorrected commission of sin, and for other just and reasonable motives known to Us. . . ."

Several ideas have been put forward to explain these secret motives mentioned by Clement XII. Mellor is absolutely certain that the motive was political, put forward in the guise of a religious issue. Thus the pope was supporting the Catholic monarchy of the Stuarts against the Protestant Hanoverians, who were defended and supported by English Freemasonry. And since the Jacobite struggle against the Hanoverians has long since lost all significance, Mellor proceeds to erase it with a stroke of his pen as a valid argument against Freemasonry.

This explanation is flat supposition, nothing more, and a risky supposition at that, destined to buttress the progressive thinkers' thesis, which aims at obtaining a revision of the papal condemnations, and yet it is announced with such assurance that it may impress the reader who is not fully versed in this complicated question.

To put it briefly, Mellor maintains that the only remaining valid motive for condemnation is that of secrecy, and then he launches into a muddled and interminable dissertation to prove that the secret is a false secret, and that at least it is a matter of past history which no longer has any meaning or value today.

At this stage of his reasoning, there is practically nothing left of the papal condemnations and the way is left free for a total revision of the policy which the Vatican has consistently upheld since 1738.

Further on in this work we devote a chapter to the study of the Masonic secret, but for the moment let us continue the history of the pontifical condemnations.

Clement XII's bull had very little practical effect on the governments of Europe, and none whatever on the French government.

> "*The Papacy was the only power which clearly recognised the peril which Freemasonry presented, and that almost from its beginning.*
>
> "*The Papacy had definitely seen the peril, and had drawn attention to it in time.*
>
> "*But her voice was not believed, and in France it was not even listened to.* The parliaments refused to ratify the pontifical bulls, and since they were not promulgated they achieved no visible effect. A world was about to vanish."
>
> (G. Bord: *La Franc-Maçonnerie en France des origines à 1815*, pp. 194-196)

Confronted with this indifference, Clement XII's successor, Benedict XIV, renewed the first condemnation on 18th May, 1751. And there again, as Mellor openly recognises, neither the pope nor the cardinals of his entourage were fanatical inquisitors.

> "In the opinion of all his contemporaries, *if ever a man was quite the opposite of a fanatic, of a persecutor, that man was Prospero Lambertini, elected Pope under the name of Benedict* XIV upon the death of Clement XII. Nor was anyone more a man of the eighteenth century. He had its keen finesse, its elegance of speech and style, and even its irony. The 'graces' which Lord Chesterfield so commended to his son as being essential: tolerance, a wonderful knowledge of human nature, in addition to his generous patronage of the arts, and all crowned by his charity—this was the Pope, by far the greatest of his period."
>
> (A. Mellor: *Our Separated Brethren*, p. 197)

After Benedict XIV, the condemnations were renewed by Pius VI, Pius VII (1821), Leo XII (1825), who described Freemasonry as "the

Church's capital enemy", Pius VIII (1829), Gregory XVI (1832 and 1839), and Pius IX (1846, 1864, 1865, 1873, 1876).

After Pius IX we come to the pontificate of Leo XIII, which marks an important date in the Church's struggle against Freemasonry. On 20th April, 1884, Leo XIII promulgated the celebrated encyclical *Humanum Genus*, which is entirely and exclusively devoted to the "Sect of the Freemasons". It is the most comprehensive and important document which the Vatican has ever published on this subject. In it Freemasonry is condemned with the utmost severity and without appeal, and yet, according even to his opponents, Leo XIII was an extremely liberal pope.

The following extracts will serve to give the reader a summary résumé of the whole work.

It begins with a preamble in which the Pope recalls the eternal struggle between the Church of Christ and the powers of darkness.

> "In our day, the partisans of evil seem to be drawing closer together and, as a body, appear to be animated with extraordinary energy, under the leadership and with the assistance of the widely diffused and strongly organized association known as Freemasonry.
>
> "Our Predecessors, ever vigilant and solicitous for the safety of the Christian people, promptly detected the presence of this dangerous enemy and its designs, as soon as it came out of the darkness in which it had been secretly plotting. Looking far ahead into the future they raised the alarm and enjoined on both rulers and people to be on their guard and not to allow themselves to be ensnared by the tricks and devices prepared for their deception."
>
> (*Humanum Genus*, tr. Rev. D. Fahey, p. 2)

The Encyclical then explains the motives for the condemnation of Freemasonry.

At the fore are the anti-Christian principles which constitute the essence of Freemasonry, and which may be described as "naturalism".

> "Their ultimate aim is to uproot completely the whole religious and political order of the world, which has been brought into existence by Christianity, and to replace it by another in harmony with their way of thinking. This will mean that the foundation and the laws of the new structure of society will be drawn from pure Naturalism."
>
> (*Humanum Genus*, ibid., p. 7)

The Encyclical explains at length in the following paragraphs what this implies.

The second motive for the condemnation of Freemasonry is the political action which flows from the first. For Freemasonry strives to introduce its principles into the laws and institutions of States.

> "In the sphere of politics, the Naturalists lay down that all men have the same rights and that all are equal and alike in every respect; that everyone is by nature free and independent; that no one has the right to exercise authority over another; that it is an act of violence to demand of men obedience to any authority not emanating from themselves. All power is, therefore, in the free people. Those who exercise authority do so either by the mandate or the permission of the people, so that, when the popular will changes, rulers of States may lawfully be deposed even against their will. The source of all rights and civic duties is held to reside either in the multitude or in the ruling power in the State, provided that it has been constituted according to the new principles. They hold also that the State should not acknowledge God and that, out of the various forms of religion, there is no reason why one should be preferred to another. According to them, all should be on the same level."
>
> (*Humanum Genus*, ibid., pp. 13-14)

The third motive is the secret methods used by Freemasonry in the political sphere. We do not propose to discuss this again here, but refer the reader to chapter 3, which deals with the whole question of Masonic secrecy.

The fourth motive for condemning Freemasonry is the breakdown in moral standards which accompanies the influence of Freemasonry in politics, and which indeed it sometimes uses deliberately as a weapon.

> "Since in general no one obeys cunning and crafty schemers so readily as those whose courage and self-control have been sapped and broken by subjection to the yoke of their passions, there have been found in Freemasonry men who have proclaimed their determination to strive skilfully and cunningly to saturate the masses with every form of vice. They hope that the masses thus debased will be like putty in their hands to carry out their future projects, no matter what may be their nature."
>
> (*Humanum Genus*, ibid., p. 12)

The fifth motive is the danger which Freemasonry represents from the social point of view, for it prepares the way for Communism—a question to which we have devoted chapter 9 of this work.

Finally, the Encyclical ended by exhorting men to look to the Church as the central focus of resistance to Masonic subversion.

"Whatever our Predecessors have decreed in view of opposing the designs and machinations of Freemasonry . . . all and each of these measures we ratify and confirm. Full of confidence in the goodwill of Christians we beg and beseech each one of them, for the sake of his eternal salvation to consider it a sacred obligation never in the least to deviate from what the Apostolic See has enjoined in this matter . . . and since it is becoming that we ourselves should indicate to you the most suitable line of conduct in the circumstances, we enjoin the following:

"First of all, tear away the mask from Freemasonry and let it be seen as it really is." (*Humanum Genus*, ibid., pp. 19-20)

What do the Masons say about this Encyclical? And what do progressive thinkers, and notably Mellor, who is their spokesman—what do they say?

Let us first of all hear Dumesnil de Gramont, Grand Master of the Grand Lodge of France, for the Masons.

"What a terrible text this Encyclical contains," he writes, "and one which our brothers ought to read frequently. Terrible and surprising too, when you consider that its author is still considered as the finest, the most clear-sighted and the most liberal of modern popes. One is overwhelmed at its vehement tone, the violent epithets, the audacity of the accusations, the perfidy of the appeals to secular repression. All the odious fables, all the absurd grievances which, not so long ago, were circulated in France by anti-masonic factions, are implicitly and even explicitly contained in this document which, we are sorry to say, seems rather to resemble the work of a pamphleteer than of a Pontiff."

(M. Dumesnil de Gramont: *La Maçonnerie et l'Eglise Catholique*, p. 18)

And what does Mellor say?

While he writes at length on Clement XII's bull, to which he devotes part of his book, Mellor becomes very silent and reserved on the subject of *Humanum Genus*—in brief, he avoids discussing it, save for two and a half pages out of the eight hundred and thirty five which his two books comprise.

The fact is that *Humanum Genus* is a dire thorn in the flesh of progressive thinkers for, this time, the motives for the condemnation of Freemasonry are clearly and precisely formulated at length, and no amount of argumentation can escape that fact. Instead, progressive thinkers prefer to avoid discussing the question; they quite simply ignore the Encyclical.

It is perfectly obvious that Leo XIII was convinced of the extreme importance of the problem of Freemasonry, for he referred to it on several occasions after *Humanum Genus*, in 1890, 1892, 1894, and in 1902. He published a double letter in 1892, one to the Archbishops and Bishops and the other to the people of Italy, which was entirely concerned with the question of Freemasonry. In this letter he renewed and reinforced the themes he had elaborated in *Humanum Genus*.

The letter began:

> "The spirit common to all former sects which have revolted against Catholic institutions has sprung up with fresh vigour in that sect which is called Masonic. . . .
>
> "Whole cities are overrun by its contagion; civil institutions are becoming more and more deeply penetrated with its inspiration. . . .

and the Pope concluded:

> "Let us remember that Christianity and Freemasonry are fundamentally irreconcilable, so much so that to adhere to the one is to cut oneself off from the other."

Finally, in a new Encyclical promulgated on 19th March, 1902, Leo XIII described Freemasonry as:

> ". . . the permanent personification of the Revolution. It constitutes a sort of society in reverse whose aim is to exercise an occult overlordship upon society as we know it, and whose sole *raison d'être* consists in waging war against God and His Church."
>
> (Encyclical: *On the 25th Year of Our Pontificate*)

To this very day the Vatican has confirmed and renewed the condemnation of Freemasonry and thus, by implication, the reasoning upon which this position is based, without the slightest deviation from its original position.

In 1906 Pius X attacked the ungodly sects.

In 1937 Pius XI drew attention to the alliance between Communism and Freemasonry in his Encyclical, *Divini Redemptoris*.

In 1946 and in 1949 the Supreme Congregation of the Holy Office published the following declaration in reply to a question from the Italian Archbishops:

> "Scottish rite Masonry falls under the condemnation decreed by the Church against Masonry in general, and there is no

reason to grant any discrimination in favour of this category of Masons." (1946)

and again,

"Since nothing has happened to cause any change in the decisions of the Holy See on this question, the provisions of Canon Law remain in full force for every kind of Masonry whatsoever." (20th April, 1949)

On 5th January, 1954, the Holy Office condemned a work drawn up by the Grand Master of the Johannine rite of Austrian Freemasonry, (B. Scheichelbauer: *Die Johannis Freimaurerei*, 1953) and on 17th January the *Osservatore Romano*, the official Vatican journal, published a long article concerned with this particular branch of Masonry, from which we reproduce the following passage:

"Surprise may have been caused in certain quarters by this serious step taken by the Church, after the statements which have so insistently been circulated almost everywhere in recent years concerning the conciliatory attitude of the Johannine lodge of Austrian Freemasonry towards the Catholic Church.

"The plea was advanced, in this connection, that the excommunication decreed against members of Masonic sects by Canon 2,335 of the Canon Law, did not affect those who belonged to the aforesaid lodge.

"If there were any need for fresh proofs to confirm that the concepts of even the Johannine rite of Austrian Freemasonry are a positive perversion of religious principles, the above mentioned publication provided the most recent and the most irrefutable demonstration of that fact.

"The author is himself Grand Master of the Austrian Johannine lodge.

"We shall confine ourselves here to a summary examination of the principle ideas expressed in the book.

"It is there asserted that 'the direct aim of Freemasonry is to bring its own members to the "Gnosis"', as being the only possible method of attaining the Divine Essence, and to overcome the existing contradiction between faith and science. Thus 'Gnosis' is nothing less than Anthroposophy, though this term is not expressly employed. Its principle dogma is Pantheism. Herein resides the 'Ars Regia', or sovereign skill, through which man acquires the knowledge of the identity of his own being with the divine being.

"It goes on to declare that Freemasonry favours tolerance in matters of dogma, seeing that no religious society, not even the

Catholic Church, is in possession of the whole truth. Although there are to be found in all religions traces of natural religious knowledge, yet the 'Gnosis' is the only true science; other systems of knowledge represent only a preparation for the true science, that is to say, the 'Gnosis'.

"No one can fail to see the gravity of such ideas and concepts, and how radically and fundamentally they are not merely at variance with revealed religion but utterly opposed to it.

"*Moreover, the placing of this book on the Index is an effective warning to Catholics not to let themselves be deceived by those who are trying to persuade them into becoming attracted to Freemasonry by claiming that there is a change of attitude on its part towards the Catholic Church.*"

On 19th March, 1950, the Most Reverend Father Mario Cordovani, Master of the Sacred Palace, published an article on Freemasonry in the *Osservatore Romano*, which has special relevance to the present issue. The following are its most essential passages:

"One might reasonably suppose that after such a tragic lesson as the last war, we should all have become wiser and that our way of living would have been given a new direction. On the contrary, to our great surprise we have to take note of the fact that nothing, so to speak, has been learned from it, that the errors and methods of the past are still being repeated, bringing dangers which are greater and easier to foresee.

"Among the things which are springing up again with renewed vigour, and not only in Italy, is Freemasonry with its ever recurring hostility to religion and to the Church. One only needs to recall the speeches delivered in Parliament by the head of Italian Freemasonry.

"What appears to be a new feature in this Masonic renaissance is the rumour circulating in various social classes that a particular rite of Masonry might no longer be in opposition to the Church, whereby even Catholics can enrol at their ease in the sect without fear of excommunication and reproach. *Those responsible for propagating these rumours must surely know that nothing has been modified in the Church's legislation relative to Freemasonry,* and if they continue this campaign it can only be in order to profit from the naivety of simple folk.

"*The Bishops know that Canon 684 and especially Canon 2,335, which excommunicates those who have given their names to Masonry without any distinction between rites, are as full in force today as they always have been; all Catholics ought to know this and remember it,* so as not to fall into this snare, and also so as to know how to pass due judgment on the fact that certain simpletons believe that they can call themselves both Catholics and Freemasons with impunity. *This, I repeat, applies to all Masonic rites,* even if some of them, in varying circumstances, declare that they are not hostile to the Church."

At this point it is worth interposing an illuminating passage from the paper *La Croix*, which on 6th February, 1964, made the following comment on Mellor's latest book, *La Franc-Maçonnerie à l'Heure du Choix*:

"It would seem that raising the excommunication which continues to hang over the whole of Freemasonry scarcely ought to encounter insurmountable obstacles. Moreover, at the cost of some minor concessions on their part, Catholics ought to be allowed to be 'initiated'. Nevertheless, these prospects affect only regular Freemasonry. The case of irregular Freemasonry is different, and in particular that of the Grand Orient of France, which in 1877 inscribed atheism into its constitution. Before anything else could be done it would be necessary for the latter to return to regularity and to the true Masonic ideal, religious and non-political. Grand Orient Freemasonry and the whole of so-called 'Rites of the Latin Obedience' find themselves at the cross-roads. Overtaken by Communism in their secular ideas they no longer represent the 'future' and seem to be doomed to disappear."

The anonymous author of this commentary has probably never even read the Encyclicals. If he had, how could he have written this article?

It is merely for us to put the question, leaving the reader to form his own conclusions.

But, to return to the passage we are quoting from the *Osservatore Romano*, the Reverend Father Cordovani, Master of the Sacred Palace, goes on to say:

"Any agreement between the Church and Freemasonry, suggesting in this way that they were two powers giving juridical form to their new attitudes, would be a resounding instance of a flagrant contradiction. The man who does not share the views of the sect and who has truly Catholic feelings will appreciate the duty of ridding himself of these views, and of not adding another banner to the disloyal standards under which the fight goes on. . . .

"But does not this rigid attitude disregard the good will of some people who would like ecclesiastical authority to recognise some small sector of Freemasonry said not to be hostile to religion and to the Church? And is it not equally opposed to the spirit of accommodation which the Church has shown in every epoch, outstripping everyone in a spirit of comprehension and generous charity?

"Only a frivolous-minded person could say that. . . .

"This modern tendency, manifest among those who would gladly bring Catholicism into harmony with all ideologies and social movements, with every advance and about-turn—is not this a sign of heresy, even if among many it is unconsciously present? . . .

"It is to be hoped that these lines will clarify the position of the great number of people who have told us that they were in need of enlightenment.

"Let everyone re-read the pontifical documents, for they daily receive confirmation from Freemasonry's own words and deeds in various countries. . . ."

(Article by the Most Rev. Father Cordovani in the *Osservatore Romano*, 19th March, 1950)

Finally, on 20th February, 1959, the Plenary Assembly of the Cardinals, Archbishops and Bishops of the Argentine, under the presidency of Cardinal Caggiano, published a long collective declaration on Freemasonry, from which we have taken the following passages:

"In the course of its plenary reunion, the Argentinian Hierarchy, confronted by various articles published in the Press by Freemasonry, felt obliged to make a public declaration to the faithful, following the recommendation of Leo XIII to 'first of all, tear away the mask from Freemasonry and let it be seen as it really is'. . . .

"On 23rd May, 1958, in an address to the 7th week of Pastoral Adaptation, Pius XII mentioned that *the roots of modern apostasy lay in scientific atheism, dialectical materialism, rationalism, illuminism, laicism, and Freemasonry—which was the mother of them all. . . .*

"In 1958, the IVth Interamerican Conference of Freemasonry, which was held in Santiago, Chile, declared that 'the Order helps all its members to obtain important posts in the public life of the nations'. After this came a dissertation on the theme of 'The Defence of Laicism', to be followed by directions as to the new tactics to be adopted by Freemasonry, which coincide with the latest instructions of the Communist International. Freemasons are to work for the triumph of laicism in all walks of life, and Communists are to subvert social order in order to create a favourable terrain in which to achieve their ends. This is how the instruction is worded: 'Intensify the campaign of laicisation through the intermediary influence of the different political parties. Try and appease the alarm of the Catholic Church at Freemasonry by avoiding direct Masonic action. Intensify the action which will unsettle the unity of the working-class movements, so that they may the more easily be stifled afterwards. *Freemasonry and Communism for the moment are pursuing the same objective in Latin America, which is why they must try and work together in the best possible way, without allowing the slightest sign of their alliance to become public. . . .*'

"Proof that this is no dream is the Second International Congress for Universal Fraternity.

"World Freemasonry and Communism are preparing for a Congress which will be held at Montevideo, called 'The Second International Congress for Universal Fraternity'. It is a Masonic Congress of Communist inspiration which aims to subordinate the Masonic ideal of 'universal fraternity' to the expansion of the Soviet Communist International. The congress will take place in Holy Week, from 26th to 28th March, and its object is to prepare for the 'struggle for human confraternity and world peace'—two themes behind which Freemasonry and Communism disguise their evil intentions. . . .

"'Marxism and Freemasonry both serve the common ideal of earthly happiness. . . . A Freemason can accept completely the philosophical conceptions of Marxism. No conflict is possible between the philosophical conceptions of Marxism and Freemasonry', asserts the Grand Master of Freemasonry in Paris.

"To achieve its ends, Freemasonry uses high finance, high politics and the world Press; Marxism, on the other hand, uses social and economic revolution against the country, the family, property, morality and religion.

"Freemasons achieve their ends by secretly subversive means, Communists by openly subversive movements. Freemasonry activates sectarian political minorities; Communism relies on mass political movements exploiting their aspirations to social justice. . . .

"Every Argentinian, and especially the young, should know that Catholicism and Freemasonry are completely contradictory and self-exclusive, like Christ and Antichrist. Also they ought to know that Liberalism or laicism, under whatever form it may take, is the very embodiment of Masonic ideology. . . .

"The Church of Christ presides over every level of the life of our country. It is present, vigilant and active in every important event in our history. Catholicism is the origin, the root and the essence of the people of Argentine. In other words, to make an attempt on Catholicism is to conspire against one's native country.

"We draw the attention of all who love their country to the two enemies of our traditions and our future greatness, Freemasonry and Communism, which are seeking the destruction of everything that is noble and sacred in our land.

"Given at the Villa San Ignacio, on 20th February in the Year of Our Saviour 1959, and signed by Cardinal Caggiano, president of the Plenary Assembly of the Argentinian Hierarchy, and by the Argentinian Archbishops and Bishops present at the reunion."

The advocates of an agreement between the Church and Freemasonry tell us that it is high time to revise and annul the Vatican's condemnations of Freemasonry, and in support of this contention they advance three reasons:

(1) The condemnations were a mistake and cannot be founded upon solid grounds of justification. The Church would win respect by recognising her error.

(2) The Vatican has never been able to formulate clearly and concisely valid motives for the condemnation.

(3) Freemasonry is profoundly evolutionary, and from having been rationalist, agnostic and anti-Christian, it is becoming spiritual in its regular obediences. Therefore the hostility with which the Church and Freemasonry have opposed each other no longer has any meaning.

The first two arguments are valueless. From 1738 to 1954 the Vatican has clearly and concisely formulated its motives for condemnation, and from the point of view of Catholic doctrine these motives are perfectly valid. The Church is not unique in this position, for numerous Catholic, Protestant, Orthodox, Moslem and atheist governments have banned Freemasonry as a secret society which is subversive of social order and incompatible with stable rulership.

The third argument can, on the other hand, at a pinch be considered valid. Everything advances in the world, and if Freemasonry really were to deny its former doctrinal and political attitudes, the former condemnations would no longer correspond to this new situation. But a very long experience has taught us that Masonry is essentially infinitely variable in its exterior manifestations according to the political opportunity of the moment. Thus we must be extremely cautious in the face of these apparent transformations, and we are justified in requiring more than the simple assertions of Mellor or the Rev. Fr. Riquet to convince us that they are real.

Only the Church can decide on the attitude it should adopt in this field, and up to the present day the Vatican has clearly indicated that there is no real justification for the modification of its condemnations.

3

THE MASONIC SECRET

SECRECY is an essential part of Masonry and Mellor recognises it as being of capital importance. Here is a brief summary of his argument.

The secrecy which Freemasonry imposes on its initiates, and which surrounds all its activities, creates an atmosphere of mystery, uneasiness and suspicion, which poisons Masonry's relations with the outside world.

It was this secrecy, to the exclusion of every other known motive, which was the basis of Clement XII's well-known condemnation of 1738, and it is this secrecy which has caused Freemasonry to be distrusted, condemned or forbidden by numerous Catholic, Protestant, Moslem and other governments throughout the world.

Now, in the days of medieval operative Masonry there was a reason for this secrecy; it existed to protect the art of those who built the cathedrals. From the moment that Masonry became speculative and transformed itself into a "société de pensée", there was no longer any reason for such secrecy.

However, apparently in the face of all logic, Freemasonry continues to impose an obligation of secrecy on its members.

Today, Freemasonry finds itself at the crossroads. If it wishes to put an end to the war between itself and Catholicism, which has raged since 1738, it must abandon this outdated notion of secrecy, for there is now no longer any justification for not discussing things frankly in broad daylight.

Mellor's argument is logical enough and would be valid if Masonry were really what he represents it to be: that is, simply a philosophical, religious, non-political society, as the Grand Lodge of England, or regular Freemasonry, as it calls itself, claims to be.

Mellor and others depict Freemasonry in colours which appease and soothe us, lulling any suspicions we may have had.

But the texts from which we shall quote reveal a picture of Freemasonry which offers us far less reassurance as to its aims and methods, its international organisation, its secrecy and its activity in international politics.

Let us then carefully examine the problem of Masonic secrecy. It is more difficult than most, for it is complex, confused and ambiguous, like everything else connected with Masonry.

Mellor asserts that secrecy is an outdated notion, that there is no longer any reason for it, and that in reality there is no secret.

The Encyclicals say exactly the opposite. In his bull of 1751 against the Freemasons, Pope Benedict XIV enumerates the motives for condemnation and justifies them. The basic motive is still the impenetrable secrecy with which Freemasonry seeks to surround itself, a result of the Masonic oath, "as if anyone had the right to take a promise or an oath to dispense him from replying to the legitimate authority seeking to find out whether, in such secret assemblies, there was nothing enacted against the State, religion and the laws."

In the Encyclical *Humanum Genus*, which was written in 1884, Pope Leo XIII deals at length with Masonic secrecy.

> "The manifold differences among the members in regard to rights, duties and functions, the elaborate hierarchical distinction of orders and degrees, and the severe discipline by which the associates are governed, all these contribute enormously to the maintenance of secrecy. Candidates for admission to the society are obliged to promise and in most cases even to take a solemn oath that they will never, at any time or in any way, make known to anyone, either the members, or the signs or the doctrines of the society. In this way, by the help of a deceitful external appearance and by a steady cultivation of a policy of dissimulation, the Freemasons, like the Manicheans in former times, leave no stone unturned to keep themselves hidden and to have as witnesses of their actions only their associates." (ibid, p. 5)

As it is, the leaders of Masonry have always regarded secrecy as an essential condition of the Order's existence and of its success. We will now quote from some Masonic texts which leave no doubt of this fact.

> "Masonry should be felt everywhere, but nowhere should it be unveiled." (Convent of the Grand Orient, 1922, p. 362)

> "The whole strength of Masonry lies in its discretion. Our enemies fear us all the more because we never reveal our methods of action." (Convent of the Grand Orient, 1929, pp. 81-82)

At the 1929 Convent of the Grand Orient, the Freemason Uhry, Deputy for the Oise, opened his report with these words:

> "Some of our brethren would like Masonry to open itself up more to public view. I beg them to hold fast to this fact: *that our Order can only keep its strength and effectiveness if it maintains its character of secrecy. On the day that we lose our peculiar character, based on discretion and secrecy, our effective action in the country will come to an end.*"

While we are discussing such a serious subject, we propose to quote from a secret Masonic document, which is extremely revealing of the international power of Freemasonry.

After the collapse of Bolshevism, the Hungarian government dissolved the lodges and published their archives. In their distress the Hungarian Masons called upon their brethren throughout the world, and it was then that the Masonic newspaper, *Latomia* of Leipzig, published the following interesting article:

> "After the catastrophe the Freemasons, who had sent another address of welcome to the Emperor, Franz-Joseph, during the war, fervently embraced the socialist republican ideology out of the noble conviction that the time had come when the Masonic ideal would be accomplished. In their writings they made active propaganda in its favour and most of the leaders were Freemasons. . . .

(The movement then rapidly degenerated into Bolshevism and when it collapsed Freemasonry was dissolved.)

> "In their distress, our Hungarian brothers turned to the North American Grand Lodges. The result was that, as Hungary was then negotiating a loan in America, the reply came back that this loan could not be considered until lawful institutions were re-established in Hungary—a clear allusion to the prohibition of Freemasonry.
>
> "Thereupon the Hungarian government was obliged to open negotiations with the ex-Grand Master. The free resumption of Masonic work was proposed to him, on condition that non-Masons should have right of access to the sessions. This was naturally refused by the Grand Master and the loan miscarried."
>
> (*Latomia* of Leipzig, No. 2/3, 1922, p. 31)

From this brief extract we may draw, among others, the following vitally important conclusions:

(1) On its own admission, Freemasonry played a leading rôle in

the Hungarian Socialist Revolution, which very quickly ended in the horrors of Bolshevism.

(2) American Freemasonry came to the help of Hungarian Freemasonry when the latter was forbidden by law in Hungary. This proves that an international liaison exists among the various Masonic bodies throughout the world; it also shows that any differences separating Continental Masonry from that in the English-speaking countries are ignored whenever the vital interests of the brotherhood are affected.

(3) International Freemasonry intervenes in the internal politics of certain countries and enjoys sufficient power to cause international loans to fall through.

(4) Freemasonry regards secrecy as such a necessary condition of its power and activity, that it prefers to be officially dissolved rather than allow a government the right to investigate its internal affairs.

Now remember that this information is furnished by a Masonic publication and is therefore indisputable.

Why is secrecy so vital to Freemasonry?

> "Freemasonry claims to have an aim which is progressive, philanthropic and humanitarian. It seeks to guide the moral and spiritual development of humanity outside and above any differences of class, nationality or creed.
>
> "Freemasonry, as described by its statutes, is an institution essentially progressive, philanthropic and humanitarian. Its aims are the search for truth, the study of morality and the practice of solidarity. It works for human betterment both materially and morally, and for the social and intellectual perfecting of man.
>
> "Its principles are mutual tolerance, respect for others and for oneself, and liberty of conscience.
>
> "Since it regards all metaphysical notions as falling exclusively within the individual decision of its members, it avoids dogmatic assertions.
>
> "Its motto is: Liberty, Equality, Fraternity.
>
> "The duty of Freemasonry is to extend to all human beings those fraternal links which already unite Freemasons throughout the world.
>
> "It recommends its adepts to propagate its ideas through their example.
>
> "In all circumstances the Freemason has a duty to help, enlighten and protect his Brother, even at the peril of his own life, and to defend him against injustice."
>
> (Edouard E. Plantagenet: *La Franc-Maçonnerie en France*, p. 41)

All this appears most attractive and perfectly innocuous. But the search for truth, the study of morality and the practice of solidarity have no need whatever to surround themselves with a rigorously kept secret.

There must then be something else. In fact, these attractive sounding principles have been very cleverly drawn up in order to conceal profoundly subversive activities under a cover of pleasing vagueness.

Mellor and the progressives are up in arms against the idea of subversion.

> "Those who insult the Order have always proclaimed that the real but concealed aim of Freemasonry was world subversion. Not only have they always maintained this idea, but some of them certainly consider that we ourselves are hand-in-glove with Freemasonry."
>
> (A. Mellor: *La Franc-Maçonnerie à l'Heure du Choix*, p. 392)

Among those who have "insulted" the order in this way must be included Pope Leo XIII, for this was precisely the conclusion he reached in his Encyclical *Humanum Genus*:

> *"Their ultimate aim (the Freemasons') is to uproot completely the whole religious and political order of the world, which has been brought into existence by Christianity, and to replace it by another in harmony with their way of thinking. This will mean that the foundation and the laws of the new structure of society will be drawn from pure Naturalism."* (ibid., p. 7)

The Pope's statements are confirmed by many Masonic authors, for example, Brother Quartier La Tente, whose name is celebrated in Freemasonry, and who said:

> *"Freemasonry has undertaken a task and a mission. It is a question of nothing less than the reconstruction of society upon an entirely new basis."* (*Two Centuries of Freemasonry*, 1917)

Again, Pope Leo XIII said:

> *"Freemasonry is the permanent personification of the Revolution; it constitutes a sort of society in reverse whose aim is to exercise an occult overlordship upon society as we know it, and whose sole* raison d'être *consists in waging war against God and His Church."* (Encyclical *On the 25th Year of Our Pontificate*, 19th March, 1902)

In this work of subversion, Freemasonry undertakes three tasks which represent three successive steps towards the final objective.

The first step is the work inside the lodges. Freemasonry gradually steeps its initiates in Masonic principles and ideas. It is a more subtle equivalent of Communist brainwashing techniques. The brethren formed in this way comprise groups active outside the lodges.

Secondly is the work of propaganda in the outside world. Freemasonry has perfected a very effective technique of occult propaganda in the world at large, which consists in spreading and imposing Masonic ideals outside the lodges, without revealing the secret source from which these currents originate. As one of the speakers at the 1922 Convent of the Grand Orient expressed it, "Masonry should be felt everywhere, but nowhere should its face be unveiled". It consists in spreading belief in the natural, inevitable and irresistible evolution of human progress.

The third step towards the final objective is in the field of political activity. The ideological propaganda, as described above, runs parallel with the political conspiracy, whose object is to seize power and place Freemasons in positions of command. As far as possible, the public is not to know that they are Masons.

All this vast field of activity is protected by two secrets: the esoteric secret inside the Masonic lodges; and the secret political action outside the lodges.

Let us now pass on to study the nature of the esoteric secret. In the first stage, new members are attracted by Freemasonry's generous and humanitarian professions of faith, and also by promises of influence and concealed assistance.

Candidates are carefully chosen and thoroughly vetted long before they are even approached. When they are received into the lodge, they are made to take an oath of secrecy, which is renewed every time they advance to a higher degree. At this point commences the second stage in the candidate's formation; as soon as he has become a Mason, a process of doctrinal formation (or brainwashing) begins, which will continue all his life.

The statements of principle are cleverly worded in vague, generous, humanitarian terms which can be interpreted in many very different ways. Cautiously, and by easy stages, a neophyte learns that these terms have a hidden meaning, a higher meaning, which he will not understand until he has undergone further initiation. In this way, he learns, one by one, of a succession of hidden meanings, which he is told are an ascent towards the Light, and in which he gradually becomes steeped. This is the purpose of the succession of different degrees; if the Mason is receptive, he climbs upward in the Masonic hierarchy, and yet he never at any time knows exactly where he stands in it, nor how many higher degrees or persons control the organisation. As in the secret Communist organisation, one is never very sure whether the titular degrees correspond to the real seat of power.

Freemasonry is therefore in a sense a succession of secret societies superimposed on one another, whose mode of operation has been slowly laid bare, at least in broad outline, by a series of patient investigators; nevertheless, it remains unknown to the public at large and, all in all, continues to be very effective.

To justify the above statements, here are a few Masonic texts emanating from highly-placed dignitaries in the Order, who themselves admit to being initiates at a high level.

> "*The Blue Degrees*", wrote Albert Pike, "*are but the outer court or portico of the Temple. Part of the symbols are displayed there to the Initiate, but he is intentionally misled by false interpretations. It is not intended that he shall understand them; but it is intended that he shall imagine he understands them. Their true explanation is reserved for the Adepts, the Princes of Masonry.* The whole body of the Royal and Sacerdotal Art was hidden so carefully, centuries since, in the High Degrees, as that it is even yet impossible to solve many of the enigmas which they contain. It is well enough for the mass of those called Masons, to imagine that all is contained in the Blue Degrees; and whoso attempts to undeceive them will labour in vain, and without any true reward violate his obligations as an Adept. Masonry is the veritable Sphinx, buried to the head in the sands heaped round it by the ages."
> (A. Pike: *Morals and Dogma*, p. 819)

The well-known English Mason, Wilmshurst, says the same thing:

> "The method in question (of Freemasonry) is that of initiation; the usage and practice is that of allegory and symbol, which it is the Freemason's duty, if he wishes to understand his system, to labour to interpret and to put to personal interpretation. If he fails to do so, he still remains—and the system deliberately intends that he should—in the dark about the Order's real meaning and secrets, although formerly a member of it."
> (W. L. Wilmshurst: *The Masonic Initiation*, 1957, pp. 4-5)

And further on he says:

> "We profess to confer initiation, but few Masons know what real initiation involves; very few, one fears, would have the wish, the courage, or the willingness to make the necessary sacrifices to attain it if they did."
> (W. L. Wilmshurst, ibid., p. 17)

For his part, Brother Oswald Wirth, so praised by Mellor, tells us:

"When Freemasonry, or for that matter any other confraternity based on initiation, prides itself on its impenetrable veil of secrecy, it is not a case of the transferable but of the intelligible content of the mysteries. One can divulge only the dead letter, not the spirit, which of its own accord reveals itself to those who are privileged to understand.

"It is a serious matter to ask for Initiation, for one has to sign a pact. Agreed, there is no external, formal, visible signature; it cannot be compared with signing one's name in blood, for being purely moral and immaterial, it demands that the man's soul be truly committed in the act. It is not, then, like driving a bargain with the Devil, in which the Evil One allows himself to be tricked; it is an agreement entered into seriously on both sides, and there is no escape from its clauses. The Initiates in fact contract into certain duties towards the pupil thus admitted to their school, yet the pupil himself is by that very fact indissolubly bound to his masters. . . .

"Note that the guides are never seen and do not thrust themselves forward. . . .

"At the basis of any real initiation there are certain duties contracted. Beware then of knocking at the door of the Temple if you are not resolved to become a new man. . . .

"*It would all be nothing more than a snare and a delusion, if you could ask to be initiated free of all obligation, without paying with your very soul for your entry into brotherly communion with the builders of this great humanitarian edifice, whose design has been traced by the Great Architect of the Universe. . . .*"

(O. Wirth: *L'Idéal Initiatique*, pp. 10-11)

Thus, there is a secret theology in Freemasonry, to use the trenchant expression of Rabbi Benamozegh, in his book *Israel et l'Humanité*, and in this context he is in full agreement with the Masonic writers from whom we have just quoted, whether French, like Oswald Wirth, English, like Wilmshurst, or American, like Albert Pike; whether "regular" or "irregular", to use Mr. Mellor's terms.

Then comes the second stage in the activities of Masonry—secret activity outside the lodges—which consists in spreading and implanting throughout the world the philosophical ideas of Freemasonry under a general cover of humanitarianism.

This work is accomplished by secret infiltration and the undercover circulation of ideas, by means of a technique admirably described for us by the Freemason Régis, when speaking at the Convent of the Grand Orient in 1928:

"Under the Grand Orient's influence, and in the calm and silence of our Temples, we should study all the most important questions affecting the life of communities, of the Nation, and of Humanity at large. Our Brethren will be thoroughly well-informed; they will leave the Temple well-instructed, fully equipped for the struggle ahead. They will leave behind them their aprons and their outward insignia of Masonry; they will go down into the city just as ordinary citizens, but each one will be thoroughly steeped in our outlook, and each, in his own profane circle, in his party or his union, will act according to his conscience—yet, I repeat, he will be saturated in the teaching he has received.

"Rich will be the result—not because it is occult, but because the influence of Masonry will gradually seep in everywhere; to the bewilderment of the profane world, the same spirit and the same unity of action will force their way to the front, and, as in a well-constructed syllogism, a certain conclusion bearing fateful consequences will gradually emerge and impose itself on its profane environment.

"Over and above all our other loyalties, a power we cannot deny governs us; that power is the spiritual power called Freemasonry.

"And why not follow these proud thoughts to their logical conclusion? Because we know more, because we have worked along sounder lines, than the mass of those who belong to profane groups, it is almost inevitable that we should take over their leadership. Let us not hide our light under a bushel; to a large extent it has already happened, and thus many profane bodies are without question receiving an infusion of our warm, living blood. I am perfectly well aware that we do, discreetly, form the élite in all the big social and political parties, and that thus we are sure of being able to control their policy. *It is our duty—I repeat, our duty—to make sure that we control the politicians who are elected*, that we right their wrongs, and show them their mistakes, and reproach them for what they have failed to do. In a word, Freemasonry should be the 'politician's conscience'."

(Brother Régis, Convent of the Grand Orient 1928, p. 256)

Finally, we come to the third stage in the work of Masonry, that of its direct intervention in politics.

This is how Leo XIII described it in his Encyclical of 19th March, 1902:

"Freemasonry is the permanent personification of the Revolution;

it constitutes a sort of society in reverse whose aim is to exercise an occult overlordship upon society as we know it, and whose sole *raison d'être* consists in waging war against God and His Church."

(Encyclical: *On the 25th Year of Our Pontificate*)

It is instructive, in this context, to compare the conclusion of the famous Pope with the following passages from the equally renowned Freemason, Oswald Wirth:

"The cause of Freemasonry became identified with the cause of the Republic, and if electoral campaigns sometimes did absorb too much time in the affairs of the lodges, the reason is that all friends of progress, seeking to strike a final blow at clericals and reactionaries, rallied together under the banner of Masonry."

(O. Wirth: *Le Livre de l'Apprenti*, p. 80)

"If at these moments of civil distress, the lodges had limited themselves to what we may call their normal peacetime occupation, they would have failed in their most sacred duty, for they would have been refusing to defend that heritage of liberties conquered by our valiant ancestors. It is to their honour that they have broken their rule, launching themselves with all haste into the political arena. They formed themselves into electoral committees to save the Republic, forgetful for the moment of that lofty humanitarian philosophy whose cultivation is the basic aim of Freemasonry." (O. Wirth: *L'Idéal Initiatique*, p. 82)

Freemasonry has played a leading part in international politics, and especially in all the revolutionary movements which have shaken Europe and the world since 1789: in 1830, 1848, and 1871 in France; in 1848 and 1917 elsewhere in Europe, to mention only the most important instances. Freemasonry boasts of having been both the inspiration and the secret ruler of the Third Republic in France (1870-1939), and it is Freemasonry which has always been in the vanguard of the struggle against the Catholic Church in France, Italy, Spain, Portugal and Austria—or, in a word, wherever the Church was the religion of the country. We do not propose to re-write that history here, nor even to summarise Freemasonry's political activities; we only mention it to remind the reader that this is a factor which must be taken into account. (For a complete study of this question, see Léon de Poncins: *The Secret Powers behind Revolution.*)

But one point which we must emphasise in this context is the secrecy surrounding all these activities.

Freemasonry is practically never mentioned in the Press; history books are silent about the power and influence of the Order, and governments and parliaments never dare debate such a dangerous subject. Reports of Masonic meetings and Congresses are not available to the public; Masonic magazines and publications are not placed in the Bibliothèque Nationale or the British Museum, although the law of the land demands it.

In general, we can say that Freemasonry has succeeded in keeping its political activities secret. But no secret can be kept indefinitely, and it is nearly always possible to discover the Masonic origins of such and such a political decision—only by that time it is usually too late to hinder it. We have chosen the following examples from history to illustrate this point:

The peace treaty of 1918 was directly inspired by Masonry. Its clauses had been worked out at a great international Masonic conference which took place on 28th, 29th and 30th June, 1917, at the headquarters of the Grand Orient of France in the Rue Cadet, Paris. This conference was attended by representatives of the leading lodges of allied and neutral countries—Italy, Switzerland, Belgium, Serbia, Spain, Portugal, Argentina, Brazil, the United States (whence two lodges in Arkansas and Ohio, unrepresented, sent cordial greetings) and so on; only the Grand Lodge of England was unrepresented. In 1936 the complete minutes of this meeting came to light and were published in their entirety, accompanied by a detailed commentary, in Léon de Poncin's: *La Société des Nations—Super-Etat Maçonnique*, from which all the information and documents in the following paragraphs have been taken.

Preparations for the Congress in June were put in hand at an earlier one in January 1917, as the minutes of the subsequent meeting relate:

> "In sending you the summary of minutes of the Conference of the Masonic Jurisdictions of the Allied Nations, which was held at Paris on 14th and 15th January, 1917, as well as the resolutions and the manifesto therein adopted, it is our privilege to inform you that this Congress decided to hold a Masonic Congress at the Grand Orient of France, in Paris, on 28th, 29th and 30th of June next.
>
> "*The object of this Congress will be to investigate the means of elaborating the Constitution of the League of Nations*, so as to prevent the recurrence of a catastrophe similar to the one at present raging which has plunged the civilised world in mourning.
>
> "It was the opinion of this conference that this programme cannot be discussed solely by the Freemasonry of the Allied Nations, and that it is a matter also for the Masonic bodies of the

neutral nations to bring what light they can to the discussion of so grave a problem. . . .

"It is the duty of Freemasonry at the close of the cruel drama now being played out, to make its great and humanitarian voice heard, and to guide the nations towards a general organisation which will become their safeguard. It would be wanting in its duty, and false to its great principles, were it to remain silent. . . .

"It is clearly understood that the Masonic Congress will confine itself entirely to the humanitarian field, and that, in conformity with our Masonic Constitutions, it will not touch on any question of a political nature.

"We would be very grateful to receive from you the assurance of your support with the least possible delay. . . ."

(Léon de Poncins; *La Société des Nations*, pp. 65-67)

The Conference opened at half-past two on 28th June, 1917, with Brother Corneau, who was President of the Grand Orient of France, in the chair. He began the meeting with a speech, in the course of which he said:

"This Masonic Congress of the Allied and neutral Nations has come at the right time. We all know the disasters of the past; now we must build the happy city of the future. It is to undertake this truly Masonic work that we have invited you here. . . .

"What are we faced with? This war, which was unleashed by the military autocracies, has become a formidable quarrel in which the democracies have organised themselves against the despotic military powers. . . .

"Thus it is absolutely indispensable to create a supranational authority, whose aim will be not to suppress the causes of conflicts, but peacefully to resolve the differences between nations.

"Freemasonry, which labours for peace, intends to study this new organism, the League of Nations. Freemasonry will be the propaganda agent for this conception of universal peace and happiness. That, my Most Illustrious Brethren, is our work. Let us set to it."

(Léon de Poncins, ibid., pp. 70-71)

Brother Corneau then gave the chair to Brother André Lebey, Secretary of the Council of the Grand Orient of France, who read out his report on the Constitution of the League of Nations, a lengthy document, in which he said:

"The great war of 1914 . . . has gradually and continually brought into definition itself the character of the struggle, which is revealed as one between two opposing principles: Democracy

and Imperialism, Liberty and Authority, Truth proving its good faith, and Falsehood plunging deeper and deeper into shady intrigues . . . (throughout the war) there is not one event which has failed to bear witness to this gigantic duel between two hostile principles. (Léon de Poncins, ibid., pp. 75-76)

"We are invited to succeed in the work which was compromised by the Holy Alliance, by reason of its principles, which are contrary to ours, and through the universal but guaranteed reconciliation of men, to make manifest the proof of our principles. We will crown the work of the French Revolution.

(Léon de Poncins, ibid., pp. 84-85)

"The more one studies the present situation, the more one realises that the abdication of the Hohenzollerns is the means of attaining the League of Nations. It is not for us, my Brethren, to define or demarcate the conditions of peace . . . but we can at least indicate the four principal points which we consider necessary:

(1) The return to France of Alsace-Lorraine;

(2) The reconstitution of Poland by the re-unification of its three separate parts;

(3) The independence of Bohemia;

(4) *In principle, the liberation or unification of all the nations which are today oppressed by the political and administrative organisation of the Hapsburg Empire into States which the said nations shall select by a referendum. . . .*"

(Léon de Poncins, ibid., pp. 95-97)

This speech was greeted with applause, and Brother Corneau proposed the nomination of a Commission to examine the conclusions of Brother Lebey's report. In the opinion of Brother Nathan of the Grand Orient of Italy, the Committee should only deal with the Charter of the League of Nations, and discuss and vote upon the articles of which this Charter is composed, which was the principal object of the reunion of the Congress.

The second session opened the following day at half-past three. The conclusions presented by Brother Lebey on behalf of the Commission were adopted by the Congress. They contained, among others, the following resolutions:

"The unity, autonomy and independence of each nation is inviolable. A people which is not free, that is to say, a people which does not possess the liberal and democratic institutions indispensable to its development, cannot constitute a Nation.

"International legislative power is to reside in a Parliament. Just as the Constituent Assembly in 1789 drew up the Table of the Rights of Man, its first care will be to draw up the Table of the Rights of Nations, the charter guaranteeing their rights and their duties."

(Léon de Poncins, ibid., pp. 106-107)

Brother Urbain proposed that these resolutions should be sent to all the Governments of the Allied and Neutral Nations, and this was adopted. Then, after the resolution of the Italian delegation had been laid before the delegates, Brother Meoni of the Symbolic Grand Lodge of Italy read the following report:

"Reality . . . shows us that there exists one unique and supreme necessity: *future humanity must be established on absolutely new foundations,* secured by the conclusion of solemn treaties which should include the creation of an international Court of law, effectively supported by an international force. *Thus, the reconstitution of Europe and the humanity of the morrow cannot be abandoned to the whim of dynasties, diplomats, and ruling class interests.*

"It is obvious that we are confronted with two diverse and antipathetic conceptions of the nature and functions of the State. On the one hand is the imperialist idea, which despises the rights of peoples and is today represented by the preying empires which unleashed the criminal aggression, and on the other hand, the democratic idea, which asserts these same rights.

"Hence the necessity, for the peace of the world, that the conception of an aggressive military hegemony be destroyed. How will this result be achieved? Doubtless, through the integral triumph of the principle of nationalities. 'National life', wrote Joseph Mazzini, 'is the means; international life is the end'. The whole destiny of Europe and of the new humanity is involved in the resolution of this problem of nationality. After the failure of the German plan will come the Federation of the United States of Europe, by liberty and by right.

"How, then, will this end be achieved?

"Firstly, by the suppression of all despotism . . . and secondly, by the regulation of international conflicts by arbitration."

Brother Meoni then read the resolution of the Italian delegation which, among other things, affirmed:

"The unflinching determination of all the Masonic Powers represented at the Congress . . . to see that nations which had been shattered or even obliterated by long centuries of despotism and militarism . . . had the right to reconstitute themselves."

(Léon de Poncins, ibid., pp. 110-115)

After discussions, this resolution was adopted, and the Congress then approved the following motions:

"This Congress sends to Mr. Wilson, President of the United States, the homage of its admiration and the tribute of its recognition of the great services he has rendered Humanity.

"Declares that it is happy to collaborate with President Wilson in this work of international justice and democratic fraternity, which is Freemasonry's own ideal,

"And affirms that the eternal principles of Freemasonry are completely in harmony with those proclaimed by President Wilson for the defence of civilisation and the liberty of peoples. . . ."

In the third motion, the Congress:

"Declares that faithful to their traditions, and like their glorious ancestors, the Freemasons today are still the devoted labourers of the emancipation of the human race,

"Warmly appeals to all the Brethren for their support in the task of bringing into being the League of Nations, which alone can guarantee the future and the liberty of peoples, and international justice and law." (Léon de Poncins, ibid., pp. 117-118)

With this passage we end the quotations from the Minutes of the Congress, but it is worth inserting at this point, as a conclusion which effectively sums up the above, Brother André Lebey's communication to the Council of the Order on 9th December, 1917.

"*It is a question of knowing which is right: good faith or lies, Good or Evil, Liberty or Autocracy. The present conflict is the continuation of that which began in 1789, and one of these two principles must triumph or die.* The very life of the world is at stake. Can Humanity live in freedom; is it worthy of it? Or is it fated to live in slavery? That is the vital question in the present catastrophe, and all the democracies have given their answer.

"There is no question of retreat or compromise. In a war in which the opposing principles are so clearly and distinctly defined, no one could hesitate as to his duty. Not to defend our country would be to surrender the Republic. Our country and our Republic, Socialism and the spirit of Revolution, these are inseparably bound together."

(Léon de Poncins, ibid., p. 62)

Weigh these texts carefully word for word, and it will be found that they actually assert the incredible theory that, while the rights of each nation are inviolable, nevertheless a people which is governed by an autocratic régime does not constitute a nation! In other words, Freemasonry accords its protection to all peoples except those who evade its own democratic and revolutionary law, and the League of Nations, denying all rights to nations whose political régime was not considered sufficiently democratic, under the influence of Masonry became an organ for control and coercion at the service of its international policy. Thus when the conflict between Italy and Ethiopia broke out, the League of Nations unhesitatingly took sides against Italy.

A number of other important conclusions flow from the revelations contained in these texts.

Firstly, as we have seen the Masonic Congress of 1917 opened by loudly proclaiming that it would not discuss any question relating to politics. But it proceeded to discuss the means of elaborating the Constitution of the League of Nations and guiding the nations towards a general organisation which would become their safeguard, the abdication of the Hohenzollerns, the principal points necessary for inclusion in the peace treaty, the establishment of future humanity on absolutely new foundations, the destruction of aggressive military hegemonies, the reconstitution of Europe in the Federation of the United States of Europe, the regulation of international conflicts by arbitration, and so on, all of which are purely matters of the highest political interest to the nations of the world. These facts cannot be denied. It is apparent, therefore, that Freemasonry lies.

Next, as we have seen, the Congress declared its desire for the suppression of all despotism. But, as we relate in other chapters in this work, Freemasonry openly prepares the way for the triumph of Communism, than which no more accomplished system of despotism has yet been devised.

Indeed, in an article published in the secret Masonic review, *l'Acacia*, in 1910, Brother Hiram recognised that:

> "*. . . We have overthrown, undermined, destroyed and demolished with a fury that at times seemed blind.*"

And why have they done this? The reason, he says, is:

> "so that we can rebuild in the best conditions with taste and solidarity. But," he goes on, "since the ground is littered all round us with ruins which are the result of our work, it is high time that we applied ourselves to learning our truly Masonic rôle as builders."

The whole tenor of the Masonic Congress of 1917 is permeated with this idea of the destruction of the ancient world, upon which a new world is to be built inspired by Masonic principles.

Finally, it must be observed that all the conclusions adopted in the course of these talks at the Masonic Congress in 1917 became an integral part of the Treaty of Versailles two years later. Most important of all was the setting-up of the League of Nations which, in the light of the documents above, appears to have been a kind of Masonic supra-State.

Freemasonry was thus the chief beneficiary, in a political sense, of the First World War. Hers were the principles and hers the men who were in charge of European politics from 1918 to 1930. Mr. Coolidge, late president of the United States of America, publicly admitted as much when, in a speech at Hammond on 14th June, 1927, he said:

> "The chief question at stake in this formidable conflict was to decide which form of government was to predominate among the great nations of the world: the autocratic form or the republican form. Victory finally remained on the side of the people."
>
> (*Reuter*, London, 14th June, 1927)

The results were disastrous. The Treaty of Versailles quickly led to a widespread breakdown of order, to revolutionary unrest, to the opposing reactions of the Fascist and Hitler régimes, to the Spanish Civil War, and finally to the Second World War.

Now, apart from the initiates who were present at the Congress in 1917, no one at that time knew anything about the secret meeting, nor of the part it played in drawing up the Treaty of Versailles. It was only many years later that I was able to obtain the official report of the Conference, which I published in the afore-mentioned book in 1936. It is a frightening thought that an occult organisation, owing responsibility to no one, can direct the course of European politics without anyone being aware of the fact.

Our second example of the Masonic origins of political decisions is taken from the Left-wing coalition, or Cartel des Gauches, which was victorious in the 1924 elections in France, and brought M. Herriot to power. The Convent of the Grand Orient that year sent him a loyal address:

> "Before we begin, allow me to send greetings from all Freemasons to our great citizen Herriot, who, although not himself a Freemason, is so successful in putting into practice our Masonic ideas."

His government introduced a series of Socialist laws which proved to be a foretaste of Léon Blum's Popular Front.

But not long after the Cartel des Gauches came to power, a most remarkable book was brought out by the Spes publishing house under the pseudonym of A. G. Michel. His *La Dictature de la Franc-Maçonnerie sur la France* provides some of the most complete documentation ever produced on the activities of Masonry in politics. Freemasonry, as will be shown from its own statutes, led the campaign which brought the Cartel des Gauches to power, and initiated in secret in the lodges practically all the laws subsequently passed by the Herriot administration. The documents we reproduce below are taken from Michel's book.

First of all, Freemasonry organised and co-ordinated the left-wing parties:

> "On the eve of the legislative elections, what is needed by the Republicans? It is *that the countersign be sent forth by the Grand Orient of France. . . . It is incumbent upon Freemasonry to give the countersign. It should be listened to; Freemasons should be the liaison agents of future victories. You can do it. It is up to you to vanquish the delegates of the National Coalition.*"
>
> (Convent of the Grand Orient, 1923, p. 315)

> "Thus we must organise the defence of the Republic. It is through the union of the Left, of which the lodge will be the cell, that we will triumph. We must bring together all republicans of good will, and even join with the Communists in adopting a programme to which all efforts can be made to rally."
>
> (Convent of the Grand Orient, 1922, pp. 236-237)

> "Surely Masonry, which brings together in its bosom republicans of all shades of opinion, is specially designated to bring to an end the divisions which exist in the *avant-garde* parties? Fraternally united on our columns, why shouldn't we be even more so outside our temples, in order to ensure the defence of Democracy and Freedom of Thought against the clerical and reactionary coalition?"
>
> (Convent of the Grand Orient, 1922, p. 266)

The next step centred round the struggle for power. Freemasonry had no illusions about its objective, which was:

> "To get rid of the present Chamber of Deputies."
>
> (Convent of the Grand Orient, 1922, p. 104)

> "The democratic idea has been imperilled by the resurgent and cunning schemes of clerical reaction. Have we any chance of hoping for a favourable intervention from our present leaders?

. . . I declare that our present leaders are visibly held prisoner by clerical and capitalist reaction. . . ."

(Convent of the Grand Orient, 1923, p. 308)

"We, who want to raise up France for the Republic and Peace, by the Republic and Peace, we are resolved to take over power from the National Coalition in order to bring the country the remedies and the well-being which it has the right to expect from a majority which has set out to restore it."

(Lecture "La Faillite ou la République", by J. Schmidt, Deputy for the Oise, given at the Lodge Action Socialiste, 7th February, 1924)

How was Freemasonry to achieve this objective? A campaign of propaganda and penetration was organised throughout the country. Michel shows from Masonic documents how the lodges were instructed to study and prepare public opinion, and to conduct what can best be described as Masonic public-opinion polls throughout the country to determine the best ways of uniting Left-wing parties to combat the clerical reactionaries.

Very considerable attention was devoted to the Press.

"The Convent of the Grand Lodge of France protests against every manoeuvre of a coalition of big papers preventing the diffusion of Left-wing papers, and thus creating a monopoly which destroys the liberty of the Press. Freemasons have a duty to employ all practical means to oppose these intolerable schemes."

(Convent of the Grand Lodge of France, 1923, p. 94)

"Circular No. 5 concerns propaganda through the Press, and asks lodges to bring to our attention the names of papers likely to publish reports of the Grand Orient, and information on their regularity, their clientele, the quantity of their circulation, and their political sympathies . . . so that the Council may send them whatever communication they think fit . . . and to enquire among the republican Press upon whose support Freemasonry could rely if necessary. . . . Our largest financial support must be reserved for the Press which is republican in outlook."

(Convent of the Grand Orient, 1922, pp. 372-374)

"The Departmental Press . . . which has preserved the flame of republican opinion . . . is the best guardian of our tradition. . . . The Convent asks the Council to draw the attention of the lodges to the experiment of the lodges in Lower Normandy, which have set up a weekly paper entirely edited by Masons, and to call upon the lodges to follow this example, following different local circum-

> stances, and set up papers throughout the whole of France produced entirely under our control."
>
> (Convent of the Grand Orient, 1922, pp. 374, 380)

Individuals were also encouraged, under the strict supervision of the Order, to produce their own propaganda.

> "When a serious, interesting and instructive work has been written by a Brother, the lodge should not hesitate to have it printed, without revealing its identity. As far as written propaganda is concerned, the Commission is of the opinion that pamphlets and tracts provide the most immediate and fruitful means through which to radiate our ideas. We must ask Freemasons to let us sift everything that they intend to say or write with our fraternal criticism."
>
> (Convent of the Grand Orient, 1922, pp. 274, 279, 385)

> "Written propaganda, coupled with the personal influence of Brethren belonging to the Press, should be increased by oral propaganda in the form of white meetings and conferences . . . public conferences, white meetings and fêtes, are regarded as a good means of propaganda by the lodges . . . they are more useful than can be imagined, for the guests are select people who become, in their turn, excellent propagandists."
>
> (Convent of the Grand Orient, 1922, pp. 269, 276, 387)

All this concerted campaign was not without its effect, and indeed in the following year we find the lodges congratulating themselves on the success of their work:

> *"Masonic propaganda, we learn with joy, is making itself felt everywhere, in the most happy circumstances. Soon we will see the awakening of republican opinion in this country."*
>
> (Convent of the Grand Orient, 1923, p. 305)

Finally, in 1924, Masonry's efforts met with success, the Cartel des Gauches came into power, and thereafter promulgated a whole succession of laws, almost every one of which had previously been suggested in the lodges:

(1) The lodges demanded the suppression of the French Embassy at the Vatican.

> "The order of the day comprised two distinct parts: the former was a protest by the Grand Lodge of France against the renewal of relations with the Vatican, for it is evident that if this renewal, as we fear, takes place, it will begin a movement of regression

against the laws of laicisation which we have had so much trouble to get passed by the Chamber."

(*Bulletin Officiel* of the Grand Lodge of France, September, 1920, p. 14, and many other sources which we have not the space to reproduce here.)

On 17th June, 1924, M. Herriot declared that "we have decided not to maintain an Embassy at the Vatican", and on 24th October, 1924, the Embassy was suppressed.

(2) The lodges requested that the law on religious bodies should be enforced.

> "The lodge *Le Travail Ecossais* of Dijon . . . demands, and with reason, that our parliamentary Brethren request the Government to apply the law and to forbid members of Congregations which are seeking to re-establish themselves in France to teach, either in groups or individually, profiting from the inertia or reactionary attitude of the present Chamber."

(*Bulletin Officiel* of the Grand Lodge of France, Convent 1922, p. 220, among others)

On 17th June, 1924, M. Herriot declared: "We have decided . . . to apply the law on the Congregations", and on 27th September, he told the French Cardinals, "As far as the religious congregations are concerned, Your Eminences should not be surprised that the Government defends the law and remains bound to it." This was followed by various enforcements of the law.

(3) The lodges desired to see the triumph of laicism.

> "It is in the defence of the school and of the spirit of laicism that we will find the programme which can and should bind together the whole Republican party."

(Convent of the Grand Orient, 1923, p. 255)

> "The question which is more than ever important today is to study and apply rapid, energetic and decisive measures to defend the work of laicisation accomplished by the Republic."

(Convent of the Grand Orient, 1922, p. 219, and other sources.)

On 17th June, 1924, M. Herriot declared: "The idea of laicisation, as we conceive it, comprises the safeguard of national and fraternal unity." This was followed by various enforcements of the law.

(4) The lodges demanded a general free pardon for all traitors and those under sentence of death, notably Marty, Sadoul (both notorious Communist leaders), Caillaux, Malvy, Goldsky and others. (See, among other sources, a Grand Conference "Pour l'Amnistie" held at

the headquarters of the Grand Orient on 31st January, 1923, *Bulletin Hebdomadaire*, No. 339, 1923, p. 13.)

On 15th July, 1924, a vote of pardon was passed in the Chamber by 325 to 185.

(5) The lodges protested against the Orders in Council (Grand Lodge of France, February to April 1924, pp. 209-210), and M. Herriot declared, on 17th June, 1924: "In order to re-establish the guarantees to which all are entitled, we ask you to suppress the Orders in Council."

(6) The lodges requested a constituency poll (See, among other sources, the Grand Lodge of France, 1922, p. 287), M. Herriot made a statement about it on 17th June, 1924, and the desired action was voted on 23rd August by 232 votes to 32 in the Senate.

(7) The lodges demanded the enforcement of the principle of laicisation in Alsace-Lorraine, in spite of promises previously given to the contrary. (See, among other sources, the 1923 Convent of the Grand Orient, p. 271.) M. Herriot made a statement on 17th June, 1924, which was followed by various enforcements.

(8) The lodges demanded the establishment of a single type of school and the monopoly of education.

> "The principle of the single type of school, whereby all children, to whatever social class they belong, are brought together under the same system of teaching, seems to flow naturally from the conceptions laid down by the revolutionaries in 1789 and 1793."
>
> (Convent of the Grand Lodge of France, 1923, p. 46)

On 17th June, 1924, M. Herriot said: "Democracy will not be completely secure in our country while the availability of places for secondary education is determined by the wealth of the parents instead of the merit of the children."

This was followed by various enforcements.

(9) The lodges requested that France should resume diplomatic relations with Soviet Russia (*Bulletin Officiel* of the Grand Lodge of France, October 1922, p. 286), M. Herriot declared, on 17th June, 1924: "We are preparing as from today to renew normal relations with Russia", and this was followed by the official resumption of diplomatic relations with the Soviet Union on 28th October, 1924.

(10) The lodges demanded that the economy should be organised so as to prepare the way for full-blooded Socialism.

> "The practical realisation of the nationalisation of industry must be pursued by every possible means."
>
> (Convent of the Grand Orient, 1923, p. 96, among other sources.)

On 17th June, 1924, M. Herriot declared: "The Government will develop the national production by all the means within its power . . . instead of suppressing the State industries, we wish to modernise them." Details of the various enforcements carried out in this field are listed on pages 74-83 of A. G. Michel's *La Dictature de la Franc-Maçonnerie sur la France.*

(11) The lodges adopted a policy of emancipation and laicisation with regard to the colonies (See the Convent of the Grand Orient of France, 1923, p. 247, among other sources), the implementation of which is described in A. G. Michel's book (ibid., pp. 91-94).

(12) The lodges expressed hostility to discipline in the Army.

> "From the point of view of the Army, no citizen ought to be called up for any time longer than is strictly necessary for his instruction. In time of war, the military Commander will be subordinate to the civil authorities . . . the military law courts will be suppressed. . . ."
>
> (Convent of the Grand Orient, 1922, pp. 142-143)

On 17th June, 1924, M. Herriot declared: "We propose to reorganise the Army . . . so as to reduce active military service in such a way that France will never at any moment find herself unprepared and weakened", and this was enforced in various ways.

(13) The lodges support the League of Nations.

> *"The League of Nations which we desire will have all the more real moral force and influence as it will be able to depend on the support of Masonic Associations throughout the entire world."*
>
> (Resolution of the Grand Lodge of France, 1923, p. 97)

> "It is the duty of universal Freemasonry to give its absolute support to the League of Nations, so that it no longer has to be subject to the partisan influences of Governments. . . ."
>
> (Convent of the Grand Orient, 1923, p. 23)

> "The principal tasks of the League of Nations consists in organising . . . the extension of a general pacifist education, relying, especially, on the development of an international language . . . the creation of a European spirit, and a patriotism loyal to the League of Nations. in short, the formation of the United States of Europe, or rather the Federation of the World."
>
> (Convent of the Grand Lodge of France, 1922, pp. 235-236)

On 17th June, 1924, M. Herriot declared: "We will do everything in our power to strengthen the League of Nations"; subsequently he achieved the recognition of the principle of arbitration by the League of Nations at the London Conference, and the League was further enhanced when M. Herriot and Mr. Ramsay MacDonald, the Prime Minister of Great Britain, attended sessions in September, 1924.

The third example of the secret, Masonic origin of a political decision is the Conference of Yalta.

In spite of belated reservations on the part of Churchill, the Yalta agreements were concluded between President Roosevelt and Stalin in the strictest secrecy and without the knowledge of the American people. (see Chapter 9).

These agreements were a complete diplomatic disaster for the West. Roosevelt yielded to Stalin, without anything being given in return, half Europe and a large part of Asia.

Since then, certain documents have been published in America showing that Benes played a large part in drawing up the details of the Yalta agreement. As a Freemason, Benes always enjoyed considerable influence over Roosevelt; both were high-degree initiates; it was Benes who convinced Roosevelt of the necessity of placing such blind trust in Stalin; and Benes was always a fervid admirer of Stalin, an admiration which eventually led to the loss of his country and indirectly cost him his life.

Let us confine ourselves to these three examples of Masonry's influence on politics, though it would not be difficult to quote others.

From all this we must conclude: it is a frightening thought that an occult organisation, owing responsibility to no one, can thus in secret direct the policies of one country or of a group of countries.

Those Presidents, Ministers and deputies who are Masons keep their membership of the Order as far as possible secret. They never advertise the fact that they are Masons when facing their constituents or their Cabinets.

Nevertheless, as Masons, they have taken an oath of secrecy, and for all practical purposes, of obedience. What will happen, then, if a conflict arises between their duty to their country and their secret loyalty to the Masonic Order—in other words, if there is a conflict between the interests of the Nation and the interests of Freemasonry? Which will win? Which will carry the most weight? For any country, such a situation is fraught with peril.

This is why so many governments, Catholic, Protestant, Orthodox, Moslem and others, have officially banned Freemasonry. The problem has arisen once more in Soviet Russia. There is a brief account of it in the Freemason Vinatrel's book, *Communisme et Franc-Maçonnerie*.

The Communists accept aid and friendship from Freemasonry

whenever they are offered, but they take good care that Communism is not infiltrated and taken over by Masonry.

"As the doctrines, policies and discipline of Communism are constantly confronted by the doctrines, morals and traditions of Freemasonry, the Freemason who is also a Communist finds himself in a dilemma—shall he remain faithful to his party and betray Masonry, or remain faithful to the Masonic ideal and renounce his party?

"On one particular point (among many others), the Communist Party can charge any member of the party who is also a Mason with perjury. At his initiation, the Freemason takes a solemn oath never to reveal anything which he may have heard, said or done. He is so bound in honour.

"To which the Communist Party replies: '*The Communist Party could never allow any of its members to join in secret activities the nature of which is hidden from the Party, all the more so if the member is a militant Party worker.*'

"This statement was published by André Fajon in *l'Humanité*, the central organ of the French Communist Party, on Friday, 19th September, 1952, in the name of the Bureau Politique of the French Communist Party."

(G. Vinatrel: *Communisme et Franc-Maçonnerie*, pp. 139-140)

Freemasonry imposes a rigid discipline on its members, and the various Grand Lodges, at least, are strict on one point: Freemasons occupying political posts owe obedience, above all else, to the orders and directives of Masonry. The Order does not always manage to obtain this unconditional obedience, but it always insists upon it as the Mason's duty.

"*As soon as a Freemason is elected to the Chamber of Deputies he has this imperative duty: to remember that he is still a Mason and that he must always act as a Mason.* But since, as we realise, many have failed to adhere to this standard, the Commission asks you to demand this oath of any Freemason seeking entry to politics: that he will join and assiduously attend all meetings of the Brethren in his Assembly, and that while he is there he will always be inspired by the purest spirit of Masonry."

(Convent of the Grand Orient, 1928, p. 255)

"When a Freemason is received into a lodge, he takes an oath. If he is a Deputy, he is responsible to his constituents, but he is also responsible to us.

"We do not want politicians who are Masons to adopt a dual attitude: one which they display in Parliament, and the other in the lodges. We do not want to see politicians having a foot in both camps: one in the lodge, and one in the Bishop's palace."

(Convent of the Grand Orient, 1929, p. 48)

"Politicians who are Masons, and who are consequently in some degree emissaries of the Order, should remain subject to it during their term of office. As politicians, they must be guided by the work of the general Assembly, but in every circumstance of their political life they have a duty to obey those principles which govern us." (Convent of the Grand Orient, 1923, p. 365)

"Those Freemasons holding public office have a duty to apply the principles of Masonry, and those of them who have been invested with an electoral mandate—either sought by themselves or approved and tacitly invested in them by their Brethren—have, for all the more reason, a duty exceeding that of all other Masons, never to forget those Masonic principles which have fashioned their personality or their political fortunes."

(Convent of the Grand Orient, 1923, p. 365)

"It is in our Lodges that our Brethren will acquire a philosophical spirit. Let us guard it lovingly, for it is the secret of political influence. Our strength lies in this silent resource of which past generations of Masons set us such an example as they worked to establish that ideal which we hold in common."

"Quite apart from the organisation of the lodges, I would like to give you a rapid summary, as I see it, of the organisation and exercise of power, such as we should bear in mind. We must exercise constant control; we must hear and question all those of our Brethren who, by their professions, touch on politics, the law or administration. . . .

". . . *Democracy must of necessity directly exercise control of power through our lodges* and through those of our Brethren who are Senators or Deputies. It is through such supervision that the organisation of a Democracy progresses. . . ."

(Convent of the Grand Orient, 1924, p. 442)

"Without seeking to intervene in party disputes, the Convent finds its trust persistently betrayed by Masons in Parliament, and condemns those who have not the courage, when voting, to apply the ideas which they display when they are in the Temples. It calls on them, in the higher cause of Masonry and the Republic, to choose between their electoral interests and their duty to Masonry." (Convent of the Grand Orient, 1930, p. 50)

We shall conclude this brief survey of the work of Freemasonry with the official report of the Extraordinary General Assembly of the Spanish Grand Orient, held at Madrid on 20th February, 1932, and on several days following.

The evidence you are about to read is of capital importance, for it provides proof of the close supervision exercised by Masonry over those of its members who occupy political posts, and of the strict obedience it demands of them—an obedience on oath to secret directives, for failing which they are liable to Masonic justice.

The importance of the last point is that Freemasonry has denied that it holds it members to account for failing to obey its directives, but this document provides irrefutable proof that this is precisely what it does do.

The document was originally published by the author in full in the *Revue Internationale des Sociétés secrètes* on 15th December, 1933. Here, we have reproduced the principal passages:

Official Bulletin of the Spanish Grand Orient, Madrid, 10th September, 1932, VIth year, No. 64, page 13:

"Decisions taken at the Extraordinary General Assembly of the Spanish Grand Orient on 20th February, 1932, and succeeding days.

"First motion on the Agenda

"(2) All Freemasons of the Spanish Grand Orient will confirm their oath according to the rank they hold; those absent or impeded will do so in any suitable way, and those present, at the first meeting of their lodge. The Venerable Master will warn the Freemasons that *they must renew their oath, verbally or in writing, to be always ready to appear before their respective judges in order to explain and justify the correctness of their Masonic conduct in every aspect of their Masonic or secular life.*

"(7) The Lodges and Triangles will file a report on each Freemason, on which will be recorded his actual work, the posts he holds or has held in the State or private enterprise, and the reasons for his leaving; as also a record of his meritorious services and Masonic achievements. This file must be specially complete and specific for those Masons holding a political post through popular vote or by Government nomination, such as councillors, deputies, etc. . . . The said files will be sent to the Grand Lodge of the district concerned, to be transmitted to the C.P. of the G.S.F.C.

"Second motion on the Agenda

"(11*a*) The Masonic authorities are bound to see to it that, as often as necessary, *Freemasons holding public positions renew their oaths to explain and justify their conduct as Masons before their superiors.* And since, in carrying out public duties, a Mason may transgress Masonic rules by act or omission, it is evident that such a Mason will be bound not only to explain and justify those actions that seem culpable or doubtful, but also to receive Masonic rules of conduct and to observe them.

"(*b*) Freemasons in public posts must be reminded of their duty of charity and fraternal tolerance, and care must be taken that this spirit of Masonic brotherhood remains above all differences of opinion which may separate them in political contests.

"(*c*) All this supervision, help and collaboration will depend on the Lodge of the Degree concerned, and should be carried out in a spirit of absolute respect for the political views of Masonic Brothers, without the slightest trace of partisan spirit, but solely for the defence of the great principles of our August Order.

"(13) In order to be able to determine correctly the immediate or remote projects of Freemasonry, this Assembly should not limit its scope merely to drawing up rules regarding certain concrete facts, but it is its business especially to ratify, recall to mind and to explain the fundamental principles which guide the whole movement.

"And this we must do in the religious, political and social spheres.

"It is the function of this Assembly to recall and explain the Masonic principles which, in these three spheres, should inspire the work of Spanish Masonry today and in the future.

"Work in the religious sphere is the most important thing. It is the foundation of all the others, since every political and social doctrine must be erected on an ethical foundation, which in turn is based on metaphysics, or an attempt to explain the order of the the world—such an explanation constituting a religion in the widest and noblest sense of the word."

From our study of the Masonic documents from which we have quoted in the course of this chapter, there emerges one very clear conclusion.

Contrary to what those who defend Freemasonry claim, it is evident that secrecy, as observed under different forms and within the different spheres of Masonry's activity, is of vital importance to the Order, for without it, Masonry would simply be just another political party among many, and it would lose its subtle and formidable efficiency, which has turned it into a first-class instrument in the service of subversion.

4

JUDAISM AND FREEMASONRY

THE affinities between Jewry and Freemasonry have often been described in works on Freemasonry, and in this respect perhaps Mgr. Jouin can claim to have revealed the greatest understanding and knowledge of this formidable problem in his remarkable works.

Mellor, nevertheless, considers that the very theme itself is absurd and iniquitous, and he ascribes its origin to the ignorance, stupidity and bad faith of antimasons.

"Antimasonry, which had not thought of mobilizing the Devil in the service of the publishers until the middle of the nineteenth century, left the Jews in peace for just a little longer. Their turn was to come, however. The Crémieux Decree of 1871 (by which Algerian Jews became full French citizens, whereas Algerian Arabs were only French subjects), the prosperity of the House of Rothschild in the world of finance, the bitterness stored up against Lord Beaconsfield (Disraeli), and the Dreyfus affair above all, revived that mental illness which flares up at certain periods of human history, dies down, then erupts again, like a volcano, and which is called anti-Semitism.

(A. Mellor: *Our Separated Brethren*, p. 263)

"The last quarter of the nineteenth century saw the birth of a neologism, *judeo-masonry*, and the rapid growth of anti-judeo-masonic writing. . . .

"A dogma was born: that Freemasons were merely puppets whose strings were pulled by the Jews. There were even caricatures to illustrate this brilliant discovery, inevitably depicting a Jew with an extraordinary nose and a fez on his head, manipulating a marionette dressed in the Masonic apron and sash.

"Some believed that Freemasonry had been made up by the Jews, as was proved by the names of Elias Ashmole, Martinez de Pasqually, the Élus Coens, and by the taste of the higher degrees in past times for the Kabbala. Some people even exhumed that old, old story according to which a Jew was at the source of every heresy. Others 'proved' Jewish origin through masonic symbolism

(Solomon's Temple, pillars J and B, etc.). The idea of a Puritan origin based on English Biblism didn't occur to anyone. The wisest people were content to accuse an 'anti-Christian union' between Jewish high finance and the Masonic politics of the Third Republic. The latter definitely existed, incidentally, but it was no less definite that the Jewish Freemasons in business circles and political committees were by no means religious Jews; quite the opposite.

"The height of bad faith was reached, beyond any doubt, with the famous legend of the *Protocols of the Elders of Zion,* which was a criminal forgery.

"The Jews at first noticed with astonishment the strange paternity attributed to them. But eventually they saw it as one more bee in the bonnet of the anti-Semites. Many, out of prudence, adopted a very careful attitude towards Masonry.

"In the twentieth century Nazi theories and the attempted genocide which they produced dealt 'anti-judeo-masonry' a mortal blow. Many decent Frenchmen who, previously, had broken out in written or spoken violence now found themselves face to face with reality, and were utterly confounded. In most of them the voice of a Christian conscience spoke a new language, much to their own surprise. They had never wanted torture of their adversary, nor extermination camps. Still less had they wanted the world made the slave of a paranoiac.

"That was the end of 'anti-judeo-masonry'."

(A. Mellor: *Our Separated Brethren,* pp. 263-265)

This passage represents a categorical assertion by Mellor; yet it is no more than an assertion, for no text, no document, and no fact whatever is adduced in support of it. It is flatly contradicted, on the other hand, by many Jewish and Masonic writers.

In a work written in 1914 and recently republished, and which, we are told, is a most important example of Jewish thinking, the Rabbi Elie Benamozegh tells us:

"*What is certain is that Masonic theology corresponds well enough to that of the Kabbala.* Moreover, a profound study of Rabbinical works in the first centuries of the Christian era provides abundant proof that the Haggada was the popular form of a secret science, whose methods of initiation bore the most striking resemblances to Freemasonry.

"Those who take the trouble to examine the question of the links between Judaism and philosophic Masonry and the mysteries in general, will, we are sure, lose some of their lofty contempt for the Kabbala."

(Rabbi Elie Benamozegh: *Israel et l'Humanité,* p. 73)

And the editors add, in a footnote at the bottom of the page:

"To those who may be surprised by the use of such an expression (Masonic theology), we would say that *there is a Masonic theology in the sense that there exists in Freemasonry a secret, philosophic and religious doctrine, which was introduced by the Gnostic Rosicrucians at the time of their union with the Free Masons in 1717*. This secret doctrine, or gnosis, belongs exclusively to the High, or philosophic, degrees of Freemasonry."

No less clear and categorical on this point is the great Jewish authority on anti-semitism, Bernard Lazare, who in his time defended Captain Dreyfus.

"What then was the connection between these secret societies and the Jews? The problem is a difficult one to solve, for respectable documentary evidence on the subject there is none. It is clear, however, that the Jews were not the dominant factors in these associations, as the writers whom I have just quoted would have it (Lazare refers to Barruel, Crétineau-Joly, Gougenot des Mousseaux, Dom Deschamps and Claudio Jannet); they were not 'necessarily the soul, the heads and the Grand-Masters of Freemasonry', as Gougenot des Mousseaux maintains. *It is true, of course that there were Jews connected with Freemasonry from its birth, students of the Kabbala, as is shown by certain rites which survive.* It is very probable, too, that in the years preceding the outbreak of the French Revolution, they entered in greater numbers than ever into the councils of the secret societies, becoming indeed themselves the founders of secret associations. There were Jews in the circle around Weishaupt, and a Jew of Portuguese origin, Martinez de Pasquales, established numerous groups of illuminati in France and gathered around him a large number of disciples whom he instructed in the doctrines of re-integration. The lodges which Martinez founded were mystic in character, whereas the other orders of Freemasonry were, on the whole, rationalistic in their teachings. This might almost lead one to say that the secret societies gave expression in a way to the twofold nature of the Jew in, on the one hand, a rigid rationalism, and on the other, that pantheism which beginning as the metaphysical reflection of the belief in one God, often ended in a sort of Kabbalistic theurgy. There would be little difficulty in showing how these two tendencies worked in harmony; how Cazotte, Cagliostro, Martinez, Saint-Martin, the Comte de Saint-Germain and Eckartshausen were practically in alliance with the Encyclopaedists and Jacobins, and how both, in spite of their seeming hostility, succeeded in arriving at the same end, the undermining, namely, of Christianity.

"This, too, then, would tend to show that though the Jews might very well have been active participants in the agitation carried on by the secret societies, it was not because they were the founders of such associations, but merely because the doctrines of the secret societies agreed so well with their own."

(B. Lazare: *Antisemitism*, pp. 308-309)

A third refutation of Mellor's assertion, showing that a large part of the very symbolism of Freemasonry is Jewish in origin, is taken from the pen of an English writer, who was probably Jewish, from a passage in which he concludes a study of this particular question:

"Although I have not, by any means, dealt with the Hebraic influences on all the symbolism of Masonry, I hope I have given sufficient illustrations to support the deduction that *Masonry, as a system of symbolry, rests entirely on a foundation which is essentially Hebraic.*"

(B. Shillman: *Hebraic Influences on Masonic Symbolism*, p. 31)

Elsewhere, the well-known historian Nesta Webster writes in her excellent work, *Secret Societies and Subversive Movements*, that

"the masonic coat-of-arms still used by the Grand Lodge of England is undoubtedly of Jewish design",

and she continues, quoting from an article by Lucien Wolf, the Jewish historian and scholar, which appeared in the *Transactions of the Jewish Historical Society of England* (vol. II, p. 156):

"'this coat is entirely composed of Jewish symbols and is an attempt to display heraldically the various forms of the Cherubim pictured to us in the second vision of Ezekiel—an Ox, a Man, a Lion and an Eagle—and thus belongs to the highest and most mystical domain of Hebrew symbolism.'

"The fact remains," she concludes, "that when the ritual and constitutions of Masonry were drawn up in 1717, although certain fragments of the ancient Egyptian and Pythagorean doctrines were retained, *the Judaic version of the secret tradition was the one selected by the founders of Grand Lodge on which to build up their system.*"

(pp. 123-124)

We will now go on to compare Jewish and Masonic texts, and in the course of our study we shall often find that there is a basic affinity between them, both in doctrine and conception.

We set out below a few examples of their fundamental connection.

Firstly, at the 1902 Covent of the Grand Orient, Brother Delpech, who was Grand Master of the Grand Orient, delivered a speech in the course of which he said:

> "The triumph of the Galilean has lasted twenty centuries. In his turn he is dying. That mysterious voice, which once cried: 'Great Pan is dead!' from the mountains of Epirus, is today proclaiming the end of that deceiving God who had promised an age of peace and justice to those who would believe in him. The illusion has lasted long enough; but the lying God is disappearing in his turn; he is going to take his place, amidst the dust of the ages, with those other divinities of India, Egypt, Greece and Rome, who saw so many deluded creatures prostrate themselves before their altars. Freemasons, we realise, not without joy, that we ourselves are no strangers to this downfall of false prophets. The Church of Rome, based on the Galilean myth, began to decline rapidly from the very day on which the Masonic association was established. From a political point of view, Freemasons have often differed among themselves. But at all times Freemasonry has stood firm on this principle—to wage war against all superstitions and against all forms of fanaticism."

Now let the reader compare this passage with another from the pen of a most distinguished Jewish writer, James Darmesteter, who was at work at the end of the first decade of the twentieth century. Like the Freemason Delpech, Darmesteter was fanatically opposed to Christianity. We quote a few typical passages from his *Prophètes d'Israel* as reproduced and commented upon in André Spire's *Quelques Juifs*, a book devoted to the modern prophets of Israel.

Darmesteter proclaims the end of Christianity. He shows us Christ, propelled by an invisible hand, rejoining in the pit of Sheol those other gods, brothers and victims of his, whom man had conceived before him and whom man had sacrificed to Christ out of obedience to his wishes.

> "And a sigh passed over that world of chaos, and Hell shuddered to the deepest fibres of its roots.
>
> "And a light shone in the night from all those burning eyes . . . and I saw a white spectre descending from afar off on high. He came—slowly, but without stopping or turning his head. It was Christ, the Son of Man, the Son of the Virgin! . . .
>
> "Hell also knew him, and Hell's thousand legions leapt forward to welcome their approaching guest. . . .
>
> "And a tremendous shout burst from the throat of the pit:

"'So you have come at last, Galilean! So here you are, stricken, just as we are; no different from ourselves!'

"'How did you fall from Heaven, Star of the Stars, Son of the Virgin? You, who used to say in your heart: I am God, world without end; I shall reign for eternity from the highest throne in Heaven, above the stars and the broken idols, and my name alone shall ring in men's ears.'

"'And now in turn your star has been cast down and broken, cedar of Lebanon, and you, the great mocker of dead gods, you too descend among the gods who live no more.'

"Little has changed in the progress of the world. Nature is unmoved by the spectacle of this great defeat, and as always happens after events which seem to exceed the limits of tolerance assigned to her, she continues, indifferent, upon her eternal course.

(A. Spire, *Quelques Juifs*, Vol. I, p. 243)

"For man is not the work of a God who existed before the world began. It is man who has created his own gods in the image of his own dreams, and who casts them down when his dream changes, content if the new dream is sweeter and offers him a nobler ideal."

(A. Spire, ibid., vol. I, p. 238)

The similarity between these two passages is so striking that one is justified in suggesting that Delpech drew his inspiration directly from Darmesteter; but whether he did or not, what does stand out is a marked identity of thought between a Jew and a Freemason who were both well-known personalities in their respective communities.

In his defence of Freemasonry, Mellor mocks the old, old story, according to which a Jew was at the origin of every heresy.

But it was Darmesteter who wrote the following passage, a truly terrible indictment, overflowing with centuries-old Jewish hatred towards Christianity, in which he stressed Israel's revolutionary rôle, published in an article entitled "Coup d'oeil sur l'histoire du peuple juif" (1880):

"The Jew championed reason against the mythical world of the spirit. It was with him that thought took refuge during the intellectual night of the Middle Ages. Provoked by the Church, which sought to persuade him, having in vain attempted to convert him by force, he undermined it by the irony and intelligence of his arguments, and he understood as nobody else did how to find the vulnerable points in its doctrine. He had at his disposal in this search, apart from the wisdom of the sacred scriptures, the redoubtable wisdom of the oppressed. *He was the doctor of unbelief; all who were mentally in revolt came to him, either secretly or in broad daylight.* He was at work in the vast laboratory of blasphemy under the great emperor Frederick and the princes of Swabia and Aragon. It was he who forged all that deadly arsenal of reasoning and irony which he bequeathed to the sceptics of the Renaissance and the libertines of the grand siècle (the reign of Louis XIV); Voltaire's sarcasm, for example, was nothing more than the resounding echo of a word murmured six centuries previously in the shadow of the ghetto, and even earlier (in the Counter-Evangelists of the first and second centuries) at the time of Celsus and Origen at the very cradle of the Christian religion."

(Quoted by A. Spire in *Quelques Juifs*, Vol. I, p. 233)

It would be easy to multiply comparisons of this kind from the copious Jewish and Masonic texts which have come to light. But to simplify our study, we will confine ourselves to the few examples from which we quote, and which in themselves sufficiently demonstrate the point we are trying to elucidate.

The relationship between Judaism and Freemasonry is most clearly summarised in the following article, which appeared in 1861 in a Parisian Jewish review, *La Vérité Israélite*. Although over a century old, it is still applicable to the situation today, and we conclude this chapter by reproducing it in full.

"The connections are more intimate than one would imagine. Judaism should maintain a lively and profound sympathy for Freemasonry in general, and no matter concerning this powerful institution should be a question of indifference to it.

"For a very long time, owing to the progress in morals and public liberty, Freemasonry has been able to abandon its rôle of a mysterious secret society, forced by the fear and tyranny of former governments to veil itself in prudent obscurity. Its principles and methods have been known to the public for so long that it cannot be difficult to understand its spirit and its aims.

"But the spirit of Freemasonry is that of Judaism in its most fundamental beliefs; its ideas are Judaic, its language is Judaic, its very organisation, almost, is Judaic. Whenever I approach the sanctuary where the Masonic order accomplishes its works, I hear the name of Solomon ringing everywhere, and echoes of Israel. Those symbolic columns are the columns of that Temple where each day Hiram's workmen received their wages; they enshrine his revered name. The whole Masonic tradition takes me back to that great epoch when the Jewish monarch, fulfilling David's promises, raised up to the God of Abraham, Isaac and Jacob, a religious monument worthy of the creator of Heaven and earth—a tradition symbolised by powerful images which have spread outside the limits of Palestine to the whole world, but which still bear the indelible imprint of their origin.

"That Temple which must be built, since the sanctuary in Jerusalem has perished, the secret edifice at which all Masons on earth labour with one mind, with a word of command and secret rallying-points—it is the moral sanctuary, the divine asylum wherein all men who have been reconciled will re-unite one day in holy and fraternal Agapes; it is the social order which shall no longer know fratricidal wars, nor castes, nor pariahs, and where the human race will recognise and proclaim anew its original oneness. That is the work on which every initiate pledges his devotion and undertakes to lay his stone, a sublime work which has been carried on for centuries."

(*La Vérité Israélite*, vol. V, p. 74, 1861)

The oneness of the human race, the goal towards which Judaism and Freemasonry work hand-in-hand, "with a word of command and secret rallying-points", is the unification of the world under Jewish law.

"Let us now examine more closely the picture of the Messianic age, when justice and brotherhood shall reign over the earth, according to Deutero-Isaiah, whom it is well to remember is the most universal in tendency of the Prophets.

"'What is certain,' writes Mr. Loeb, 'is that with or without the King-Messiah, the Jews will become the centre of humanity, with the Gentiles, after their conversion to God, grouped all around them. The unity of the human race will come about through religious unity. That is to say, if I understand the meaning of the words correctly, the Messianic age will be marked by the triumph of Jewish exclusiveness, in which the reign of justice means the strict observance of the law of Yahweh and his Prophets, the law of the poor; in a word, Jewish law. . . .'

"This is purely and simply imperialism, political, social and religious imperialism. To be quite sure, we have only to follow Isidore Loeb's guide to the description of messianic times in Deutero-Isaiah:

"'The nations will gather to pay homage to the people of God; all the fortunes of the nations will pass to the Jewish people, they will march captive behind the Jewish people in chains and will prostrate themselves before them, their kings will bring up their sons, and their princesses will nurse their children. The Jews will command the nations; they will summon peoples whom they do not even know, and peoples who do not know them will hasten to them. The riches of the sea and the wealth of nations will come to the Jews of their own right. Any people or kingdom who will not serve Israel will be destroyed. The chosen people will drink the milk of nations and suck the breasts of rulers; they will devour the wealth of the nations and cover themselves with their glory. The Jews will live in abundance and joy, their happiness will have no end, their hearts will rejoice, they will flourish like the grass. The Jews will be a race blessed by God, they will be the priests and ministers of God; the whole people will be a righteous people. The descendants of the Jews and their name will be eternal; the least among them will multiply a thousand-fold, and the most lowly will become a mighty nation. God will make an eternal covenant with them; he will reign anew over them, and their power over men will be such that, in a hallowed phrase, they will march in great strides over the high places of the earth. Nature herself will be transformed into a kind of earthly paradise; "it will be the golden age of the earth. For I, the Eternal One, love justice and hate plunder and iniquity; I shall faithfully give them their reward".'

"The dream of the poor, their ideal of justice, is no more humble, nor any less resplendent, than that of the Prophets. Yet there is a difference: the poor man is fiercer.

"'It cannot be denied,' says Isidore Loeb, 'that the poor man goes too far in his hatred of the foe and in his thirst for revenge. At certain moments his anger becomes almost insensate, and he breaks out into curses which makes us shudder. He desires to do evil for evil to the foe with his own hands; he will declare war upon him and triumph over him; he will call upon the God of vengeance for help; his own eyes will witness the fall and punishment of the foe; he will mock his enemy, and his feet will trample in the blood of his foe. . . .'

"'Psalm CIX is nothing less than a long cry of hatred and vengeance against the foe.'"

(After quoting the text, Mr. Loeb adds: "It is a curse in all its horror.")

"As for the final result of the messianic revolution, it will always be the same: God will overthrow the nations and the kings and will cause Israel and her king to triumph; the nations will be converted to Judaism and will obey the Law or else they will be destroyed and the Jews will be the masters of the world.

"The Jews' international dream is to unite the world with the

5

SATANISM, NATURALISM AND FREEMASONRY

A NUMBER of the opponents of Freemasonry have linked the Order with Satanism and have attributed the doctrinal inspiration which animates the spiritual life of Freemasonry to supra-human origins, to a force of Evil.

Mellor strongly rebukes this point of view, and claims that it has been invented by the anti-masons.

> "The Catholic faith accepts the existence of a Spirit of Evil and its intervention in human behaviour. The normal form of this intervention, temptation, is not the only one. It emerges from the Scriptures, and it is unanimously accepted by the Fathers, councils and theologians that in addition there exists a second, more tangible, kind of intervention, called diabolical possession. We have neither the competence nor the intention of examining it, and on this question we would refer the reader to the works of specialist theologians, particularly the well-known and rightly praised studies by Father J. de Tonquédec. Nevertheless we need this reminder in order to note how the antimasonic elucubrations on the Devil's account are merely the caricature of a genuine branch of theology.
>
> (A. Mellor: *Our Separated Brethren*, p. 255)

> "Until the middle of the nineteenth century no one took it into his head to accuse Freemasons of being Luciferians or Satanists—not even writers like the Abbé Fiard, who saw the Devil all around; not even Barruel. Such an imputation would in any case have brought ridicule on their books.
>
> "Let us bring counter-proof: it is well known that Luciferians and Satanists have existed ever since the Middle Ages.[1] It does not appear that they were ever recruited from among the Masons, and we should be hard put to it to quote from one serious docu-

[1] The Luciferian is a worshipper of the fallen Archangel, considered as the source of Good; God, under the name of Adonai, is considered as the source of evil; in his view Lucifer was unjustly condemned. The complete Satanist, if he existed, would be a worshipper of Evil in itself.

ment dating from before the mid-nineteenth century having any pretensions to the contrary. . . .

"The idea that the Devil lurked among the higher degrees was very tempting to nervous minds, haunted with medieaval visions. Everything that we know about the higher degrees in the eighteenth century contradicts their theory. . . . (A. Mellor, ibid., p. 256)

"In 1867, Mgr. de Ségur, the son of the good Countess *née* Rostopchine, a prelate admirable for his spirit of charity and apostolate among the poor, started what was to be the long series of a whole inept literature. . . .[1]

"His book ran to nine editions in three months (30,000 copies), thirty-six editions in less than five years. He launched the legend, which was to prosper, of the 'inner lodges', where he stated that Black Masses were celebrated, and which the publisher, in his foreword, claimed had sentenced the author to death. . . .

(A. Mellor, ibid., p. 257)

"In 1894 Dr. Bataille, a doctor with the shipping lines, whose real name was Hacks, published *Le Diable au XIXe siècle*, an enormous quarto volume of close on one thousand pages. Many illustrations: nothing but devils everywhere. One of them—no doubt he wanted to see just how far the credulity of the public would stretch—depicted the *Quadrille maçonnique, exécuté par les initiés de l'Ordre des druides*. He reproached Taxil for his insufficient anti-Semitism!

"Taxil tricked even a respectable colonial bishop, Mgr. L. Meurin, Bishop of Port Louis (Mauritius). (A. Mellor, ibid., p. 258)

"Mgr. Meurin was far from being an uncultivated man, and there is no doubting his good faith, but he did establish the most fantastic connections between the 'discoveries' which he thought he had made in the course of his reading. He was a frenzied interpreter, literally intoxicated by Taxil. . . .

(A. Mellor, ibid., p. 259)

"This deluge of follies continued to pour down until the Second World War. Then came the Nazi occupation. Real atrocities made people forget verbal extravagances and the ferment of the imagination. The antimasonry of the nineteenth and early twentieth centuries was now dead.

[1] His doctrine was more uncertain. His *Jesus vivant en nous* was placed on the Index by an order of the Holy Office dated June 30, 1869. (The author submitted—Notes by A. Mellor.)

"In 1948 Jules Boucher published an excellent treatise on *Le Symbole maçonnique,* in which, not uncharitably, he is content to say:

"'It would be too easy to multiply the quotations from Catholic authors which evince gross antimasonic fanaticism. We shall not be so cruel.'

(A. Mellor, ibid., p. 231)

"This nonsense, incidentally, has not yet disappeared in some regions, it would appear.

"According to a very reliable witness, the furniture of a lodge was being sold one day, and an old peasant woman came up, very curious, to the Master's chair, asking to see the slot where the Devil put his tail whenever he took his seat!

(A. Mellor, ibid., p. 262)

". . . The old anti-Masonic school considered that Freemasonry consisted of Luciferian coteries guided by the Devil himself, and assisted by a strange general staff of Jews, occultists and radical politicians. Some had even got to the point of allowing that there were interconnections between these groups and spy circles."

(A. Mellor: *La Franc-Maçonnerie à l'Heure du Choix,* p. 414)

Finally, Mellor asserts that the Encyclicals have never linked Freemasonry with Satanism.

But, in spite of his claims, the Encyclicals, while they say nothing of Black Masses, do insist that Masonic doctrines are inspired by Satan, and one can hardly accuse Leo XIII and other modern Popes of being the victims of mental illnesses in the form of an obsessional psychosis—terms which Mellor is rather too ready to apply to people who defend traditional values.

Let us refer to the Encyclical *Humanum Genus.*

"After the human race, through the envious efforts of Satan," it begins, "had had the misfortune to turn away from God, who had created it and bestowed on it the supernatural life of grace and other heavenly gifts, it became divided into two distinct and mutually hostile camps. One of these steadily combats for truth and virtue, the other for all that is opposed to virtue and truth. The former is the Kingdom of God on earth, namely, the true Church of Jesus Christ, and all who wish to belong to it sincerely and in a manner worthy of salvation must serve God and His Only-Begotten Son with all the vigour of their minds and all the strength of their wills. The latter is the kingdom of Satan, under whose sway and in whose power are all those who, following the baneful example of their leader and of our first parents, refuse to obey the divine and eternal law, and in many ways either show contempt for God or openly revolt against Him. . . .

"From what we have already set forth, it is indisputably evident that their (the Freemasons') ultimate aim is to uproot completely the whole religious and political order of the world, which has been brought into existence by Christianity, and to replace it by another in harmony with their way of thinking. This will mean that the foundation and the laws of the new structure of society will be drawn from pure Naturalism. . . .

"In this mad and wicked design, the implacable hatred and thirst for vengeance with which Satan is animated against Our Lord Jesus Christ becomes almost visible to our bodily eyes."

(ibid. pp. 1, 7, 14)

This Encyclical is dated 1884. In 1892, in a letter to the Italian people, Leo XIII returned to the subject.

"The war of which we speak is directed against both Heaven and Earth.

"But whence does it originate?

"It comes especially from that Masonic sect of which we spoke to you at length in the Encyclical *Humanum Genus*, on 20th April, 1884, and more recently, on 15th October, 1890, when we addressed the Bishops, clergy and people of Italy.

"They (the Freemasons) . . . conceived the Satanic idea of substituting Naturalism for Christianity.

"Let us remember that Christianity and Freemasonry are fundamentally incompatible, so much so that to adhere to the one is to cut oneself off from the other.

"The maxims of the Gospel cannot be reconciled with those of the Revolution; Christ cannot be reconciled with Belial, nor the Church of God with the Church that is Godless."

In a new Encyclical, promulgated on 19th March, 1902, Leo XIII returned again to the subject of Freemasonry:

"Freemasonry is the permanent personification of the Revolution; it constitutes a sort of society in reverse whose aim is to exercise an occult overlordship upon society as we know it, and whose whole raison d'être *consists in waging war against God and His Church. . . ."*

On 20th February, 1959, the assembly of the Bishops of Argentina published a collective statement on Freemasonry, from which we have selected the opening paragraphs:

"In the course of its plenary reunion, the Argentinian Hierarchy, confronted by various articles published in the Press by Freemasonry, felt obliged to make a public declaration to the faithful, following the recommendation of Leo XIII to 'first of all, tear away the mask from Freemasonry and let it be seen as it really is. . . .'

"The Popes, the supreme and infallible mentors of civilisation, realising what a danger the sects represent to the world, have from the very first pointed it out, and unreservedly denounced this satanic conspiracy against humanity.

"From Clement XII, in his Encyclical *In Eminenti* of 1738, down to the present day, the Sovereign Pontiffs have repeatedly condemned the Masonic sects, and the Code of Canon Law, Canon 2,335, states: 'Those who join the Masonic sect or any other similar association . . . incur excommunication. . . .'"

The doctrines and aims of Freemasonry were set out by Pope Leo XIII in these terms:

"The immortal Pontiff, Leo XIII in his Encyclical *Humanum Genus*, condemned Freemasonry in these terms: 'Alongside the Kingdom of God on earth, the true Church of Christ . . . there exists another kingdom, that of Satan, under whose sceptre are found all those who refuse to obey God's eternal law and who seek in a multitude of ways to act without reference to God or even directly against Him. . . .' The Pope warned us that: 'in our age all who favour the second of these two camps seem to have made an immense coalition, instigated and aided by a particular society, that of the Freemasons . . . they rival one another as to who can be the most insolent towards God's august Majesty. Publicly and openly they work for the destruction of Holy Church; their aim is, if it were possible, to rob the Christian nations of every one of those benefits which they owe to Our Saviour Jesus Christ'."

(*Verbe*, August 1961)

Now let us allow Masonic texts to speak for themselves.

"Senator Goblet d'Aviella, of the Belgian Grand Orient, made the following remarks in a speech to the Loge des Amis Philanthropiques de Bruxelles on 5th August, 1877:

"'Tell the neophytes that Masonry is not as foolish people imagine, a convivial get-together, a kind of helping-hand to one and all; it is not even a purely benevolent society, nor does it even understudy the rôle of our electoral associations. Tell them that if it does indeed aim to do good, it is good in the widest sense of the word, and that if it does engage in politics, it does so to bear in mind questions of principle of which contemporary politics represent only a partial and secondary application. *Tell them that Freemasonry is above all a school for the popularisation of knowledge and the perfecting of men's minds; it is a kind of laboratory in which the great ideas of the time combine to assert themselves, in order that they may spread through the outside world in a practical and tangible form. Tell them, in short, that we are the philosophers of Liberalism.* Tell them all that, as far as Masonic secrecy permits. . . .'

"Masonic progress is the kind of progress which takes a man obedient to God and to those claiming to be his representatives on earth, and makes of him a morally-emancipated freethinker.

"Camille Pelletan's father, a Deputy for Paris under the Second Empire, was speaking to the Legislature in 1867 in favour of people's Libraries and the freedom to read whatever one wished. He ended: 'Thus shall we bring to birth the final flowering of human progress—the man who is his own king and priest, answering only to his own will and conscience.'

"Words so completely revealing as these call for no comment; the only comment required is a comparison with what is certainly the most ancient Masonic text in the world.

"In the Bible, the book of Genesis, it is written (III, 1-5):

"'Now the serpent was more subtle than any beast of the field which the Lord God had made. And he said unto the woman, Yea, hath God said, Ye shall not eat of every tree of the garden?

"'And the woman said unto the serpent, We may eat of the fruit of the trees of the garden. But of the fruit of the tree which is in the midst of the garden, God hath said, Ye shall not eat of it, neither shall ye touch it, lest ye die.

"'And the serpent said unto the woman, Ye shall not surely die; for God doth know that in the day ye eat thereof, then your eyes shall be opened, and ye shall be as gods, knowing good and evil.'

"Mr. Pelletan said: 'Man is his own king and priest, answering only to his own will and conscience.'

"The serpent said: 'Man shall be as God, knowing good and evil.'

"Where is the difference?"

We have taken the above texts from a remarkable lecture on Freemasonry delivered in Paris in March, 1932, by Maitre Colmet Daage, a barrister of the Court of Appeal.

We shall now quote a text from Oswald Wirth which assumes special importance in this context. Oswald Wirth, a 33rd degree initiate of the Grand Lodge of France, held an eminent position among Masons, having inspired a revival of spiritualism and symbolism in French Masonry, and being also the founder and editor of the review, *Le Symbolisme: Organe Mensuel d'Initiation à la Philosophie du Grand Art*. He was the author of many books on Freemasonry.

Marius Lepage, his disciple and successor as editor of *Le Symbolisme*, is the Worshipful Master of the Volnay Lodge at Laval, and it is in association with Lepage that Mellor and Father Riquet are leading the campaign in favour of closer relations between Catholicism and Masonry.

Mellor praises Oswald Wirth very highly in his books:

> "Secondly, rationalism had to face an attack from inside Masonry itself. This attack was a revival of symbolism. A man of noble mind, Oswald Wirth, whose reforming role we noted in our previous book, realised at the end of the nineteenth century that the anti-symbolists had led Masonry along the wrong path, and founded a group whose object was to restore and honour the study of Masonic symbols. . . .
>
> "The Scottish lodge, Travail et Vrais Amis Fidèles, became under the master's direction the heart of this renewal, and we can realise today that Wirth's work has been of immense influence. Without Wirth, the more intelligent members of the Grand Orient would no doubt have ended up resembling a society like the Rationalist Union, while the less intellectual members would have gravitated to various 'Freethinkers' associations.
>
> (A. Mellor: *La Franc-Maçonnerie à l'Heure du Choix*, p. 148)

> "Oswald Wirth's influence, however, was most effective in certain Grand Orient lodges which were isolated from the mainstream of rationalism. Oswald Wirth himself was indifferent on matters of the respective merits of lodges and the like. As we were able to emphasise in our previous book, the chief seat of this influence was the Volnay lodge at Laval, whose Worshipful Master was for many years Marius Lepage, spiritual son of Oswald Wirth and his successor as editor of *Le Symbolisme*. (He was to leave the Grand Orient in May, 1963)."
>
> (A. Mellor, ibid., p. 151)

We shall now let Oswald Wirth speak for himself. In his book *L'Idéal Initiatique*, he explains to us the significance of a Masonic initiation:

> "It is a serious matter to ask for Initiation, for one has to sign a pact. Agreed, there is no external, formal, visible signature; it cannot be compared with signing one's name in blood, for being

purely moral and immaterial, it demands that the man's soul be truly committed in the act. It is not, then, like driving a bargain with the Devil, in which the Evil One allows himself to be tricked; it is an agreement entered into seriously on both sides, and there is no escape from its clauses. The Initiates in fact are contracting certain duties towards the pupil thus admitted to their school, yet the pupil himself is by that very fact indissolubly bound to his masters. . . . (O. Wirth: *L'Idéal Initiatique*, p. 11)

". . . Note that the guides are never seen and do not thrust themselves forward. . . .

"At the basis of any real initiation there are certain duties contracted. Beware then of knocking at the gate of the Temple, if you are not resolved to become a new man. . . .

"*It would all be nothing more than a snare and a delusion, if you could ask to be initiated free of all obligation, without paying with your very soul for your entry into brotherly communion with the builders of this great humanitarian edifice, whose design has been traced by the Great Architect of the Universe. . . .*

(O. Wirth, ibid., p. 10)

"When the candidate, by his good name, has given proof of the moral integrity required, his first duty is one of discretion: he must undertake to keep silence in the presence of non-Masons, for, as an Initiate, he will be entrusted with secrets which should not be divulged. . . .

"The minor mysteries met with in the Convents are in fact only symbols of much deeper secrets, which the Initiate will discover for himself as he follows the course of the Initiation. . . .

(O. Wirth, ibid., p. 8)

"If the Hermetist's great work is not accomplished in us, then we languish for ever in the ranks of the profane and our dull lead will never change to shining gold. But is anyone so simple-minded as to expect such a miracle? The ceremonies of Initiation are only symbols. They are a visible and external sign of our internal acts of will, which are meant to transform our whole moral personality. If only our outside person is affected, then the whole operation has failed; lead remains lead, even though it appears to be gold from the outside. . . . (O. Wirth, ibid., p. 12)

"When Freemasonry, or for that matter any other confraternity based on initiation, prides itself on its impenetrable veil of secrecy, it is not a case of the transferable but of the intelligible content of the mysteries. One can divulge only the dead letter, not the spirit, which of its own accord reveals itself to those who are privileged to understand. . . .

(O. Wirth, ibid., p. 36)

"From all this there emerges a Masonic faith expressing itself in action and not tied to any one opinion. *Masonry is the Church of Human Progress* and whatever influence she has in the world is due to her undying convictions, which offer Masons a vision of a better, more enlightened, more brotherly future for Mankind. . . .

(O. Wirth, ibid., p. 56)

"Now the strength of Freemasonry lies in the collective will of its members. When they meet it is only to work, and since no energy is wasted, every lodge is a seed-bed of moral and social change.

"But do not ask the vast majority of Freemasons to give reasons for what they do. They act by instinct, following shadowy traditions which for centuries have exercised their suggestive influence.

"Nevertheless there does exist a Masonic doctrine, even if nowhere explicitly formulated in words, which is to Freemasonry what Christianity is to the Christian Churches; we may call it the science of Masonry. . . .

"Now the Great Architect, no doubt because he is less transcendant than the God of the theologians, refers to an entity which does undeniably exist, for the constructive work of Freemasonry has, as its origin and inspiration, an ideal which gives birth to an immense energy. A *force superior to themselves impels Masons and co-ordinates their efforts with an intelligence far exceeding that possessed by any one individual among them*. Such is the hard fact which emerges and before which we bow our heads. Let every man interpret it as he pleases. . . ."

(O. Wirth: ibid., p. 58)

"In the book of Genesis, these ideas are expressed by the myth of the Earthly Paradise, a place of happiness in which primitive man had only to live, as do animals, or children who have not yet come to the age of reason.

"The beguiling serpent, who incites us to eat the fruit from the tree of knowledge of good and evil, symbolises one particular instinct. He breaks away from the conservative instinct and represents both a nobler and a subtler impulse, whose purpose is to make man aware of his need to rise in the scale of beings.

"This secret spur is the promoter of all progress, and of all the conquests which enlarge the sphere of action both of individuals and of groups.

"That explains why *the Serpent, inspiring disobedience, insubordination and revolt, was held accursed by the ancient theocracies, while at the same time he was honoured among the initiated*, who considered that there could be nothing more sacred than those aspirations which lead us ever closer to the Gods, who are seen as rational powers, charged with bringing order out of chaos and with governing the world.

"The object of the ancient mysteries was to make men like unto gods. The mystery took on more of the divine nature as it rose morally and intellectually further and further beyond the level of common humanity. The programme of Initiation has not changed even in our own day; the modern Mason, too, also becomes more divine, but he realises that he can only become so if he works divinely, that is, by completing the unfulfilled task of creation. Raised above the level of man's animal nature, the Builder, by carrying out the divine plan, himself becomes a god, in the ancient sense of the word." (O. Wirth: *Le Livre du Compagnon*, p. 74)

Oswald Wirth believed that man, by giving free rein to his noblest aspirations, is on the path to achieving his own divinity, without the help of any divine power outside himself.

This conception is at the opposite pole from Christianity. As G. Bord so clearly expresses it:

"From a Christian point of view, the Freemasons represent human pride, the spirit of evil, the revolt against God."

(G. Bord: *La Franc-Maçonnerie en France des origines à 1815*, vol. I, p. 5)

Many similar texts can be found in French and European Masonry. This, for example, is what Dr. Raymond Corbin wrote in a book entitled *Symboles Initiatiques et Mystères Chrétiens* (1929), which opens with a preface by the famous Freemason, André Lebey:

"Throughout all history, in India, in Egypt, in the mysteries of Pythagoras or Alexandria, the system of initiation has been constructed on reason; the Christian Church has only collected them together. The system which the initiates' own reason had built up in a symbolic but scientific fashion, through geometrical or numerical calculations, the Church has made into a mystery which she declares to be beyond our understanding; she forbids reason even to try to explain it, and yet it is human reason's own creation or invention.

"To set a barrier on understanding, to cherish obscurity; these are vitally necessary for Christianity; how could she shelter her own authority behind that of a God, if she herself admitted that that God was only the work of a man?

"A symbol becomes a dead thing when congealed by the dogmas of a religion and turned into a Christian mystery, although it may sometimes have an imposing appearance, like a gigantic oak beneath whose bark there is no sap.

"The Church has everywhere sought to fashion a symbol into reality; the bread of the Eucharist, symbolising the fruits of the earth made to blossom by the sun, has become for her the very body of God; wine has become His blood; from the fulfilment of these two principles she has created a God in three Persons.

"These are formulas attributed by some philosopher to the symbols of initiation, and which have thus acquired a permanent character.

"Since they are final, and regarded as God's own revelation, all that they teach man is to submit without understanding; they compel him to shun any new interpretation, in other words, to shun all progress.

"*One day, when humanity is more knowledgeable and more enlightened, it will look at these fables which the Church has made into dogmas, and these principles which the Church declares to be immutable, and it will find them too crude, too full of errors. On that day, the religions of the world will dissolve and disappear. . . .*"

(Dr. R. Corbin: *Symboles Initiatiques et Mystères Chrétiens*, pp. 102, 111)

Let us now turn to Masonry in the English-speaking world, said by Mellor to be regular and religious. We soon find that many of its best-known writers—Pike, Wilmshurst, Buck, Stewart, and others—say exactly the same thing, as the previous authorities from whom we have just quoted, and that the Vatican, therefore, has very serious reasons for making no basic distinction between the different rites or obediences of Masonry.

Here, for example, is what Thomas M. Stewart says in his book *Symbolic Teaching; or, Masonry and its Message.*

"Passing under a domination exclusively sacerdotal and traditional, and losing thereby the intuition of things spiritual (a gross, yet subtly presented distortion, on the part of Masonry which, while reducing everything to a purely naturalistic level of materialism, nevertheless claims to be spiritualising matter—*author's note*), the Church fell an easy prey to that which is the besetting sin of priesthoods, Idolatry; and in place of the simple, true, reasonable Gospel (to illustrate which, the history of Jesus has been expressly designed) fabricated the stupendous and irrational superstition which has usurped his name. Converted by the exaltation of the letter and the symbol, in place of the Spirit and the signification, into an idolatry every whit as gross as any that preceded it, Christianity has failed to redeem the world. Christianity has failed, that is, not because it was false, but because it has been falsified. And the falsification generally has consisted in removing the character described under the name of Jesus, from its true function as the portrait of that of which every man has in him the potentiality, and referring it exclusively to an imaginary order of being between whom and man there could be no possible relation, even were such a being himself possible."

(T. M. Stewart: *Symbolic Teaching*, p. 187)

We must return to primitive truth. Thus Masonry

"will lay the foundation for a grander civilisation that will secure social order, because it will be an organization of individuals actuated by a desire to do right under the Light furnished by untrammeled reason and conscience. Thus shall Justice be Universal and want and misery unknown." (T. M. Stewart, ibid., p. 12)

However, in its march towards the light, Masonry encounters a powerful enemy: the Catholic Church.

"Masonry is a world-wide institution; it teaches independent thinking, and is the only world-wide institution that stands in the way of the Poltico-Ecclesiastical schemes of the Hierarchy at Rome; which is in the control of the Catholic Church, and dominates the good people of that Church who honestly and faithfully follow their misguided leaders. (T. M. Stewart, ibid., p. 58)

"Down through the ages two forces have been engaged in a deadly conflict, a conflict that concerns all the past, a conflict that enthralls the present with evil forebodings and which bodes no good to the future. . . .

"The one force finds today its nucleus for a universal, undogmatic, and unfettered manifestation in our grand Masonic, world-wide institution.

"The other force finds its field of operation in an organised body that seeks to maintain itself without regard to the largest measure of individual liberty and enlightenment.

"Upon one side stands an institution that has 'from time immemorial and through a succession of ages' given LIGHT to all its votaries.

"Upon the other is entrenched an organization that champions ignorance, superstition and fear, and that dominates and controls the reason and conscience of its communicants."

(T. M. Stewart, ibid., p. 31)

This is what Buck says in his book, *The Genius of Freemasonry*:

"What our ancient brethren in the Greater Mysteries called 'the Immortal Gods', were simply perfected by this normal human evolution. . . .

(J. D. Buck, ibid., pp. 28-29)

"First a mollusk, then a fish, then a bird, then a mammal, then a man, then a Master, then a God.

(J. D. Buck, ibid., p. 43)

"The theologians who have made such a caricature or fetish of Jesus, were ignorant of this normal, progressive, higher evolution of man. Hence, the theologian has created an impassable gulf between the man Jesus and the Christ; or between man and God.

(J. D. Buck, ibid., p. 29)

"There has been a tendency, at certain times and in certain directions, to 'Christianize' certain Masonic degrees. Any sectarian or religious bias given to any degree in Masonry is wholly un-Masonic and wholly opposed to the real Genius of Freemasonry.

(J. D. Buck, ibid., p. 34)

"*The Mason everywhere is an enemy of Popery, because Popery seeks to deny, control, or abrogate every right of citizenship. It denies man's right to Life, Liberty and the Pursuit of Happiness. Masons are made out of Free men and not out of slaves. There are, and there can be no free men where Popery has control.* This principle of Freedom lies at the back of Masonry, as it underlies the foundation of this government.

"*It is necessary that the basis, the real Genius of these two Institutions, should be clearly understood and accurately distinguished; for they are exact opposites and are antagonistic to the last degree.*"

(J. D. Buck, ibid., p. 67)

W. L. Wilmshurst, who occupies an important position in English Freemasonry, expresses himself in more cautious terms than his fellow Masons across the Atlantic, but his ideas are similar. He explains to us that Freemasonry is the revival of the ancient Gnosis, the notorious heresy which was a synthesis of the pagan theosophies, against which the early Fathers of the Church waged such a bitter struggle. (See W. L. Wilmshurst: *The Masonic Initiation.*)

It is very interesting in this context to bring forward the testimony, based on his own personal experience, of an ex-Freemason, the writer J. Marquès-Rivière. He left Masonry following the scandals brought to light by the eruption of the Stavisky affair in France (see Chapter 10), and the bloody riots which ensued. He describes the life of the lodge, with its atmosphere of initiation, through which he had himself lived, in his various books.

> "Freemasonry's resistance to the passage of time, and its survival through the vicissitudes of two centuries, are in fact a unique attraction in a body which claims no basis in Divine Revelation. A past of such length presupposes some permanent and unchanging body of doctrine underlying all the varied interpretations of successive generations of adepts.
>
> "If this sect confined itself to party politics, one could leave it to the various parties to look after their interests in their own way. Yet behind all Masonry's feasting and postures, and even clowning, there is something else—something exceedingly formidable, which pulls the strings of all these puppets.
>
> "There is a peculiar flavour, almost a bouquet, throughout Freemasonry. It is an atmosphere of silent foreboding, secret and esoteric . . . a feeling of mystery pervades the sect, forming its attitude, nourishing all its spiritual life.
>
> "Freemasonry speaks of initiations, of spirituality, of mysticism, of religion, of setting man free. Thus it enters, at least nominally, into the realm of Metaphysics. From long experience from within, I have learned that its chief object is a strange reversal of those traditional values which form the very essence of all spiritual life. I have obtained evidence at first hand of the existence of, not exactly a secret plot, but of a whole habit of thought which is anti-traditional, anti-spiritual and anti-Christian. I am the first to admit that this attitude of mind is unconscious, that it is not openly admitted or easily seen. I would agree that there is much good faith and good will in it, and that these qualities are sometimes very moving. But that is not enough.
>
> "What we must flee (in Freemasonry) is a whole world, a whole doctrine, a whole way of thought, a whole hierarchy, a *whole heretical Church. The dangers are great; the risks are fearful. I am not exaggerating if I speak of spiritual death.*

"The utopian idea of man's being sufficient to himself is a form of monstrous, superhuman, truly diabolical egoism. For such an idea to take shape under the collective, rational forms of the present age, one needs to suppose a supernatural origin in order to understand it at all. There is in all this . . . a profound mystery of iniquity, a bitter and terrible spiritual revolt, known to few, but intoxicating many.

"This spirit, born of the Renaissance, dominated the lodges as established by Anderson, who was the spiritual successor of the anti-traditionalists. It reigned supreme over the corrupt society of the eighteenth century, and mastering the popular conscience, it provoked that hideous butchery, that riot of the unchained Beast, the Revolution of 1789. Rising Phoenix-like from its ashes, adopting a thousand different masks, it has ever since reigned supreme over western civilisation."

(J. Marquès-Rivière: *La Trahison Spirituelle de la Franc-Maçonnerie*, pp. 103, 213, 224, 252)

For his part, a German writer, Baron von Stotzingen, has given us a clear summary of Masonry's essence—the worship of humanity.

"In the last analysis, the leaders of Freemasonry mean by this that man is his own master and that there exists no authority either below or above him. Expressed in another way, Humanism means the moral and spiritual autonomy of a mankind liberated from any superior authority; this is fundamental to all true Freemasonry.

"In this conception, of course, no place is left for a personal God outside this world. Nor can there be room for any form of stable government, resting on a divine basis. Carried to its extreme, this idea must end in total anarchy, and in the war of every man for himself against all his neighbours. For without a moral order resting on a divine basis, no legal, social or political form has any real foundation.

"It is true that in many countries Freemasonry does not draw the fundamental conclusions from its own basic principles. In any case, most Freemasons have no suspicion of what those conclusions would be. But this in no way affects the root of the problem.

"When the essence of Freemasonry is defined in this way, we can easily understand why it has such affinities with Liberalism. We can even say that Freemasonry is organised Liberalism, Liberalism's general staff. Nevertheless Liberalism confines itself to recognising the Humanist principle, but rejects its consequences. Socialism, the heir to Liberalism, is much more logical; it unhesitatingly follows its own principles right through to their conclusion, and puts them into practice whenever it can.

"Not only does Masonry's Humanist principle lead to the Revolution; it actually is the Revolution. It expressed itself politically in the 'Rights of Man' in the French Revolution of 1789.

"The spiritual relationship which links Freemasonry with Liberalism and Socialism explains the apparently astonishing fact that the rich Freemason or Liberal is found, in spite of everything, in the same camp as the working-class Socialist—at war with the Conservative conception of the world.

"When we learn more of the profound essence of Masonry, we understand yet another of its relationships: that linking the lodges with the Jewish world. The modern Jew almost without exception, inclines towards a liberal view of the world, a view moving further and further away from any solid basis in positive religion . . . and in the writings of Jewish leaders today there recur the same phrases persistently employed by Freemasonry.

"So it is perfectly logical that at an early period Judaism should have turned towards Masonry, and thanks to its remarkable adaptability, it has gained increasing influence in Masonic circles. It is scarcely an exaggeration to say that today most of the lodges are under Jewish influence and that they form Judaism's spiritual shock-troops.

"*If we look again at the deepest essence of Masonic thought, we realise that the Humanist principle is basically nothing more than the ancient 'Non Serviam', which since the Fall has haunted the mind of man, in perpetual conflict with his better self.*"

(Freiherr von Stotzingen: *Die Freimaurerei und Ihre Weltanschauung*)

To conclude our study at this particular point, we shall show, from original texts, how similar conceptions unite Freemasonry, Judaism and Communism.

Here is the evidence of a Jewish writer of Hungarian origin, who has published very interesting works on Communism and anti-Semitism in Soviet Russia. Fetjö begins by showing us that Karl Marx declared war upon God.

"Before anything else, we must rid ourselves of this myth about God, Karl Marx tells us. I will never weary of repeating: God is the great evil. It is the ghost of God which prevents us from carrying through to the very end of our efforts to bring into existence that vision of which religion is only an abortive dream: the reign of justice and happiness, paradise upon earth.

"The number one exploiter, capitalist and robber of humanity is

God. He it is who is the foundation and moral source of every inequality and evil that exists. He is the great obstacle. Only if we socialise God can we socialise society and humanise man. No task is more important or more urgent, than to arouse man to rebellion against the illusion called God. This will be the revolution to end all revolutions, the last judgment which will unite the good and abase the wicked. As long as the ghost of God haunts the minds of men, there will be no happiness, no real joy, no peace, no tranquility. *With Marx, war is declared against the ghost of God.*

"*It is the most radical of all programmes of revolt.* God was in the beginning man's dream of power, perfection and security. Into this vision the poor puny creature put the very best of himself, his ideal, his glory, the fullest essence of his being. To be like God: that was the dream of Adam and Prometheus, a desire both secret and forbidden—forbidden because desired. To be like God: there lies salvation, Paradise, man's original impulse, the reaping of the harvest, the religion of pleasure and joy.

"How right was Adam in wishing to eat the apple! It was his right and his duty. Far from being blameworthy, his action prefigured the future action of humanity. The whole system of dialectics is contained in it. Would you forbid a poor man to gather dead wood? He will take live wood for his own. Who can prevent him? Who can prevent man, this 'fourth estate', who in himself is nothing, from desiring everything? Who can prevent us, we who are without rights, without property, from taking our pleasure, from reigning, governing, possessing? Only a conscience steeped in mysticism, that turning aside from man's first vision in alienation, the religious ideal which states that God exists but closes all access to God. . . .

(F. Fejtö: *Dieu et son Juif*, pp. 93, 134)

"Religion binds man, it ties him to his past, it paralyses him. . . . To the devil with this teaching of resignation which 'deflects man from fighting for his own interests'. Salvation is not to be found in Heaven, nor in happy idleness: it lies in the future, here upon earth, in the fight for the future and for the earth. *The true Gospel is not a message of humility. It says: man is fully grown; he is his own father. He has no more need of a mystical or any other kind of paternalism.*

"*Louis XIV said: 'I am the State'. But Marx cried: 'We are God. . . .'*

(F. Fejtö, ibid., p. 94)

"We the disinherited of all races, the proletariat, this chosen people. It is through the proletariat, and by ridding himself of all feudal or bourgeois shackles, by shedding all mystical notions, that man will attain to God's stature, loving himself with a love that is infinite. He will expel the Philistines from Canaan, settle himself in the Promised Land, work in joy, feed according to his needs, and develop the forces of production; and having duly chastised the wicked and the landowners, and driven out feudalism, he will cause peace and justice to reign at last."

(F. Fejtö, ibid., p. 95)

Then he shows us the Jewish elements in Marx's ideas.

"Thus Communism, clothed afresh in scientific, dialectical disguise, revived the idea which haunted the Jews of old, that of concrete, material and immediate salvation here on earth.

"Marxism has been linked with German philosophy, with the English economists, and with utopian ideas from France. But in Marx, at the very roots of his thinking, there is a certain 'pathos', a feeling of revolt whose 'judaic' character seems to me beyond question. Marx starts with an attack on religion, and with the most radical criticism of the works of God. He unhesitatingly 'unmasked' religion, and behind its images he found unbared the pathetic spectacle of economic interests.

"God is an illusion. Religion (and here Marx is in perfect agreement with the anti-Christian Nietzsche) is a turning-aside, a deviation, proposing dubious comforts to the alienated man, instead of harnessing his energies.

"With Marx, a 'family quarrel' becomes general, even global. *God is put on trial, in the name of all mankind; he is found wanting; all his attributes of omnipotence and omniscience are now taken over by man, the whole man, the new God, whose Church will be the Communist Party. . . .*" (F. Fejtö, ibid., pp. 134-135)

As we can see, these ideas very closely resemble those advanced in the authoritative studies on the nature of Freemasonry from which we have quoted above and in other chapters in the present work.

"The Jew is patient. He has been patient. . . .

"But patience has its limits. He has complained at last. He has complained to God against God. That is his everlasting suit. You will completely fail to understand the Jew, his torments and his exaltation, if you do not understand that his people are the plaintiffs. His is the people which stands up to claim its due, to denounce God for his injustice. (F. Fejtö, ibid., p. 56)

"People at all costs want the world to believe that in this trial, it is the Jew who is the defendant, whereas all the evidence suggests that it is the Jew who has taken the case to court. He is made to seem at a disadvantage, as the accused, whereas in fact it is he who is the plaintiff.

"For how many thousands of years has the chosen people been at odds with God? The Jews are the people who are angry with God, and for whom this family quarrel has become an obsession.

"You above any other are the jealous people. That is your truth and your falsehood, it is your curse. . . .

"In truth, the terms of the covenant clearly bear the mark of your own particular spirit. You it is who are jealous; you it is who demand of God that he shall have no dealings with other peoples, and that he repudiate all his other progeny.

"All or nothing was your motto, not his. Tyrannical children, you would have him all to yourselves. On the pretext of making him your only Lord, your only Master, your only King, you worked unceasingly to bring him down to your level, to dominate him, to make him the slave and instrument of your national expansion. . . . (F. Fejtö, ibid., p. 106)

"Nothing could be less generous or more possessive than your love of God.

"To put it quite simply, you wanted to be like him, to substitute yourselves for him, to take his place. Nothing less than that!

"You are a jealous people. God is with you! And with you alone, solely for you, by your favour. . . .

"It is not a covenant between equals, it is slavery. It is not a contract, it is dictatorship. . . .

"And then there sprang up in your soul, from the depths of your collective conscience, that quarter where no man dares to venture once the night has fallen, this unutterable, monstrous dream, to make him disappear in one way or another and to substitute yourselves for him, to become like him, to be God.

"You didn't take long to transform yourselves from Adam to Cain and to kill Abel, the best among you, the one whose offering had been accepted. (F. Fejtö, ibid., p. 109)

"And in that again is your sin. Our sin. It is the original sin, which you have made every effort to deny, to turn into a phantom, a myth, an illusion.

"No water on earth can slake our thirst. We are like a wounded beast running from one fountain to another in a fever, but always in vain. We are a gaping sore which never heals. We are a void crying to be filled, but which nothing will ever fill. For this reason and for no other we have become eternal nomads. We cannot remain in one place. Our happiness is always elsewhere."

(F. Fejtö, ibid., p. 111)

One basic conclusion emerges from studying all these texts: the position is that we are confronted by a war of religion, a war whose spirit has been admirably described by the Jewish poet, Heinrich Heine, in his fascinating, terrifying and prophetic book, *Lutèce*, published in 1843:

"The great mass of the public is still much concerned with the incessant war which the clergy continue to wage against the University. The dispute itself will not so soon be resolved, for it has roots in a centuries-old opposition, an opposition which we must perhaps see as the final and fundamental reason for all the unrest of French political life.

"The true meaning of these disputes is nothing more nor less than the ancient struggle between philosophy and religion, between the free exercise of reason and the belief in divine revelation, a struggle which simmered constantly in both the nobility and the bourgeoisie, and in which the rationalists gained the victory in the 1790's. Yes, quite often actors who survived the tragedy which overtook the French state and politicians, whose memories of the times are most vivid, quite often they have let slip in my hearing an admission that, when all was said and done, it was hatred of the Church which caused the French Revolution; and that the throne had been destroyed because it protected the altar. In these men's opinion, a constitutional monarchy could already have been established under Louis XVI, but it was feared that the orthodox King would not have been able to remain faithful to the new Constitution, out of pious scruples of conscience. They feared that his religious convictions were dearer to his heart than his own worldly interests, and so Louis XVI fell victim to this fear, this preoccupation, this suspicion. He was suspect in their eyes; that was his crime, and in those days of terror it was punishable by death.

"Although Napoleon had re-established and favoured the Church in France, his haughty, arrogant will was regarded as a sufficient guarantee that the clergy could never, in his time, advance too many pretensions, still less succeed in dominating the State. He kept as tight a grip on the clergy as on the rest of us, and the grenadiers who marched with rifles at the side of religious processions seemed not so much a guard of honour for the Church as her prison escort. The powerful, iron-sceptered Caesar wished to reign alone, and everyone knew that he would not share his power even with Heaven itself. At the beginning of the Restoration there was more cause for anxiety, and the rationalists again felt secret shivers of fear. But Louis XVIII was a man without religious convictions, a wit who composed bad Latin verses and ate good *pâté de foie gras*. The public were reassured. They knew that he would not risk his crown and head to win Heaven. The less he was respected as a man, the more they trusted him as King. His frivolity was itself a guarantee against even the suspicion that he might favour the black hereditary enemy of liberal France. Had he lived, the French might not have brought about another revolution. That happened only in the reign of Charles X, a king deserving of the highest respect as a man, and whom, everybody was already convinced, would sacrifice all worldly goods for the salvation of his soul. They knew that he would fight with knightly courage and to his last breath for the defence of the Church against Satan and the Gentile revolutionaries. *They drove him from his throne precisely because they considered he was a man of nobility and integrity. So he was, just as Louis XVI had been;* but in 1830, this suspicion was enough to send Charles X to his ruin, and it is also the real reason why his grandson has no future in France.

"It was lucky indeed for the July Monarchy that, by chance and the circumstance of the time it escaped this deadly suspicion. . . ."

(H. Heine, *Lutèce*, Paris 1855)

Heinrich Heine not only wrote lucidly, but showed great vision and insight where the Revolution was concerned. For Heine, famous throughout the world as the admirable and lovely poet of the *Intermezzo*, Heine was also a hate-crazed revolutionary and a fanatical Communist; this is what he tells us himself and loudly proclaims for all the world to read in his *Lutèce*, a book which consists of a selection of articles originally published in the *Augsburg Gazette* between 1840 and 1843:

"I have not described the storm itself. I have described the great storm-clouds which bore the approaching tempest, advancing dark and menacing across the sky. I have made frequent and exact descriptions of those sinister legions, those titans buried underground, who lay in wait in the lowest ranks of society; I have hinted that they would arise from their obscurity when their hour was come. These shadowy creatures, these nameless monsters, to whom the future belongs, were then usually only looked down on through lorgnettes; from this angle they resembled fleas gone mad. But I have shown them in their greatness, in their true light, and seen thus, they resemble if anything, the most fearsome crocodiles and gigantic dragons that have ever emerged from the foul abyss.

"Communism is the secret name of this tremendous adversary which the rule of the proletariat, with all that that implies, opposes to the existing bourgeois régime. It will be an appalling duel. How will it end? That is known to the gods and goddesses in whose hands lies the future. For our part, all we know is that, however little talked-of at present, however miserable an existence it drags out in concealed attics on wretched beds of straw, Communism is nonetheless the dark hero, cast for an enormous if fleeting role in the modern tragedy, and awaiting only its cue to enter the stage.

"There is an approaching rumble of hard times filled with upheavals. Any prophet wishing to write a new Apocalypse will have to invent new monsters so frightful that the old symbolic beasts in St. John would appear in comparison no more than cooing turtle-doves and gracious cupids. The gods hide their faces out of compassion for the poor insignificant human creatures, their wards for centuries, but perhaps also out of fear for their own fate. The future smells of Russian knouts, of blood, of impiety and of violent blows. I advise our descendants to have good thick skins on them when they are born into this world.

"I made this statement, that the future belongs to the Communists, with a feeling of extreme horror and fear. Alas! It was no disguise. Only with fear and terror can I think of the age when those dark iconoclasts will come to power. With callous hands they will mercilessly smash all those marble images of beauty, so dear to my heart: they will shatter all those fantastic toys and trifles which poets used to love so well; they will destroy my laurel-woods and plant potatoes in their stead; the lilies of the valley, which toil not, neither do they spin, yet even Solomon in all his splendour was not arrayed like one of these—these they will uproot from the soil of society, unless they can take up spindle in hand and work. The same fate will befall the roses, those idlers beloved of the nightingale. The nightingales themselves, mere singers producing nothing will be hunted down. Alas! My own Book of Songs will go to the grocer to make cones through which to pour coffee or snuff for the old women of the future. Alas! All this I can see, and I am filled with unutterable sadness when I think of the destruction with which my verses are threatened by this conquering proletariat; they too are doomed to perish with all the old Romantic world.

"*And yet, I frankly admit that this same Communism, so hostile to all my interests and to everything I hold dear, exercises a fascination over my soul which I cannot gainsay.* Two voices rise up within my breast in its favour, two voices which will not be silent, though they are at bottom perhaps no more than temptations of the Devil—but whatever they are, they possess me and no power of exorcism can silence them.

"*And I cry out: this old world society has for a long time been judged and found guilty. Let justice be done! Let it be destroyed,* this old world in which innocence has perished, in which selfishness has prospered, in which man has exploited man. Let them be rent in twain from top to bottom, these whited sepulchres, homes of lies and iniquity. *Fiat justitia, pereat mundus. . . .*"

(H. Heine: *Lutèce*, Paris 1855)

It was the same fanatical, revolutionary spirit that possessed Benes, when he proclaimed, on the eve of catastrophe: "Rather the Anschluss than the Hapsburgs."

In other words: rather invasion, and the ruin of my political ambitions; rather exile and death, rather the triumph of Hitler's Germany; anything rather than the restoration of a Catholic Monarchy in Austria.

And it was the same fanatical revolutionary spirit which filled Léon Blum, and which was so evident in a leading article which he wrote in *Paris-Soir* on 14th November, 1939—a newspaper which at that time had a circulation of over a million copies. Léon Blum was criticising the German-Russian agreement of August 1939 signed by Stalin and Ribbentrop, an agreement which hastened the Second World War, which was to prove so disastrous for Blum's own country, France.

He showed, clearly and rightly, that in August 1939, in the world situation as it then was, Stalin, like the god Janus in former times, was master of both peace and war.

By signing the Germano-Russian Pact with Ribbentrop, Stalin was automatically setting in motion the events which led to the Second World War, and this he realised beyond all possible doubt.

Léon Blum gave vent to his bitterness against Stalin, reproaching him for acting only in accordance with Russia's material and imperialistic interests.

"I say material interests, since I deliberately rule out of his plans any hint of that immense ambition for revolution in which lay the greatness of Communism twenty years ago. Stalin's interests are his personal desire for power and the interests of imperial Russia, just as they were conceived under the Czars."

This text reveals a great deal of the basis of Leon Blum's thinking. The Pact between Russia and Germany in August 1939 unleashed the Second World War and led France into a fearful disaster. None of this matters to Léon Blum, the man who had twice been France's Prime Minister, for neither his country, nor his race, nor his traditions, nor his religion were at stake. Stalin's really serious crime, in the eyes of Léon Blum, thinking as a Jewish international revolutionary, was that he betrayed the spirit of world revolution. Exactly the same accusation was brought against him by Trotsky, and it led to his duel to the death with Stalin.

Trotsky, the cosmopolitan, messianic, Jewish figure-head, the demoniacal magus of world revolution, set against Stalin, the Asiatic, the man of steel, the cold, implacable agent of Soviet imperialism.

"Permanent revolution" versus "Socialism in one country".

The problem is thus a veritable war of religion; the greatest religious war of all time, for it covers the whole world, and there is not one single country on the face of the globe which can escape it.

6

REGULARITY AND IRREGULARITY IN MASONRY

THE school of thought in favour of reconciliation between Freemasonry and the Catholic Church constantly urges the idea of Masonic Regularity and Irregularity.

According to their tenets, and Mellor is of their persuasion, there is "Regular" Masonry, of which the Grand Lodge of England is the archetype, and "Irregular" Masonry, of which the Grand Orient of France, at the head of the Grand Orients of Europe and Latin America, is the archetype.

The question of Regularity and Irregularity in Masonry has been the subject of endless discussion between the different Masonic obediences.

What is it all about? Mellor gives us the following definition of Masonic Regularity:

> "The term Regularity can be understood in two ways. There is regularity of origin and regularity of principles.
>
> (A. Mellor: *La Franc-Maçonnerie à l'Heure du Choix*, p. 61)

> "Regular origin is where an obedience or, within an obedience, a lodge has been legally constituted and consecrated. The English rule is that a new Grand Lodge, to possess regular origin, must be founded by another Grand Lodge itself of regular origin, or by three other lodges of regular origin.
>
> "Nevertheless, an obedience can become irregular. As soon as it repudiates one or several of the essential conditions of its Masonic nature, it becomes profane in the literal meaning of the word. It loses its Masonic quality. The example of this instance usually quoted is that of the Grand Orient of France, which by erasing the name of the Grand Architect of the Universe from its Constitutions in 1877, became in the eyes of all regular Freemasonry a pseudo-Masonry whose principal Landmark had been decapitated, a Masonry Masonic only in name.

"The regularity of principles is thus the juridical state created and preserved by conformity to the former. . . .

"There is one obedience whose regularity is not contested by any other, and that is the United Grand Lodge of England, sprung from the Grand Lodge of London, which was founded in 1717. This is the mother Grand Lodge of all others, the Mecca of Masonry. (A. Mellor, ibid., p. 64)

"Round this kernel cluster the obediences which are 'recognised' by the United Grand Lodge, or in other words, those that are regular according to its definition of the word. Thus, at least in principle, all these obediences recognise each other. It is this enormous bloc, united from the English point of view of regularity, although comprising lawful internal differences, which we will lump together under the heading of Regular Freemasonry.

"Outside this bloc, or to be more precise, outside this agglomeration of obediences, we find other Masonic powers which, since we are following the attitude of the Grand Lodge of England, for the sake of clarity we have grouped under the heading of the Irregular Freemasonries. The use of the plural is justified by reason of the profound differences between them.

"Finally, there is a branch of Freemasonry whose originality and particularity merits a heading on its own: the Scottish Rite. This rite is not an obedience in the administrative sense of the word, but rather a body of obediences following the Royal Art (Freemasonry) in their own fashion. One could almost say that it is an Order within the Order. The word 'rite' moreover, in this context, ought not to be considered synonymous with ritual, but as indicative, to be more exact, of a branch of Masonry.

"The idea of regularity would seem to be a difficult criterion in this instance. Can the Scottish Rite be included in regular Freemasonry? Yes, if one takes it on its historic merits. No, if one accepts the English criterion, for there are some 'Scottish' obediences which the Grand Lodge of England recognises, and others which it regards as irregular, such as the Grand Lodge of France. As an extra complication, the 'Scottish' obediences do not all recognise each other.

"A former Grand Master told me one day that the Scottish Rite was a 'great Power'. He was right.

"We do not wish to class the Scottish Rite with irregular Masonry, but since we cannot include it in the 'regular' bloc, which denies its regularity, we have chosen to describe the Scottish Rite as non-typical Freemasonry. Will this term shock some people? We cannot judge the question of Masonic truth. For that matter, does such a thing as Masonic truth exist? Yes, it certainly does, from the English point of view, but what would be the reply of nine out of ten real Scotch Masons to this question?"

(A. Mellor, ibid., p. 65)

As can be seen from the above, Mellor himself hesitates to assert the principle of Masonic regularity. Elsewhere, he adds:

"*There is a universal Freemasonry, if by this term one understands not the organic but the spiritual entity of which the Order is composed (the English Craft).*

"But, contrary to an all too prevalent error, Freemasonry is not —unlike the Church—subject to an administrative unity, even of a federal kind.

"If it knows no magistracy, this is precisely because it has no papacy.

"When one talks about the Masonic institution, that is only a manner of speech, for, historically, Freemasonry has not been instituted. . . .

(A. Mellor, ibid., p. 55)

"The different sovereign powers or bodies in Masonry are called obediences. The Grand Lodge of France or the Grand Orient, for example, are called obediences. From the eighteenth century onwards they have excommunicated each other in the most ecclesiastical manner. They have their heresies and their schisms. But that poses a problem, for the existence of heresy presupposes the existence of orthodoxy. If Masonry has no magistracy, where does Masonic orthodoxy reside?

"The Grand Lodge of England and those who have interpreted its attitude (the 'doctrine' as the jurists would say) have replied by stating that there exist in principle certain basic, traditional and immemorial assumptions, the Landmarks.

(A. Mellor, ibid., p. 56)

"The list of landmarks has varied from one epoch to another, from one Masonic authority to another, from one author to another. . . .

(A. Mellor, ibid., p. 57)

"As we shall see later on, agreement on the Landmarks was never reached either between Masonic authorities or between authors depicting the 'doctrine'. In 1921, as a result of rapprochements begun in the First World War, the International Masonic Association was formed; twelve obediences joined it, and it published a declaration aiming at achieving doctrinal unity. . . .

"The agnostic inspiration of the Grand Orient of France was

visible in this document—there was no reference to the Grand Architect of the Universe. No criterion of regular origin.

(A. Mellor, ibid., p. 58)

"The reaction of the Grand Lodge of England was inevitable, and on 4th September 1929 it sent an eight point memorandum to all the obediences in relation with it." (A. Mellor, ibid., p. 59)

This step marked a clear regression from the gnostic rationalism of Anderson in 1723, and a return to a diffuse form of Christianity.

"In 1938 Oswald Wirth published his resounding work, *Qui est régulier?* and in 1956, pushing latin logic to its extreme limits, a Mason as traditionalist as Marius Lepage, in his *L'Ordre et les Obédiences,* challenged the very concept of regularity itself."

(A. Mellor, ibid., p. 60)

The principle of regularity as maintained by the English is hotly disputed by the other Freemasons.

Here, on this subject, is the point of view of the Grand Orient of France as presented by Brother Corneloup, Grand Commander of Honour of the Grand College of Rites, in his book *Universalisme et Franc-Maçonnerie,* written in 1963:

"The Grand Lodge of London and Westminster, founded in 1717, rapidly set about extending its jurisdiction. In 1726 its head proclaimed himself Grand Master of England; it swarmed to the continent, and especially to France, the home of numerous Stuart supporters and Orange diplomats, many of whom were Freemasons.

"The first French lodges seem to have been opened by them, at an uncertain date, but definitely before 1728. Once the example had been set, they were quickly copied.

"Originally the obedience was called the English Grand Lodge of France, but despite the descriptive adjective, which was not abolished until 1756, it behaved as if it was an independent power, and not a provincial Grand Lodge coming under the jurisdiction of London. The English were distinctly annoyed about it, as can be seen from the minutes of the Grand Lodge of England from 1734 onwards. . . .

"The bitterness clearly reveals that London considered that it was the mother Grand Lodge, and that all the others were subsidiaries whom it wanted to keep in its dependence, the sign of a strong desire to set up universality to its exclusive profit.

(J. Corneloup: *Universalisme et Franc-Maçonnerie,* p. 83)

"The conservative and conformist spirit—an intransigent form of conformity, though ostensibly traditional—of the Old Masons is clearly visible in this attitude. The latter were to triumph, in 1813, in their struggle against the Moderns, when they bequeathed the same spirit to the United Grand Lodge of England.

"Two hundred years after this struggle broke out, we still find as lively a spirit of hostility, though couched in less truculent terms, on the part of the Grand Lodge of England with regard to French Masonry, apparently concentrated against the Grand Orient of France, but equally apparent against the Grand Lodge of France.

"The lodges had received accepted Masons from the beginning of the seventeenth century. With the rise of speculative Masonry, authority passed into the hands of accepted Masons, who rapidly took precedence over operative Masons; the latter found themselves outnumbered by a flood of new recruits, fewer and fewer of whom belonged to the 'craft'.

"The atmosphere in the lodges was entirely different; it became concerned with philosophical and sometimes even crypto-political preoccupations, disguised under a laudable spirit of tolerance, at least in theory. . . ." (J. Corneloup, ibid., p. 43)

However, within the interior even of English Freemasonry, agreement did not prevail over strife between Ancient and Modern. There was veiled but obstinate opposition to the Constitutions of Anderson, and to put an end to it a recast of the 1723 constitutions was envisaged.

"It was from 1734 onwards that it was decided to prepare a new edition of the Constitutions, perhaps in order to put an end to certain opposition. The need for it was all the more pressing after the affray with the Stewards (in 1735). The most severe criticisms, from both Catholic and Reformed ecclesiastics were directed against the total absence, in the 1723 obligations, of any regulations of a religious character and of all reference to traditional prayers. (J. Corneloup, ibid., p. 47)

"All the modifications described below were introduced in answer to these criticisms. . . . And if it took four years to make the alterations, that was because hard bargaining was necessary, not only to obtain an assurance of appeasement from the 'clandestine' party, but also to appease the philosophers of the school of tolerance and universalism, who were hanging back in the face of an evident regression.

"The appearance, in 1738, of the second edition, set the seal upon the tacit agreement between the two parties.

"On 20th May, 1751, six lodges numbering seventy members

resolved to create a new Masonic body, and on 17th July the statutes of 'The Most Ancient and Honourable Society of Free and Accepted Masons' were drawn up. On 5th December, 1753, the Society set itself up as a Grand Lodge, with Brother Turner as Grand Master. . . .

(J. Corneloup, ibid., p. 48)

"In 1756 a third edition of the Constitutions of Anderson was published, from which all the amendments of 1738 had been deleted. How do you explain this return to the 1723 text if you reject my thesis?

"Henceforth, the rivalry between the two Grand Lodges became more acute and the argument took a violent turn, as I have indicated. The 'Ancients' were content to pin their loyalty and respect for religion on the 'Old Charges'; the 'Moderns' emphasised their philosophical, universal outlook. . . .

(J. Corneloup, ibid., p. 49)

"*If, in place of 'Ancients and Moderns' one inserts, according to present-day terminology in the English-speaking world, the words 'Regular and Irregular', then these lines become as relevant today as when they were written, one hundred and seventy-one years ago. . . .*

"The universality of the Ancients, and alas often also of Moderns, led astray by passion, is that of an ambitious sect rigidly entrenched in tradition.

"The seed of the universality of the Moderns is apparent in Article I of the Constitutions—a religious universality (in the etymological sense of the word) which tends to unite all Brethren of goodwill. But, just as we find today that the most intractable defenders of tolerance lack precisely this virtue when it thwarts them, so the Moderns forget their principles when they think that it is in their interest to do so. Thus George Payne, former Grand Master of the Moderns introduced the Bible into the lodge, prior to 1740, on the pretext that operative Masons should take their oath on this book. Such a decision limited the universality of Masonry to the followers of the Judeo-Christian religions, and contravened the spirit of universality. . . .

(J. Corneloup, ibid., p. 50)

"However, the philosophical spirit continued to animate the first Grand Lodge of England during the second half of the eighteenth century and became even more clearly felt, as can be found by comparing the opening paragraphs of the historical account in the successive editions of the Constitutions.

(J. Corneloup, ibid., p. 51)

"The third edition is far more bold and precise. It is founded on a distinct philosophy of scientific rationalism. It proves that the leaders of the Moderns thought that the opinion of the circles from which they drew their new members had developed sufficiently to enable them to neglect henceforth the precautions they had taken in 1723. And the effrontery of those few words: 'Ourselves, with all the other animals.' Even today, that would be sufficient for the editors to be accused of materialism and atheism.

(J. Corneloup, ibid., p. 52)

"The fact is that we are confronted with two organisations, sprung from the same stock (operative Masonry), and palpably born at the same time and in the same country, but which have evolved differently because one developed in powerful middle-class, intellectual and aristocratic surroundings, and the other in a much more democratic climate. (J. Corneloup, ibid., p. 55)

"The two Grand Lodges struggled together mercilessly for more than a century.

"However, they became reconciled to each other and prepared to unite. What catalyst effected this change of heart? My answer is: the fear of the French Revolution and its consequences.

"French Freemasonry did not have the active rôle in the preparation of the Revolution which certain writers have attributed to it. But the Freemasons did contribute to the expansion of the ideas which led to the collapse of the Old Régime.

"The English aristocrats, even the Masons, feared for their privileges. It is one thing to formulate philosophy in a lodge, but it is quite another to overturn the social order.

"When Napoleon Bonaparte became Emperor, the Sacred Union seemed more necessary than ever; his victories and the continental blockade shook Albion. It is from this era in England that the unwritten but real triple alliance dates, between the Monarchy, the Church of England and Freemasonry—an alliance which to this day has been very effective. It was in this climate that the Ancients and Moderns came together. . . .

(J. Corneloup, ibid., pp. 56-57)

"*On 23rd November, 1813, the two Grand Masters prepared and signed a treaty of Union, which was immediately presented to the two Grand Lodges, who ratified it on 1st December in the same year*. The union was celebrated on December 27th, and the Duke of Sussex was elected Grand Master of the new obedience, which was called the United Grand Lodge of England.

(J. Corneloup, ibid., p. 13)

"*The first and last phrases of the 1723 document are almost identical. But between the two, what an upheaval in the spirit of the text.* Six words appeared in the Ahiman Rezon as well as in the Constitutions of Anderson: 'Leaving to each his own opinion'. Their suppression signified the rejection of liberty of conscience. In 1717 the word God was only used in the title; but it is repeated twice, once after another, in the 1815 text, and it is laid down that, under pain of exclusion, every Mason must believe in the Glorious Architect, and not only believe in him, but adore him, which means practising a religion. And the United Grand Lodge of England was later even to lay down that the God in whom one must believe is not the vaguely-defined God of certain spiritualist philosophies, but the personal God of a revealed religion.

"After that, the United Grand Lodge of England could go on and celebrate the universality of Freemasonry; it could even, priding itself on being the Mother Lodge from which all others have sprung, claim to put this universality into practice to its own profit, with the right to dominate the whole of Masonry. As far as we are concerned, it has become dogmatic and intolerant, and has fallen to the rank of the 'handmaiden of the Church', the obedient servant of the Church of England.

(J. Corneloup, ibid., pp. 58-59)

"What is know as 'universality' assuredly has little in common with universalism."

(J. Corneloup, ibid., p. 59)

In 1921 a serious attempt was begun in Switzerland to unite all Freemasonry throughout the world with the creation of the International Masonic Association, which sprang from the Masonic Information Office, set up in Switzerland in 1901 by members of the Grand Lodge 'Alpina', which supported their endeavours.

"The twelve founder members were, in the order in which their delegates signed: the Grand Lodge of New York; the Grand Lodge of Vienna; the Grand Orient of Belgium; the Grand Lodge of Bulgaria; the Grand Lodge of Spain; the Grand Orient of France; the Grand Lodge of France; the Grand Orient of Italy; the Grand Orient of the Netherlands; the Grand Orient of Portugal; the Swiss Grand Lodge, 'Alpina'; and the Grand Orient of Turkey. In 1923, 38 Masonic obediences belonged to the International Masonic Association, with roughly half a million members.

"The United Grand Lodge of England did not take long to react against this step. As a result of its pressure, directly or indirectly, the Grand Lodge of New York and the Grand Orient of the Netherlands shortly withdrew their affiliation.

"*In 1929, the United Grand Lodge of England took a step of capital importance by publishing its Fundamental Principles for the Recognition of Grand Lodges. It is obvious that this confirms and aggravates the dogmatism of 1815. Despite its affirmations, the United Grand Lodge of England has repudiated the spirit of 1723* and can no longer claim to be the continuation of Masonry as established by Anderson. Liberty of conscience is ignored. The Grand Architect of the Universe henceforth ceases to be a symbol; he is God, and uniquely God. Not just any God, but the God of a revealed religion, the personal God of Israel, Christianity or Islam. And the Bible becomes the first Great Light, to which all are bound, the Volume of the Sacred Law (V.S.L.).

"But it is not only the Mason's liberty of thought which is at stake. The independence of the obediences is also at issue. London claims the right to lay down Masonic law; the United Grand Lodge of England claims to dominate the Masonic world, to be the sovereign judge of the authenticity of the different Masonic powers, and to impose its law upon them. Confident in its powers of intimidation, which it has skilfully cultivated, and owing to the pusillanimous ignorance of the leaders of the different obediences, who are afraid of the least suggestion of a rupture, it abitrarily fixes the criterions for regularity in such a way that it can always, in the last resort, make a decision according to its sole good pleasure.

"You just have to read the last condition, the most arbitrary. Who codified the landmarks, the customs and the usages? *Of the landmarks alone, how many lists have been drawn up which do not agree, either as to the number or the text? Not even the experts agree among themselves.* That is to say, if London has decided to delete such and such a Grand Lodge from its records, whatever the sacrifice the victim consents to, it will still be in vain, for out of the arsenal of the landmarks, customs and usages an argument will always be found to condemn it.

(J. Corneloup, ibid., p. 80)

"But what is their aim, or rather, their dream?

"They want to make the Mother Grand Lodge the unique sovereign authority over the whole of Masonry throughout the world, in order to condemn every group suspected of being able to overshadow it, to qualify every independent obedience as irregular and schismatic, and above all, to destroy, or at the very least to isolate enemy number one: the Grand Orient of France, which for 190 years has been regarded as a dangerous rival."

(J. Corneloup, ibid., p. 128)

In conclusion, Corneloup remarks:

"Let us not become hypnotised by tearing ourselves apart over such sterile, irritating and often insoluble issues, such as landmarks, regularity and recognition." (J. Corneloup, ibid., p. 146)

Such is the point of view of the Grand Orient of France, which, we may say in resumé, refuses to limit the principle of regularity to those branches of Masonry alone which accept the tutelage of the United Grand Lodge of England.

Brother Teder, from his real name Detre, who represents a particular branch of Freemasonry, Martinism, goes much further. He does not recognise the regularity of the United Grand Lodge of England, and only accepts as regular the ancient Freemasonry, which was Christian in inspiration. His point of view is set out in a little pamphlet, which was published in 1909, entitled: *L'irrégularité du Grand Orient de France.* Although he only represents a chapel within Freemasonry, we have quoted the following pages from his work since he throws valuable light on the origins of modern Freemasonry:

"I have shown from authentic documents that, from its introduction into Europe by monks until the advent of the reign of James I of England, British Masonry was purely Roman Catholic, and that its Grand Masters, of whom I have provided the official list, were drawn exclusively from the Court, the Nobility or the Prelacy. . . .

"Despite the birth of the distinctive Masonry of William of Orange in 1694, *the ancient British Masonry preserved its ancient statutes under the Protestant Kings and remained Roman Catholic;* proof of this is to be found in the precious Masonic documents which I propose to publish, and which escaped the mad orgy of destruction at the hands of the innovators of modern Masonry in 1717.

"The war between France and England had just terminated. On 4th January, 1717, the two countries signed a treaty by virtue of which the Pretender, the son of James II, and his followers, were expelled from France, and the usurped Protestant succession to the throne of England was recognised by France. All this was carried out. . . .

"Then, one month after this treaty had been signed, according to the most creditable Masonic authors, four lodges from London detached themselves from the ancient British masonry and founded what was called the Grand Lodge of England.

"As the members of these lodges were obviously Masons and,

as such, had conformed to the ancient Statutes at their initiation, and sworn fidelity to God, the King and Holy Church, consequently by violating them they became perjured rebels, and by founding their own Grand Lodge, they precisely constituted in the eyes of ancient Masonry an irregular body of the first degree.

"I am not concerned with whether their reasons were just or not, nor with the right of any man, be he the Protestant sovereign, to found his own branch of Masonry, which is regular from his point of view, and irregular from everybody else's. I am also not concerned with the various acts of reconciliation which took place between the various Masonic bodies in England in 1813. I am only interested in the brutal fact of February 1717, which happened just one month after the Anglo-French treaty had been signed on 4th January.

"The next fact I want to note is in 1720, when *all the Masonic documents that could be collected, the study of which would have enlightened the men who were going to enter the new Masonry, were burnt.* Only in 1723, at the date when its Constitutions were published, did the Grand Lodge begin to keep a register of its deliberations, without saying why or how it came to be born.

"If one examines the 1723 Constitutions, one finds that they contain a history of Masonry, and the enumeration of the Ancient Duties and General Regulations, etc., of the 'Most Ancient and Honourable Fraternity', all, supposedly, 'drawn from its General Archives and faithful traditions of several centuries. . . .'

"Who is the author of this work? A Presbyterian clergyman, Doctor G. Anderson. But Gould, the historian of the Grand Lodge of England, tells us in his *History of Freemasonry*, that Anderson only became a Mason in 1721, that is to say, one year after the most valuable Masonic documents had been committed to the flames.

"Now, I suggest that it is an absolute fact, and I am in a position to prove my theory, that there are a multitude of misrepresentations or radical errors in Anderson's work which, moreover, the celebrated Lenning described as a rhapsody and an imposture. However, it goes without saying that the great work was accepted by the author's friends, or the people who constituted the Grand Lodge, and that what he had written became an article of faith before which all newcomers inclined, without seeking to discover the sources in which Anderson said he had delved.

"Where are the archives of which Anderson spoke? Nowhere, and he could not even have known those that, according to official chroniclers, were burnt by some scrupulous brethren. As to the registers of the Grand Lodge of England, they do not begin until 1723.

"Between 1717 and 1723 are the six years comprising the real origin of 'modern' English Masonry, but in the 1723 Constitutions this period is passed over in silence.

"Since English Masonry existed long before 1717, where are the documents by virtue of which the four little London lodges, which apparently founded the so-called Grand Lodge of England, believed themselves entitled to do what they are said to have done? Nowhere. . . .

"I am astonished that in a country where the Bible has been so closely criticised in order to discover its meaning, that nobody has yet conceived the idea of criticising Anderson's fables with a view to discovering the imposture relative to the true origin of the Grand Lodge of England. . . .

"*A little further on I will refer again to Anderson, and then, relying on documentary evidence, I will prove that this man, who well before 1717 had been chaplain to the Masonic guilds of London, was simply a traitor to this ancient corporation, and that he used some of its papers. . . .*

"If they were burnt in 1720, there are others still in existence from which it is easy to throw a complete light on the obscure origins of the Grand Lodge of England. . . .

"That the origin of French Masonry is hidden from the profane amidst other things, that may be. But it should be hidden from Masons should only be allowed on condition that it is proved that these men, to whom the Light is promised, and who want to know whence they come and whither they are going, are only fit to be surrounded by darkness, and to serve as the blind and unconscious instruments of an occult power which they ought to ignore.

"Before 1717, an ancient Masonry, as I have said, undoubtedly existed in France, and it had to come to an agreement with the ancient Anglo-Scottish Masonry, introduced into our country by the Stuarts and their followers in 1688-90. To that branch of Masonry belonged all the illustrious Irish, Scottish and English who ardently defended the ancient dynasty and found death in 1708, 1715 and 1745-46, either on the battle-fields of England, or under the axe of Protestant Kings who protected the new brand of Masonry. Others were exiled to America.

"Thus it is clear that if ancient English Masonry could rightfully consider the modern English system of 1717 as irregular, we can say that the lodges founded in France by the Duke of Richmond, which were regular in the eyes of the irregular Grand Lodge of London, were absolutely irregular from the point of view of the ancient Franco-Scottish Masonry. . . .

"*In any event, the origin of modern French Masonry, as well as of modern English Masonry, stinks of irregularity.*"

(Brother Teder: *L'Irrégularité du Grand Orient de France*, 1909)

Teder's thesis is similar to René Guénon's more recent ideas. This remarkable thinker and orientalist was a member of the Theba lodge as a young man; later he left Freemasonry, and towards the end of his life—he died in Cairo not long after the Second World War—he wrote articles in an anti-Masonic review, signing himself The Sphinx. He considered that the only valid form of Masonry, from the point of view of initiation, was the ancient journeyman's operative Masonry.

However, the really important factor in Masonry is not so much the historical circumstances of its origin, as its essence and the spirit which animates it.

Mellor and others would like us to believe that English Freemasonry, in their eyes the only regular form, is religious and non-political.

In reality, there was an ancient Catholic Masonry, about which little is known, and which gradually fell into abeyance.

During the eighteenth century, and under the influence of philosophical ideas, a profound evolution transformed what remained of the Masonic spirit and organisations. On top of this was grafted the struggle between the Scottish Catholic dynasty of the Stuarts and the Protestant Hanoverians.

The alliance of philosophical rationalism with the Protestant freedom of conscience gave birth to the new form of Masonry.

And behind all this stood a more ancient, profound and secret influence, that of the gnostics.

In 1717, it was decided at London to codify the statutes of the new Masonry. This work was given to two men: Désaguliers and Anderson. The former, Désaguliers, is regarded as an occultist, and Anderson as a libertine. In 1720 they held a vast *auto-da-fé* in the course of which they destroyed what remained of the ancient Masonic archives, and thus they were left with a clean field in which to create an entirely new constitution.

This was done and promulgated in 1723, and it is called the Constitutions of Anderson. It is the charter of the new Masonry, whence all the contemporary versions have issued, for the new Masonry has indeed sprung up throughout the whole world.

English Freemasonry described itself as the sole regular version and has always claimed to govern universal Masonry.

In fact this claim has encountered two major difficulties:

(1) Disagreement within the Grand Lodge of England itself.

(2) The independent attitude of foreign Masonries, which considered that they had come of age, rejected the protection of the Grand Lodge of England, and, above all, evolved in a distinctly revolutionary and anti-religious sense.

The Grand Orient of France led this movement, followed, with some reserve, by the Grand Lodge of France, and became the guide of the Grand Orients of Europe and South America.

Freemasonry in the United States, while maintaining its union and friendly relations with the Grand Lodge of England, occupies an intermediary position between English Freemasonry and the Grand Orients of Europe. Some of its branches are nearer the English conception, and others the European.

The revolutionary and anti-Christian tendencies of Grand Orient Freemasonry, as well as of the Grand Lodge of France, are too well known for us to dwell on them here.

Let us, on the other hand, examine the differences which, despite an exterior appearance of calm, have continually agitated English Freemasonry.

English Freemasonry in 1723 was in no way Christian; it was rationalist, vaguely deistic and secretly gnostic. The latter source of inspiration is still active, but it has encountered the conservative, traditional spirit of England. Most English Freemasons were men who were scarcely concerned with philosophical or metaphysical preoccupations. The revolutionary and anti-Christian inspiration which constituted the essence of contemporary Freemasonry everywhere, encountered a veiled and instinctive resistance in English Masons. The pact which Freemasonry tacitly concluded with the Protestant monarchy, to fight against Catholicism, which it considered its principal enemy, contributed to restrain the revolutionary tendencies of English Freemasonry, whereas they developed freely in Europe and South America, and rather more timidly in the United States. In short, the revolutionary virus in Freemasonry is more or less inactive in England, where Freemasonry is more an excuse for social reunions than an organisation claiming to remake the world.

However, this does not prevent numerous English and American authors, such as Wilmshurst, Stewart, Buck, Pike and others, from whom we have quoted in the course of this book, and who are all high initiates, from writing learned studies on Freemasonry which are without exception anti-Christian and anti-traditional. They do not conceal their contempt for the conservative attitude of English

Masons, who completely fail to understand the real spirit of Freemasonry; they still provisionally tolerate the Protestant monarchies, but on condition that they are solely honorary without any real power, and they suggest, albeit in guarded language, that this situation will be changed at the first favourable moment. Thus Brother Carter of New York is correct in saying:

> "When a society, such as Anglo-Saxon Masonry, admits into its ranks not only members of the multiple Protestant sects . . . but also Unitarians, Jews, Mohammedans, and others, the followers of the various religions have some reason for considering that it is a rival in the true sense of the term, which if it does not for the moment supplant the other religions, at least tends to weaken them by reducing them all to the level of Deism pure and simple.
>
> "I do not think that the new creed is very efficacious in this sense, for the majority of those who profess it do not take it seriously.
>
> "*If Anglo-Saxon Freemasonry took its beliefs seriously, little as they are, it would produce all the consequences which the opponents of the Order attribute to it.*"
>
> (*Annales Maçonniques Universelles*, December 1931, p. 252)

It is generally considered that Freemasonry and Protestantism co-exist happily, and that it is only Catholic intolerance which is responsible for drawing down on itself the hostility of Freemasonry, which is essentially tolerant by nature. But this is not always the case; far from it. On several occasions, in various countries, Protestant governments have forbidden Freemasonry, considering that a secret state within the state constituted a permanent source of danger.

But this is not all. On the religious and doctrinal level, theologians and writers of the various Protestant Churches have violently criticised Freemasonry. Mellor himself admits that in England, it was Protestants who first sounded the alarm against the rise of Freemasonry, well before Barruel and Clement XII. Again, in Germany it was Protestants such as Eckert who first drew attention to the sect. Recently in England, two Protestant clergymen, the Rev. Walton Hannah and the Rev. Penney Hunt, have published two very serious and well-documented books against Freemasonry. The Rev. Penney Hunt's arguments can be summed up in the following passages, which we have taken from his book:

> "I am not attacking individual Masons. Many, perhaps most, enter the Society having not the remotest idea of the significance of its religious ritual. Many never trouble to understand it. They knew that leading ministers and Bishops belonged to it, and thus it

seemed absurd to suppose that there could be anything associated with the Order that would imperil one's loyalty to one's Church. So far from attacking such Masons, I would rather appeal to them to look at my evidence and to find out, ere it is too late, the kind of influence that is unconsciously working upon them with disastrous consequences to their Christian life.

(Rev. Penney Hunt: *The Menace of Freemasonry to the Christian Faith*, 5th edition, pp. 5-6)

"Freemasonry is simply Theosophy. It is the perpetuation of the worship of the old pagan gods of ancient Egypt, Greece, India . . . the contention is that God revealed himself ages ago, long before the Christian era, to the whole world; the various myths and legends of every race, including Christianity, are only local variations of the same revelation. . . . (Rev. Penney Hunt, ibid., p. 8)

"In the Middle Ages, the old superstitions passed over into Europe. The Jewish Kabbalists were among the principal agents in spreading these things. And modern Masonry is the great conservator of this pagan religion.

(Rev. Penney Hunt, ibid., pp. 42-43)

"In 1717 a wave of Deism was sweeping over England, and so Masonry reorganised itself and the Christian element was cut out. *Any Masonic writer who pretends that Masonry can be harmonized with Christianity is violating the constitutions he has sworn to accept.* (Rev. Penney Hunt, ibid., pp. 16-17)

"It is generally assumed that one of the chief recommendations of the Craft is the honour shown in every lodge to the Bible. The open Bible, on which are placed the Square and Compasses, is part of the essential equipment of every lodge. At least so the outsider is led to believe. But everything in the lodge is symbolical. A square does not mean a square. It symbolises something else. Similarly, if the Bible is there, it cannot mean the Bible. That would be taking things far too literally. *Everything* is symbolical. The Bible stands symbolically for *anything* anybody likes to think is inspired. . . . It is when we compare the *contents* of the Bible with the contents of Masonry that the contrast is so enormous that it is blasphemous to have the Bible in the lodge at all . . . there is no compatibility between the two conceptions. A man may hold the one or he may accept the other position, but only a mentality that is absolutely rotten with sophistry can pretend to hold both.

(Rev. Penney Hunt, ibid., pp. 34-37)

"In his *Meaning of Masonry* (p. 146), Wilmshurst writes: 'A Master Mason is no longer an ordinary man, but a divinized man. God has become man, and man has become divinized.' It is said that there is a Christian interpretation of the Masonic ritual. Well, *this is it.*

(Rev. Penney Hunt, ibid., p. 52)

"The future of Protestantism is in the balance. Is she so afraid of falling foul of a few official representatives that she prefers to allow her young men to be roped into this pagan religion? And does she realize that Masonic theology is more and more taking the place of the Gospel in the pulpit?"

(Rev. Penney Hunt, ibid., p. 41)

After the publication of this book, the Methodist Church forbade its members to belong to Freemasonry.

And this is what the Rev. Walton Hannah has to say, in his book *Darkness Visible*:

"I am firmly convinced that for a Christian to pledge himself to a religious (or even, to avoid begging the question, to a quasi-religious) organization which offers prayers and worship to God which deliberately exclude the name of our Lord and Saviour Jesus Christ, in whose name only is salvation to be found, is apostatic. I am also quite aware that there are many Christians, and even Archbishops, who are also Masons who do not see it in that light, either because they do not take their ritual very seriously, or because they allow other considerations, such as the good works, the benevolence, and moral uprightness of the Craft, to outweigh the clearly pagan implications of its formulae.

(Rev. W. Hannah: *Darkness Visible*, pp. 18-19)

"Christianity is a faith revealed by God to man, and not a system worked out by man of ascent to God.

(Rev. Walton Hannah, ibid., p. 41)

"*Masonry is not so much a religion as a rival to the Church as a moral guide. But there is more in it than this. There are in the Masonic workings distinct elements of a religion in a far more supernatural sense of the word, a religion that is entirely non-Christian.*

(Rev. Walton Hannah, ibid., p. 30)

"The great Masonic authority Albert Pike wrote: 'No man or body of men can make me accept as a sacred word (Jahbulon), as a symbol of the infinite and eternal Godhead, a mongrel word, in part composed of the name of an accursed and beastly heathen god, whose name has been for more than two thousand years an appellation of the Devil.' The fact that Anglican bishops and clergy see no inconsistency in forming groups of three to recite this word almost as an incantation is really staggering.

(Rev. Walton Hannah, ibid., p. 35)

"For the Christian who accepts the revelation, however, to revert to pre-Christian types and shadows for spiritual or moral light, and in so doing to ignore our Lord altogether and exclude all mention of Him in an unofficial and man-made system of worship and moral betterment is to dishonour the Incarnation by ignoring it and by going behind Christ's back.

(Rev. Walton Hannah, ibid., p. 42)

"Most Masons do not take their ritual seriously, and certainly do not read the works of Ward, Wilmshurst or Waite. They would not understand them if they did (p. 30). . . . But although Masonry does in a sense represent religion at a pre-Christian level, it also claims to impart a light, spiritual and moral, which shines nowhere else. Furthermore, there are today two deadly enemies to the divine supernaturalism of the Church. One of them is humanism. The other is the increasing popularity of a pseudo-mystical occultism which finds expression in spiritualism, theosophy, and other less desirable manifestations. (Rev. Walton Hannah, ibid., p. 45)

"Rome is remarkably well-informed about Regular Masonry. The plea that Rome has condemned English Masonry on false and mistaken grounds, then, is based either on ignorance or muddled thinking." (Rev. Walton Hannah, ibid., pp. 67, 69)

Walton Hannah then gives a list of the Protestant and other Churches which have condemned Freemasonry, and concludes with the remark that:

"The majority of Christians throughout the world have condemned Freemasonry as incompatible with the claims of Our Lord and Saviour. No Church that has seriously investigated the religious teachings and implications of Freemasonry has ever yet failed to condemn it." (Rev. Walton Hannah, ibid., p. 78)

Certain Lutheran and Presbyterian Churches have declared that Freemasonry is incompatible with Christianity, and have forbidden their members to join it, such as the Presbyterian Churches of Scotland (in 1927), and Ireland and America (at the Rochester

Assembly General, in 1942). Similarly, the Synod of the Dutch Reformed Church in the Cape, South Africa, banned Freemasonry in 1942.

The Vatican has never yet accepted the theory that there are two different types of Freemasonry, the one regular, and more or less religious and non-political, and the other, irregular, revolutionary and anti-religious. The Pontifical condemnations have always specified all Freemasonry without distinction, and on 19th March, 1950, the Very Reverend M. Cordovani, speaking in the name of the Holy Office, laid specific emphasis on this fact. (see pp. 36-38).

To conclude, the theory of regularity and irregularity is simply not consistent with the facts, and is advanced for motives of political opportunism.

In practice, the Grand Lodge of England itself, guardian of Masonic regularity, has varied its own principles since 1723, and the Constitutions of Anderson have been recast several times, in 1738, 1784, 1813 and 1929.

In law, the theory of regularity is only applicable to revealed religion.

It would be justified if Freemasonry was a religion and if it was the guardian of a theology. In this case, the idea of regularity, far from being an argument in favour of rapprochement with the Catholic Church, would present an insurmountable obstacle.

Freemasonry has no apparent theology, but is there an occult theology? Is this even possible? This is the essence of the problem we have to resolve, and to which no solution has been found to date. It is a basic question, a matter of capital importance and of prodigious interest, for it lies at the root of all modern political thinking. No detective story could ever produce such a formidable and mysterious enigma.

7

OCCULT THEOLOGY AND GNOSTICISM

THE question we have to resolve is whether there is or can be such a thing as an occult theology secretly animating Freemasonry. For guidance in this baffling and intricate problem let us refer to the work of the celebrated Rabbi, Elie Benamozegh. In his *Israel et l'Humanité*, which is generally regarded as an outstanding contribution to contemporary Jewish thought, and which was re-published in 1961, under the auspices of Doctor Modiano, who is the President of the Representative Council of the Israelites of France, and the Grand Rabbi Toaff of Livourne—both very eminent personalities—Rabbi Benamozegh tells us:

> "*What is certain is that Masonic theology corresponds well enough to that of the Kabbala. . . .*"

and the editors, Doctor Modiano and the Grand Rabbi Toaff, add in a footnote at the bottom of the page:

> "To those who may be surprised by the use of such an expression, *we would say that there is a Masonic theology in the sense that there exists in Freemasonry a secret, philosophic and religious doctrine, which was introduced by the Gnostic Rosicrucians at the time of their union with the Free Masons in 1717.* This secret doctrine, or gnosis, belongs exclusively to the High, or philosophic, degrees of Freemasonry."
>
> (Rabbi E. Benamozegh: *Israel et l'Humanité*, p. 73)

We need hardly emphasise the importance of such an assertion, and of the personalities to whom we are indebted for this revelation.

This is what the Freemason, Wilmshurst, has to say in his book, *The Masonic Initiation*.

> "Modern speculative Freemasonry had a beginning in the early years of the eighteenth century, but only in the sense that in 1717 originated that which afterwards developed into, and now subsists as, the English Masonic constitution. Masonry itself existed long before that time, and in two forms: exoterically, in the

operative building guilds, and esoterically, in a variety of communities of mystics and occultists, having no relation to the practical building trade but often using builders' terminology for symbolical purposes of their own. (W. Wilmshurst, ibid., pp. 183-184)

"All through the Christian centuries, behind the activities of public elementary religion and the official work of the Church, can be traced evidences of this higher, esoteric, more abstruse and difficult work of mystical Masonry.

(W. Wilmshurst, ibid., p. 188)

"No one can read English or European history from the period of that memorandum onward (Henry VI) without realising that *to that history there has been an inner side not cognised or treated of by academic historians*, or without feeling behind the march of external events—and as it were connected with or even directing them—the concealed presence of minds more than normally capable, initiates possessing and wielding the very powers testified to in Henry VI's memorandum. The lives and literary remains of such men as, to name no others, Paracelsus, Abbot Tritheim, Basil Valentine, Jacob Boehme, George Johan Gichtel, Thomas Vaughan and Elias Ashmole, provide above-surface indications of a strong current of sub-surface activity, a current of which no record exists or is ever likely now to be made. *But to that current one must look for the perpetuation of the secret Masonic science*, and to its projection, in a highly diluted and elementary form, into publicity in modern speculative Masonry.

"The religious reformation of the fifteenth century was the first great episode in a far-reaching revolutionary movement in the intellectual, social and political life of the West, a movement the end of which is not yet. Amid the intensifying unspirituality and materialism of the times and the impending disintegration of public instituted religion, *a decision seems to have been come to by some far-seeing enlightened minds to put forward the old mystical Gnosis* and tradition in a simple form and to attempt to interest a small section of the public in it." (W. Wilmshurst, ibid., pp. 190-191)

The American Freemason, Stewart, tells us:

"Students of Masonry soon learn that but little progress is made in its study from the historical standpoint. Why? Because the real secrets of Masonry are locked up in symbolism, and not in history."

(T. M. Stewart: *Masonry and its Message*, p. 50)

On 5th January, 1954, the Holy Office condemned a work drawn up by the Grand Master of the Johannine rite of Austrian Freemasonry, (B. Scheichelbauer: *Die Johannis Freimaurerei*, 1953), and on 17th January the *Osservatore Romano*, the official Vatican journal, published a long article concerned with this particular branch of Masonry, from which we reproduce the following passage:

"Surprise may have been caused in certain quarters by this serious step taken by the Church, after the statements which have so insistently been circulated almost everywhere in recent years concerning the conciliatory attitude of the Johannine lodge of Austrian Freemasonry towards the Catholic Church.

"The plea was advanced, in this connection, that the excommunication decreed against members of Masonic sects by Canon 2,335 of the Canon Law, did not affect those who belonged to the aforesaid lodge.

"*If there were any need for fresh proofs to confirm that the concepts of even the Johannine rite of Austrian Freemasonry are a positive perversion of religious principles, the above mentioned publication provided the most recent and the most irrefutable demonstration of that fact.*

"The author is himself Grand Master of the Austrian Johannine lodge.

"We shall confine ourselves here to a summary examination of the principle ideas expressed in the book.

"It is there asserted that 'the direct aim of Freemasonry is to bring its own members to the "Gnosis"', as being the only possible method of attaining the Divine Essence, and to overcome the existing contradiction between faith and science. Thus 'Gnosis' in nothing less than Anthroposophy, though this term is not expressly employed. Its principal dogma is Pantheism. Herein resides the 'Ars Regia', or sovereign skill, through which man acquires the knowledge of the identity of his own being with the divine being.

"It goes on to declare that Freemasonry favours tolerance in matters of dogma, seeing that no religious society, not even the Catholic Church, is in possession of the whole truth. Although there are to be found in all religions traces of natural religious knowledge, *yet the 'Gnosis' is the only true science; other systems of knowledge represent only a preparation for the true science, that is to say, the 'Gnosis'.*

"No one can fail to see the gravity of such ideas and concepts, and how radically and fundamentally they are not merely at variance with revealed religions but utterly opposed to it.

"Moreover, the placing of this book on the Index is an effective warning to Catholics not to let themselves be deceived by those who are trying to persuade them into becoming attracted to Freemasonry by claiming that there is a change of attitude on its part towards the Catholic Church."

Now let us return to Masonic texts.

> "'Masonry', says Albert Pike, in *Morals and Dogma*, 'is the descendant of that higher science held by the ancient teachers of those ancient religions that once illuminated the minds of men.'
>
> "Considering the fact, that these ancient faiths taught a secret as well as an open doctrine, as did Christianity in its early day; we come to the mysteries handed down from generation to generation, in secret traditions; given to those ready to receive and to properly impart them.
>
> "This science was known as the Gnosis.
>
> "The Gnostics derived their leading doctrines and ideas from Plato and Philo; the Zendavesta of the Persians; the Kabbalah of the Hebrews; and the sacred books of Egypt and India; and thus introduced in the early days of Christianity, that which formed a large part of the ancient teachings of the Orient."
>
> (T. Stewart: *Masonry and its Message*, pp. 55-56)

and Wilmshurst for his part writes

> "The Masonic system was devised three centuries ago, at a time of general unrest and change, as a preparatory infant-school in which once again the alphabet of a world-old *Gnosis* might be learned and an elementary acquaintance made with the science of human regeneration."
>
> (W. Wilmshurst, *The Masonic Initiation*, p. 218)

T. M. Stewart puts it summarily when he says that once the world was illumined by the Gnosis. Then the Fathers of the Church, who worked unceasingly on the priests, persuaded these torturers to massacre the wise and fair Hypathia who was a High Initiate. Thus they succeeded in extinguishing the light, and plunged humanity into the obscurity of the dark Christian ages. But the Gnosis secretly lived on, and was transmitted in the dark, uninterrupted, by subterranean channels. Today, it has found new life in Freemasonry, and sets out to capture the world.

In 1945 a secret Masonic document entitled *La Massoneria* was published in Florence, Italy, for circulation only among the lodges, which confirms the true character of Freemasonry, and which clearly reveals that Catholics who defend the Order are unwise, to say the least, in associating themselves with the strategy which it has elaborated for the profane world today. The following extracts are taken from this document:

"The Rose-Croix naturalist, John Theophilus Désaguliers, and James Anderson, a Protestant minister, and others, held a meeting on 24th June, 1717, in London, which was attended by the members of the four lodges which were active at that time.

"*The aim of this reunion was to unite the Fraternity of the Free and Accepted Masons with the Alchemist Society of the Rose-Croix, so that the Rose-Croix could shelter their alchemistic research and their gnostic and rationalistic ideas behind the respectable facade of the Fraternity*, and to procure for the Free and Accepted Masons the advantages which alone the rich, influential and ambitious adepts of the Rose-Croix could bring them, in view of the menace of certain decadence which threatened the ancient Fraternity.

"The Assembly unanimously accepted this union. Thus, on 24th June, 1717, out of this compromise, was born Freemasonry. And it was thus that there disappeared for ever the Fraternity of Builders, the Fraternity of Free and Accepted Masons, and that *Freemasonry, the workshop of pure Gnosticism, took up a stand against the Christian Church, the workshop of falsified and corrupted Gnosticism.* (*La Massoneria*, p. 14)

". . . In 1723, Anderson drew up the Constitutions of the Free and Accepted Masons, and they were accepted.

"The appellation Free and Accepted, recalling the Church of Saint Paul, was retained in order to remove any suspicion as to the real aim of the infant Freemasonry, which has always been to work for the triumph of pure Gnosticism and liberal rationalism throughout the entire world.

"In order to give the impression that the new Masonry was simply the continuation of the Fraternity of the Free and Accepted Masons, the titles, the ceremonies and the details which Masonry had received from the Fraternity of Builders were rigorously respected. Only one modification was adopted: the degree of Master was constituted separately and was distinct from the Companion degree. *Under the name of Apprentice, Companions and Masters, the army of pure Gnosticism set out to conquer the world.*

"*. . . The duty of the Knight Rose-Croix is to combat the bastard Gnosticism inherent in Catholicism, which blinds the eyes of faith, turns hope into a pedestal, and charity into egoism.* (ibid., p. 69)

"*Freemasonry alone possesses the true religion, which is Gnosticism. All the other religions, and especially Catholicism, have taken what is true in their doctrines from Freemasonry. They possess only absurd or false theories.*

"The secret teaching of the supreme leaders of Freemasonry may be summed up in these words: to establish all the rights of Man . . . to claim for Man the possession of all these rights, the privation of which constitutes a usurpation against which all means of action are permissible. (ibid., p. 177)

"*Freemasonry, which is simply a revolution in action, a permanent conspiracy against religious and political despotism,* did not assume its symbols itself, as do the Princes and priests in Society. However, the Princes and priests, who were unable to overcome the Institution which is hostile to them, and which is so formidable in its organisation, endeavoured at various epochs . . . to belong to Freemasonry and to introduce into it customs, formulas, titles and legends which would have warped the spirit of the Institution and which, instead of fostering liberal and democratic doctrines, would rather have encouraged religious or aristocratic tendencies.

"Confronted by these dangers, the leaders of Freemasonry closed up the ranks of the true Brethren, and in order to secure if not the protection, at least the tolerance of the powers of this world, they let them take part in the work in the lodges, only revealing what it was opportune to uncover. Thus, seeing that Freemasonry, so apparently insignificant, was turning itself into some sort of society entirely devoted to good works and charity, the powers of this world believed that in fact religion and politics were not connected with it. The paradoxical situation which this attitude produced serves as a protective veil under which Freemasonry can act everywhere in shadow and in secret, in order to attain its truly sublime ends." (*La Massoneria*, Florence 1945)

The reader will appreciate that here it is a question of an ultra secret document, drawn up in exultation after the re-opening of the lodges at the end of the Second World War, and destined only to initiates of the high degrees of the Order.

Clear confirmation of its divulgations may be found in "Le Livre du compagnon", Part I of Oswald Wirth's book, *La Franc-Maçonnerie rendue intelligible à ses adeptes*. In the Chapter on the Gnosis, he says:

"Companion is synonymous with associate. One could not be a Companion without having been Companions at work, and without constituting with them a collective unit from the psychical point of view. This collectivity reacts on the individual in such a way that the general light reflects in him to the degree in which he has shown himself capable of receiving it.

"Thus every real initiate enjoys an illumination which enables him to master the Gnosis, or the Knowledge characteristic of every person who has succeeded in penetrating the Mysteries of Initiation.

"One cannot over-emphasise this point: the alert Thinker can discern a supreme teaching which runs through all our symbolism. If we are able to grasp its most profound significance, our judgment will be illumined with a radiant clarity of understanding. *It is then that, possessing the Gnosis, we will be able to claim that we know the meaning of the letter G.*"

Hence the vital necessity of secrecy to protect this work of occult interpretation.

"The Apprentice must have undertaken to keep silence in front of the profane, to submit to the laws of Freemasonry, and to love his brethren.

"The Companion is not content to renew his first obligation on these various points, for one has a right to demand more from an instructed Mason more than one could from a beginner.

"Thus the Companion has to redouble his discretion and to beware, in particular, of trying to explain to Apprentices things they would not understand. Each spirit must be left to evolve in its own way, without attempting to cut short the paths of understanding which the intellect must traverse.

"By reason of the fact that a secret is scrupulously kept, one is also assured of the advantages of fidelity from those in whom it has been entrusted. The Mason, who fails to keep his promised discretion automatically cuts himself off from the Order and renounces all the intellectual and moral benefits of the fraternity of initiation. Now the whole strength of the Companion lies in his participation in the soul of Freemasonry. *Thus in him silence assumes a capital importance, all the more because he is called to act in the spirit of initiation, that is to say, in a veritable conspiracy of thought and will.*"

(O. Wirth: *La Franc-Maçonnerie rendue intelligible à ses adeptes*, pp. 56-58)

In his remarkable work *Les Sociétés Secrètes et la Société*, one of the most comprehensive and well-documented studies of Freemasonry that have ever been written, N. Deschamps cites an ancient Masonic document dated 1535, the Charter of Cologne, which reveals that from this period there were anti-Christian influences, Gnostic in origin, which had secretly begun to penetrate Catholic Freemasonry. After a long period in the dark, they finally gained the upper hand in the eighteenth century. As Deschamps says:

> "The birth and the development, in the bosom of Christian society, of secret societies such as Freemasonry, whose most fundamental idea is the negation of Christianity and of all social order constructed upon its principles, is one of the phenomena most worthy of the attention of the philosopher and historian."
>
> (N. Deschamps: *Les Sociétés Secrètes et la Société*, 4th edition, 1881, vol. I, p. 281)

In the Middle Ages and at the time of the Renaissance,

> "The Freemasons in Germany and Italy were overwhelmed with favours by the Sovereign Pontiffs, and there is not a trace of heresy or hostility against the Church in the Statutes of Strasbourg of 1462, or as revised in 1563.
>
> "However, in 1535 we come across a document which reveals the existence of an order, under the name of Freemasons, whose anti-Christian principles are absolutely in harmony with those of modern Masonry. This time it is no longer a question of builders protecting their arts. How this secret association took the name of the Masonic Guilds is a problem which history has not yet resolved. We are suddenly confronted with an indisputable fact which throws the greatest light on events in this troubled period.
>
> (N. Deschamps, ibid., p. 317)

> "The oldest and most authentic document of the Masonic lodges, known as the 'Charter of Cologne', dates back to the year 1535, and it reveals the existence, already going back some time, perhaps even two centuries, of one or several secret societies, which eked out a clandestine existence throughout the various States of Europe, in direct antagonism with the religious and civil principles that formed the bases of their constitutions.
>
> "Through this antagonism and its universal character, this sect simulated a counterfeit character of the Church and her divine works—a posture which is the essence of works inspired by the Devil.
>
> "Gradually, as one advances into modern times, Masonic documents become commonplace; the legends which run like threads through the rituals of the lodges, and which seem to refer to their different layers, demonstrate the successive filiation through which

the doctrines at the basis of Freemasonry passed before the eighteenth century.

"In its exterior organisation it resembled the great Guilds of Masons, which, like the Guilds of Mercers and Lombards for the merchants and bankers, united men skilled in the art of building throughout the various countries in Europe, owing to the large and prosperous community which Catholicism had created among all the members of the Christian republic.

"The legend of Hiram and of the Temple of Solomon is perhaps contemporary with these corporations. But beside it are others no less considerable, connected with the destruction of the famous order of the Knights Templar, whose voices are like a prolonged cry of vengeance against the ecclesiastical and civil powers whose duty it was to suppress the Order. Mingled with these memories and rites are other signs and ceremonies which take us back to the great heresies of the Middle Ages, the Albigensians, the Cathari, the Patareni, and their ancestors, the Manicheans and the Gnostics.

"*Gnosticism, Manicheanism, the Albigensians and the Templars, these are the sources whence Freemasonry has sprung.*"

(N. Deschamps, ibid., pp. 282-283)

While on this subject it is not inopportune to notice that Jewish influences were active among these heresies, as Deschamps remarks, quoting a passage from the renowned French historian, Michelet:

"The nobility of the South of France, says Michelet, which was hardly any different from the middle-class, was entirely composed of Jewish or Saracen children, people whose outlook was quite different from that of the ignorant and pious knights of the North. They were supported and greatly admired by the highland people, and they treated their priests just like peasants, dressing up their wives in consecrated vestments, beating the clerics and making them sing Mass in mockery. One of their pastimes was defiling and smashing images of Christ, breaking their legs and their arms. They were looked upon with favour by the princes precisely because of their impiety, which rendered them insensible to ecclesiastical censure. Impious as the modern world, and as wild as savages, they weighed cruelly on the country; robbing, holding people to ransom and cutting their throats at will, they waged a terrible war. Women in the highest society were as corrupt as their husbands or fathers, and the poems of the troubadors were simply amorous impieties.

"Finally, this Judea of France, as Languedoc has been called, not only recalled the former by its bitumen and olive-groves; it also had its Sodom and Gomorrah, and it was to be feared lest the vengeance of the Church gave it its Dead Sea. Nobody will be surprised that oriental beliefs, Persian dualism, Manicheanism and Gnosticism should have penetrated this country. Every doctrine had taken root there, but Manicheanism, the most odious in the whole of Christendom, eclipsed all the others."

(Michelet: *Histoire de France*, vol. II, p. 404, quoted by N. Deschamps, ibid., pp. 298-299)

Deschamps himself concludes on this subject:

"Before showing how sixteenth-century Freemasonry arose out of the ruins of the Order of the Knights Templar, we will demonstrate the identity of modern Freemasonry's doctrines with all these heresies, revealing the various forms which have shrouded the organised opposition to the work of Jesus Christ, or in other words, the Church of Satan, to call it by its true name, from the very beginning of the Christian era. Having been overcome several times by the faith of the Catholic peoples, the same enemy is mustering its forces behind the disorders of the great schism of the West, and the separation of the Christian world in two by Protestantism, and it is challenging the Church with a new struggle, universal in principle, and with the whole world as its stage, in which it masks itself in the form of a secret association. Gradually, as its success in the modern world increases its boldness, it is lifting this mask of its own accord."

(N. Deschamps, ibid., p. 283)

The gnostic origin of Freemasonry is difficult to prove historically with absolute certitude, but Masonic methods of initiation are still completely identical with the Gnostics'.

This is what the Freemason S. Hutin says in his book *Les Gnostiques*:

"The gnoses do not have the appearance of new religions; they claim to possess esoteric knowledge of any given religious tradition, such as, for example, Judaism, Christianity or Islam. Most of the time, the Gnostics set up schools of initiation, 'mysteries', and conventicles jealously reserved to a privileged few; their proselytism is generally subtle and insinuating:

"They only disclose these mysteries to the initiate, writes Hippolytus of Rome, the historian of heresies, after they have given them a plausible appearance in their eyes: they only confide in them when they have enslaved them and, holding them in a state of suspense for some time, they prepare them to blaspheme the true God, while they burn with curiosity to learn what has been promised them.

"Even when the Gnostic freely talks about it, his apparent proselytism veils a whole secret doctrine (written or oral), which is gradually communicated to the candidates as they mature, by progressive revelation. Gnostic esoteric knowledge applies much less to the doctrines (which are easy enough to pick up, after all), than to the practices of which they are the foundation—sacramental rites and rites of initiation, magic formulas, 'passwords' destined to open a free passage to illuminated souls when they ascend to the transcendant world.

"Many historians still consider that Gnosticism is a monument of weird and incoherent dreams and strange myths and fantasies bereft of any interest whatever to the philosopher, and that it is really nothing more than a particularly degenerate branch of the alarming attempt to reconcile contrary religious principles in the first and second centuries of the present era.

"If this point of view of the Fathers of the Church is still widely held, Gnosticism is regarded under quite a different light by contemporary 'occultists' and 'theosophists'. According to them, instead of perverse or raving heretics, we are dealing with men who possessed the art of amazing initiations, men who had been initiated into oriental mysteries and who held the key to occult knowledge unknown to mere mortals, and which had secretly been transmitted to rare 'masters'; *Gnosis is total knowledge, incommensurably superior to faith and reason, and Gnosticism is derived from original, primeval wisdom, the source of the various particular religions.*

(S. Hutin: *Les Gnostiques*, p. 5)

"The extreme diversity of Gnostic speculations cannot be denied. Yet it is easy to discover that an undeniable sort of 'family feeling' exists among the various forms of Gnosticism, despite the many differences and opposing principles which it displays.

(S. Hutin, ibid., p. 6)

"If Gnosticism was simply a series of doctrinal errors in which certain Christian heretics indulged in the first three centuries of this era, its interest would be purely archeological. But it is much more than that. The Gnostic attitude was to re-appear spontaneously without any direct transmission, and this particular type of religiosity presents certain disturbing affinities even with the most 'modern' aspirations. The 'Gnosticism' as described by the heresiographers constitutes the characteristic example of a religious ideology constantly tending to re-appear in Europe and the Mediterranean world at moments of great social and political stress."

(S. Hutin, ibid., p. 8)

The Gnostic heresy was very widespread throughout the Roman world in the first centuries of Christianity, and the Fathers of the Church relentlessly fought against it. It was an oriental theosophy of unorthodox Jewish origin, which once again brings us back to the many affinities which unite Freemasonry and Judaism.

In August-September, 1930, *Le Voile d'Isis* published a special issue devoted to Gnosticism, in which was reproduced an important article by one Michael Nicholas, first published in the *Nouvelle Revue de Théologie* at Strasburg in 1860. The author gives a clear exposition of the nature of the Gnosis, and brings out the Jewish influences which assisted in its diffusion:

"The first thing to notice is that those of the Apostles who had occasion to attack it regarded it, not as an error born in the bosom of the Church, but as a foreign philosophy which brought trouble upon the faithful by seeking to win them to itself and to turn them away from their faith. This is clearly evident from the way in which they speak about it.

"Elsewhere, he (St. Paul) expresses himself more clearly, *he describes their system as Judaic myths, and he points out that the adherents of these erroneous ideas belong principally to the circumcision, or in other words, to the Jewish nation.* This is cheap sophistry. It must be combated. Better still, they must be won to the Truth.

"There is thus every sign that here we are confronted with Theosophists who are not members of the Church, but who wish to act upon the Church and win her over to their doctrines—Theosophists who have found a few distant relations in the Christian faith with their own ideas and who, accommodating their language to Christian beliefs, claim to be the genuine interpreters of the Master's teaching. This is one of the most marked characteristics of Gnosticism. From its inception until the time when it had completely developed, it assimilated accepted doctrines everywhere, incorporating them into its own system and gathering, in the course of the long route it has traversed, Jewish dogma, Greek philosophy, Parseeism, Buddhism, and receiving in its Pantheon, Hermes, Saturn, Zoroaster, Pythagoras, John the Baptist, Jesus Christ, and even Epicurus and Mazdak, (the founder of the fifth century sect advocating communal ownership of property and women—*author's note*). *One would say that this Theosophy aspires to universal spiritual domination, and that it seeks to substitute itself for all known systems, as their universal, legitimate heir, by absorbing them all into itself.*

"They looked upon themselves as the depositaries of the doctrine of which Christianity, in their eyes, was only the popular and inaccurate form, and they considered that they were destined to accomplish the spiritual education of men whose eyes had not yet been opened, according to them, to anything more than imperfect clarity. . . .

"This division, which is evident in all the Gnostic schools, could only tend to nothing less, as Neander remarks, than the establishment of an order of affairs similar to the mysteries of pagan antiquity. *There was nothing more contrary to the spirit of the Christian religion, to the teaching of Jesus Christ, and to the preaching of the* Apostles.

"*Gnosticism has its roots in the Jewish sect; it was born among the Judeo-Samarians, and it is in Palestine, and more particularly in Samaria, that its cradle must be sought.* A flood of circumstances converge to prove it to us. It is first met with in Samaria, and it is there at least that it first appears with Simon the Magician, to whom it is ascribed. When subsequently it is found at work outside Palestine, it is in those places where the children of Israel abound, in Alexandria, in Asia-Minor, and in Syria. In the first decades of the Christian era it did not appeal to the pagans; it was only later, when it had been decidedly rejected by the Jews, and when it took on considerable proportions by borrowing large sections of doctrine from very different origins, and thus became a well-developed theosophical system, that it turned towards them, and even then it was to the Jews and Christians who had both, like itself, sprung from Judaism, that it appealed in preference."

(Article by Michael Nicholas in the *Nouvelle Revue de Théologie*, Strasbourg, 1860, and reproduced in *Le Voile d'Isis*, August-September 1930)

This theosophical attitude is common to all the branches of Freemasonry, and if there is one point on which the Vatican has never varied, it is that the Pontifical condemnations specify the whole of Freemasonry without any distinction of nationality, Rite or Obedience. The modern texts from which we quote below specifically confirm this point:

"Scottish rite Masonry falls under the condemnation decreed by the Church against Masonry in general, and there is no reason to grant any discrimination in favour of this category of Masons", (1946);

and a little later,

> "Since nothing has happened to cause any change in the decisions of the Holy See on this question, the provisions of Canon Law remain in full force for every kind of Masonry whatsoever." (20th April, 1949.)

and finally, on 19th March, 1950, the Most Reverend Father Mario Cordovani, Master of the Sacred Palace, wrote an article entitled "The Church and Freemasonry", which was published in the *Osservatore Romano*, and from which we have selected the following passages:

> "Among the things which are springing up again with renewed vigour, and not only in Italy, is Freemasonry with its ever recurring hostility to religion and to the Church. One only needs to recall the speeches delivered in Parliament by the head of Italian Freemasonry.
>
> "What appears to be a new feature in this Masonic renaissance is the rumour circulating in various social classes that a particular rite of Masonry might no longer be in opposition to the Church, whereby even Catholics can enrol at their ease in the sect without fear of excommunication and reproach. *Those responsible for propagating these rumours must surely know that nothing has been modified in the Church's teaching relative to Freemasonry, and if they continue this campaign it can only be in order to profit from the naïvety of simple folk.*
>
> "*The Bishops know that Canon 684, and especially Canon 2,335, which excommunicates those who have given their names to Masonry without any distinction between rites, are as full in force today as they always have been; all Catholics ought to know this and to remember it,* so as not to fall into this snare, and also so as to know how to pass due judgment on the fact that certain simpletons believe that they can call themselves both Catholics and Freemasons with impunity. This, I repeat, applies to all Masonic rites, even if some of them, in varying circumstances, declare that they are not hostile to the Church.
>
> "But does not this rigid attitude disregard the good will of some people who would like ecclesiastical authority to recognise some small sector of Freemasonry said not to be hostile to religion and to the Church? And is it not equally opposed to the spirit of accommodation which the Church has shown in every epoch, out-

stripping everyone in a spirit of comprehension and generous charity?

"Only a frivolous-minded person could say that. . . .

"This modern tendency, manifest among those who would gladly bring Catholicism into harmony with all ideologies and social movements, with every advance and about-turn—is not this a sign of heresy, even if among many it is unconsciously present?"

(Article by the Most Rev. Father Cordovani, in the *Osservatore Romano*, 19th March, 1950)

Arthur Preuss, who was a Catholic, concluded a remarkable study on American Freemasonry with this paragraph:

"Masonry is one throughout, but not by virtue of the rite, which is only an accidental unity, nor by virtue of its jurisdiction, which similarly is simply a matter of conscience, nor by virtue of its exoteric members, for they are maintained in ignorance of the Art. *Masonry is one in its real, esoteric spirit; it is one in its aim and its object; it is one in its light and its doctrines, one in its philosophy and its religion; and in this way it forms a family, a corporation, an institution, a fraternity, an order, a world, which tends by its universality to substitute itself for the Catholicism which was established by Christ.*"

(A. Preuss: *Etude sur la Franc-Maçonnerie Américaine*, p. 302, from the authorised Fr. tr. by Mgr. Jouin, from the 2nd American edition, 1908)

For his part, and with all manner of oratical precautions, the Freemason G. Vinatrel tells us in his book *Communisme et Franc-Maçonnerie*, which was published in 1961:

"*One talks of 'Freemasonry'. Freemasons among themselves talk of 'Obediences' and also of 'The Order'. Thus they recognise that there are several Freemasonries throughout the world, but that the Masonic spirit is one.*

"The Obediences spring from various sources of inspiration. Certain of them, under the influence of the Grand Lodge of England, are deist. The belief in a principal creator, the Grand Architect of the Universe, is accompanied by faith in the revealed truth, such as may be found in the Bible and various other sacred books (the Koran, the Vedas, and others). In fact it is the Protestant spirit, in the diversity of its beliefs and the unity of its faith, which predominates. These Obediences have a supplementary motive for considering Communism as opposed to Freemasonry. Along with the Catholic Church, they condemn atheism.

"Certain Latin American and European Obediences, notably the Grand Orient of France, the Grand Orient of Belgium, and others, are rationalist in inspiration.

"They do not compel their members to believe in the Grand Architect of the Universe, which they are content to acknowledge as an indeterminate symbol, an unknown guardian power. They do not consider that the Bible bears the specific stamp of Revelation. To them it is simply one sacred book, among many others, attesting to the wisdom of men and to Tradition, without attempting to discover what it represents or what lies hid in its pages.

"The Grand Orient of France, contrary to what is generally believed, has not banned the Bible from its altars, or the Grand Architect of the Universe from its lodges. Its members are free to invoke him or not, according to the rite which they have chosen (French Rite, Ancient and Accepted Scottish Rite, etc.).

"This diversity, however, is no obstacle to the profound unity of Masonic thought. All Freemasons throughout the world demand Tolerance for the ideas of others.

"All Freemasons adopt the celebrated motto which was bequeathed by the Grand Orient to the Great French Revolution: 'Liberty, Fraternity, Equality'. This slogan has raised up the peoples. In turn it was adopted by Latin America and then by revolutionary China. The Russian Revolution in February 1917 spoke the same language."

(G. Vinatrel: *Communisme et Franc-Maçonnerie*, p. 78)

How can it possibly be doubted? How can it conceivably be imagined that Freemasonry could have subsisted, unless it is held together by a supple but firm bond of unity, under a leadership from above which is highly efficacious and absolutely occult?

8

FREEMASONRY AND THE REVOLUTION OF 1789

A WHOLE school, of which Mellor is a supporter, maintains that Freemasonry played no part in the preparation and development of the French Revolution in 1789. This is what Mellor says on the subject:

> "Partisan history generally sees in eighteenth century Freemasonry the mother of the French Revolution. The legend did not originate in the lodges, far from it. The Revolution forced the lodges to lie low and guillotined the Freemasons. . . . The real reason for which it boasts this accomplishment is that Barruel, an emigré Jesuit, made it the theme of his *Memoirs illustrating the History of Jacobinism*, published in London in 1797."
>
> (A. Mellor: *La Franc-Maçonnerie à l'Heure du Choix*, p. 22)

> "*Barruel can be considered as the father of modern antimasonry.* The brand which had existed before him was short-lived. On the other hand, his sowed the seeds of lasting hatred; and of all those who wrote against Masonry, it was he who did it most harm. *By accrediting the idea—shown now to be historically false—that the Revolution was the daughter of Freemasonry he was blindly believed by all and sundry.* The opponents of Masonry based their dogma on the famous theory of the alleged conspiracy, and the Masons gloried in a revolution which not only had they neither prepared nor waged, but which had guillotined the best among them and closed the lodges. To compare Barruel with Pascal would of course be absurd, but it is possible to compare the blow which he dealt to Freemasonry with the blow which the *Lettres Provinciales* dealt to the Society of Jesus. He caused his adversary immense harm, and it can even be said that it has never fully recovered from it. He was the fountain-head for generations of anti-masons."
>
> (A. Mellor: *Our Separated Brethren—the Freemasons*, pp. 249-250)

For his part, Roger Priouret has recently devoted a whole book called *La Franc-Maçonnerie sous les lys* (Grasset, 1953) to absolving Freemasonry of any responsibility for the Revolution of 1789.

Other historians, whose testimony is more numerous and valuable, support the opposite argument. Among these, we must mention principally the remarkable works of Augustin Cochin and Gustave Bord.

Apart from the case of Barruel, the pet aversion of Mellor and progressives, to which we will return in another chapter, two Catholic writers, Gustave Bord and Augustin Cochin, whose importance no-one disputes—indeed it is recognised by the Freemasons themselves—have made extensive investigations into the position of Freemasonry in 1789. Similarly, a writer who was himself a member of Grand Orient Freemasonry, Gaston Martin, has published a highly documented historical study on this subject, and his conclusions agree with those of Gustave Bord and Augustin Cochin. The only difference is that Martin extols the work of the French Revolution, whereas the latter protest against it, but they are in almost complete agreement regarding the important rôle played by Freemasonry in this great tragedy. Furthermore, all three authors refer us to their sources, which is something that Mellor never does.

Now, it is interesting to note that one will search in vain in Mellor's works for any mention of these three authors; the name of Augustin Cochin does not appear and those of Gustave Bord and Gaston Martin are only mentioned in passing, without any reference to their works. The reader who only has Mellor's books to hand would remain totally unaware of the name of Augustin Cochin and would only know of the existence of the other two without knowing anything about what they have written. The same is true of another contemporary author, Bernard Fay.

Nevertheless, in accordance with our method of inquiry, we will summon as the principal witness on this question the evidence of a Masonic writer, the historian Gaston Martin, a member of the Grand Orient of France. For, regarding the role of Freemasonry in the preparation of the French Revolution, his remarkable work, for which he won the Arthur Mille prize of 4000 francs, provides us with clear and plentiful documentation. Gaston Martin accuses all the opponents of Freemasonry of bad faith; which cuts short all discussion. He says:

"Freemasonry is not subversive, it respects the king, religion and the law", "but it may be wise to add that this obedience objects to passivity. Laws are worthy of respect, but they are not untouchable."

(G. Martin: *La Franc-Maçonnerie Française et la Révolution*, p. 43)

Enlightened souls, Masons await the opportunity to modify the laws and, in fact, propagate principles that destroy them.

All this is thus a verbal dispute.

Freemasonry proclaims and spreads a new system of political, social and religious ideas; these ideas constitute a different civilisation, radically hostile to the old; for Freemasons it is, by definition, superior, and Freemasonry is constantly seeking to build it up. We believe, on the contrary, that it is evil and dangerous, and, since to establish this new civilisation it is first necessary to destroy the old one, we are therefore compelled to say that Freemasonry is destructive.

Gaston Martin investigates the rôle of French Freemasonry in the preparation of the Revolution.

It consists of three phases:

(1) The elaboration of revolutionary doctrine.
(2) The propagation of the doctrine.
(3) The active participation of Freemasonry in the Revolution.

Let us first examine the way in which revolutionary doctrine was elaborated. The close link between the Freemasons and the French Encyclopaedists is now known to us. Did Freemasonry inspire the philosophers or did it borrow its doctrines from them?

The Freemason Amiable (quoted by G. Martin) supports the first theory, Gaston Martin the second. This point is therefore not clearly elucidated.

The philosophers had worked out an abstract doctrine. From 1773 to 1788 Freemasonry brought these doctrines into focus and made their practical application possible; a work which Martin summarizes thus:

"In this way there emerged little by little the doctrine which was to become that of the States-General. The Masons of Saint-Brieuc were right in saying that it was all in the philosophers; those of Rennes were not wrong in stating that it was nevertheless Masonry which made it the instrument of political and social emancipation that it was in process of becoming."

(G. Martin, ibid., p. 97)

For this doctrine to have a practical political application, two conditions were necessary:

"Firstly, the support of the majority of the nation for its demands.

"And, secondly, a sufficient force to surmount the impediments which would not fail to come from those whose interests it would injure.

"Masonry worked successfully in support of these two conditions.

"It campaigned to secure the support of the majority of the nation, to secure a force (through which to act) it took an active hand in elections; at the same time it strove to disarm the hostility of rival forces."
(G. Martin, ibid., p. 98)

The campaign was initiated in Masonic circles, with the following result:

"*The fundamental principles of Masonry ended by becoming part and parcel of the mentality of all Masons; they were no more just an acquired philosophical idea, but became a way of feeling, often also a way of being.*" (G. Martin, ibid., p. 120)

The foundation of the Grand Orient in 1773 and the re-organisation of the Nine Sisters Lodge (of which Voltaire was a member) marked the beginning of a new phase: the campaign outside the lodges.

"The methods of propaganda used by Freemasons to spread abroad the reforming truths they wanted to diffuse in the outside world can be divided into three categories: the Press, propaganda by word of mouth, and the instructive spirit of the club."
(G. Martin, ibid., p. 126)

The balance-sheet of Masonic action in the field of ideas thus established that:

"1. *Masonry was the best propaganda instrument for spreading philosophical ideas;*

"2. *If it did not create the revolutionary doctrines, Masonry nevertheless elaborated them;*

"3. *Freemasonry, in this transformation of society by means of ideas, was not content to adapt principles to individuals. Very quickly it devoted itself to finding practical means of realizing its ideas. . . . It was on this account the true creator, not of principles, but of revolutionary practice;*

"4. *Finally, apart from this rôle, Masonry established itself as the great propagandist of the newest beliefs.*"

Therefore,

"Masonry well and truly, and almost despite itself, bore the weight of this constituent revolution; for it had not only, indeed, preached its doctrines; it had also prepared its leaders and, imprudently perhaps, supported certain practices deriving from the Old Régime, which, put into effect very quickly overtook their Masonic inspiration and foreshadowed the days of August and September 1792."

(G. Martin, ibid., p. 145)

The second phase in the rôle of French Freemasonry in the preparation of the Revolution lay in the propagation of revolutionary doctrine.

The Freemasons controlled the elections of March-April 1789.

"They were in many ways part of its work, and we must now examine this point in detail."

Freemasonry was a primary influence on the drafting of the *cahiers de doléances*, or lists of grievances which the people had been asked to send in from all over the country in 1789.

"The identity of the draughtsmanship has struck even the least critical scholars . . . and so some were led to try and discover if the *cahiers* were not based on models that had been circulated from district to district."

This investigation led very quickly to the discovery that instructions, or general models of the *cahiers*, had been distributed throughout the country.

"*We cannot help but be struck by the fact that all these instructions were of Masonic origin.*"

The result was that half the deputies elected to the States-General were Freemasons and G. Martin summarises their influence thus:

"*A bloc was formed in the third state that was led by Masonry,* and we will see in a minute how and by what means this came about. This group was cohesive, it had a very clear understanding of its aims, it had experience of parliamentary debates, and a discipline at the beginning that was almost perfect. In numbers it represented almost half the Assembly and the great majority belonged to the Masonic order. But it would have been powerless if the old misguided ideas of voting by order had been maintained. It therefore worked on deputies of other orders who were impressed by its unity and determination, and owing to the Masonic elements amongst them, it succeeded in disrupting them between 5th May and 23rd June. *It thus brought about the capitulation of the king and the triumph of the reform. It is difficult in these conditions to overestimate the services rendered by Masonry to the nascent Revolution.*"

(G. Martin, ibid., p. 185)

The deputies were actually closely supervised by means of an organisation called the "bureau de correspondance" according to the details revealed by G. Martin:

"*The Freemasons did not cease to direct parliamentary opinion*, and the 'bureau de correspondance' was the link between the Masonic lodges, the public and the deputies."

And elsewhere he writes:

"*No less important was the financial help given by Masonry to the work of reform*. Such an upheaval could not be put into operation successfully without vast expense. However Masonry did not limit its help to time and intellectual activity but gave its money too."

(G. Martin, ibid., p. 195)

For Masonry possessed powerful financial resources.

"The two main ways in which it spent its resources appear to have been in the printing and distribution of pamphlets which served as models for the *cahiers* and in the equipment of groups of young people who helped both to bring about the triumph of the new ideas and to maintain order during the rural anarchy at the beginning of 1789."

The Freemasons also supported many charities, some of which obviously enabled them to acquire influence over the populace by playing on their ignorance and prejudices.

"What is absolutely certain", says G. Martin, "was the fact that, in the event of trouble, the mob, having forcibly demonstrated in favour of reform, would be supported financially by the Masonic lodges."

(G. Martin, ibid., p. 198)

Thus,

"by subsidizing hand bills, by publishing posters, by aiding victims of the civil war and by financing opposition, *Freemasonry secretly but effectively aided and abetted the electoral campaign which led to the convocation of the States-General.*

(G. Martin, ibid., p. 204)

"In the meantime, the assembly of the Estates-General was getting itself organized at Versailles. There again the rôle of Masonry was to be preponderant."

The closely organized group of Masonic deputies succeeded in dominating the assembly.

"From as early as the end of May, the theory of a Masonic society of representatives had become a reality. But it was not to stay closed like a temple, as the non-Masonic deputies might have been tempted to set up in opposition to it a group which could easily have become hostile. It was enough that the leaders were Masons, and that the spirit of the club was Masonic, for the principle to be safeguarded and the necessary concentration (of force) established."

(G. Martin, ibid., p. 208)

The third phase is the active revolutionary rôle played by Freemasonry in the French Revolution. This is a dangerous field, as G. Martin knows better than anyone; consequently he deals with it in a much vaguer manner.

He shows us how Freemasonry introduced popular leaders whom it thought it could employ usefully, and inversely, how Masons were sent to harangue the people.

"Their Masonic background was unknown to those they harangued: often they were clever enough to convince their audience that it had initiated action itself; they controlled it without imposing themselves."

(G. Martin, ibid., p. 226)

Freemasonry, not content with tirades only, organized the proletariat as well, but with the object of maintaining order as much as to uphold its principles.

Little by little, with the help of their network, the Masons invaded the royal government, succesfully introducing the ideas of reform, and finally they penetrated the army.

"Nevertheless Freemasonry would have perhaps experienced much more difficulty in achieving the practical realisation of its doctrines had it not received, during the last years of the century, the support of a large section of the army. Historians who have drawn our attention to this fact seem to have grasped but imperfectly the root cause of it, which was the spread of lodges in military circles. . . .

"*The Old Régime collapsed partly because the French army and its officers did not attempt to come to its aid. Here again the consequences of Masonic propaganda surpassed the expectations of its military promoters. By the help it brought to the incipient Revolution, Masonry in the army formed an essential element in the triumph of the new ideas; it may even be suggested that without it, the great work would have been seriously compromised.*"

(G. Martin, ibid., p. 274)

G. Martin, who brings his study to an end before the outbreak of the actual Revolution, concludes with these words:

"The importance of Masonry in the Revolution must not be underestimated. Doubtless the great majority of romantic legends —daggers, traitors and cloaks of operatic repertory—have neither foundation in, nor the consistency of, truth, and Masonry has rightly pointed out the bad faith of those who accuse it of such childish absurdities. But, apart from these pathetic and deliberate falsehoods, the fact remains that *Masonry was the recognized or hidden soul of all the popular and social movements which as a whole constituted the Revolution*. Masonry created the need which transformed into creative action the potentialities for emancipation which, without it, would either have remained latent or miscarried from lack of co-ordination and the impotency of spasmodic and divergent efforts." (G. Martin, ibid., p. 284)

One objection is frequently raised when the rôle of Freemasonry in the Revolution of 1789 is discussed:

It is absurd, people say, to attribute an important part to Freemasonry in the preparation of the Revolution, since the Revolution caused the lodges to be closed and numerous Masonic leaders finally fell victim to it.

This argument, though apparently logical, is in fact absolutely invalid. All the successive revolutions since 1789 have backfired against their instigators, who have generally ended by killing one another.

Gaston Martin answers this objection in his book. He deals successively with the rôle of the nobility, the clergy, and the army in Freemasonry.

Firstly the nobility:

"Whether attracted by the novelty, a taste for mystery, or a false air of worldy masquerade and comic opera, Masonry—that 'sentimental gathering', as le Forestier called it, and which is all it would appear to be to a superficial observer, Masonry attracted a number of men about town even from the Queen's entourage.

(G. Martin, ibid., p. 104)

"*The Abbé Barruel, whose abundant documentation cannot be disputed,* perfectly understood that the membership of such nobles as Mgr. de la Rochefoucauld, Worshipful Master of the Lodge of the rue du Coq-Heron, was a stumbling block to his thesis. His explanation only confirms our deductions on this matter.

"To the honour of the unfortunate Duke de la Rochefoucauld, we hasten to say that the Revolution at least made him recognize his error. He had become Grand Master of various Masonic lodges; he was the instrument of Condorcet and of Siéyès, who used his money for the great enterprise. When he perceived the disorganisation to which France was on the point of succumbing after the reign of the first Constituent Assembly, his enthusiasm for the cause cooled, and he actually renounced it. We do not wish to make any other point; for it is obvious that neither the nobility which supported reform, nor the bourgeois Third Estate, foresaw the democratic evolution of the movement which they were preparing. As it developed, Freemasons left the order in increasing numbers."

(G. Martin, ibid., p. 105)

Next the clergy:

"It was above all in the regular and lower clergy—the figures quoted by Léonce Maître are very indicative in this respect—that the Masons abounded. Through them the Masonic ideal reached a double public: middle-class youth, taught by the former, and the parish priests and curates in the country, who belonged to the second category, and through whom could be reached the best-educated of the country folk. . . .

(G. Martin, ibid., p. 108)

"This philosophic action on the part of the regular clergy did not escape the attention of the ecclesiastical authorities, who expressed concern about it repeatedly. They hoped the regular clergy would observe stricter conformity to their traditional duties. But this they visibly failed to achieve.

"*The influence of the regular clergy was therefore considerable in the propagation of the Masonic idea*; it was all the greater because it was less the result of regular dogmatic preaching than of daily doses mixed with the very substance of their teaching.

"The parish priests could not help but exert an immense moral influence at a time when they were almost the only people who could capture the popular imagination. Charitable works, civil matters, and education all came to them; the presbytery was town hall, hospital and often also the school and study; the country could only see through the eyes of its priests; if one compares this fact with the high number of Masonic priests, one will not be surprised by the almost unanimous support that the countryside gave to the principles of the *cahiers*.

(G. Martin, ibid., pp. 109-111, 112)

"Scarcely two years later, after these events, most of these priests recovered themselves, and, fearing a formal schism, returned to tradition; this was the moment when the religious insurrection began, the origin of the wars of the Vendée; but for the moment in France 'there existed a proletariat of the clergy and this proletariat also was turning towards the lightening horizon.' The illumination of the horizon came from the flame lit in the temples, a flame which coloured the as yet indistinct plans, shrouded in the mists of the future."

(G. Martin, ibid., p. 113)

And finally the army:

Gaston Martin provides us with precise information about the penetration of the lodges into the framework of the army, and he adds:

"It would be useless to conceal the gravity of such an attitude. Those who approved displayed unheard of ingenuousness, when they subsequently deplored the scant success of their attempts to stop the movement which had been unleashed. The officers and men who took part in it had only two courses open to them: either to follow to the end the reform that was the whole purpose of Masonry, or to cut themselves off, aware of their powerlessness to arrest the torrent whose eruption they had provoked. Doubtless the majority adopted the second solution; but we have limited our study to the preparation of the Revolution, not to its ulterior development, and in 1789 there was no perceptible crack in the Masonic bloc of the young army.

"When the split took place between the left wing of the Constituent Assembly and the aristocratic right; when the army saw its ranks crumble away through emigration, the N.C.O.s of the Old Régime formed the framework on which the patriotic forces were reconstructed: Hoche, Marceau, Kléber, Augereau, and others. Whether or not they belonged to lodges, they had been infected by their spirit, which had invaded nearly all the regiments and whence they drew their unflinching zeal, which they were to bring a little later to the defence of the Republic. It has not been remarked upon sufficiently that the sans-culotte army only owed its fighting strength to this amalgamation, and that it was because it could be straddled that it triumphed. (G. Martin, ibid., p. 274)

"*The Old Régime collapsed partly because the French Army and its officers did not attempt to come to its aid. Here again the consequences of Masonic propaganda surpassed the expectations of its military promoters.*

"The military lodges were a fine instrument of national emancipation, and if we are to summarize their rôle and importance concisely, we would say that:

"1. *The first effect of Masonic propaganda in the army was to disrupt the loyal troops.* It opposed the doctrine of the army, strictly in the service of the King, with that of a national force which owed primary loyalty to the general will. It therefore smashed in the hands of the aristocrats the one certain instrument of repression which, had it been used in 1789, would very likely have been sufficient to have stifled the nascent Revolution.

"2. The Masonic ideal opened the way for certain obscure or inexperienced army leaders to reflect on their future and change their vocation. While, for example, Dumouriez was a mediocre recruit, one could not say the same of La Fayette, de Canclaux, or many others.

"3. Finally, and especially, from 1788, the admission of N.C.O.s prepared the ranks of the revolutionary army which was to stand up to the coalition of Monarchist Europe. It was from the military lodges that they drew the ideas, well aware of their value, of which they were to become the indomitable defenders and the proud propagandists.

"Thus no more in this respect than in any other, did the work of French Masonry display anything resembling a conspiracy.

"The military lodges functioned to the knowledge of all the established powers. The officers who belonged to them for the most part emigrated during the troubled period of 1791-1792.

"By the help it brought to the incipient Revolution, military Masonry in the army formed an essential element in the triumph of the new ideas; it may even be suggested that without it, the great work would have been seriously compromised."

(G. Martin, ibid., pp. 275-276)

The texts we have reproduced above are written in clear and simple language. There is really no need to pass comment on them, for they are self-explanatory. However, it would be simplifying matters too much to say that Freemasonry was the sole animating force behind the French Revolution; such large and complex movements cannot be explained by one cause alone. Freemasonry was only one of the elements involved in the Revolution, but it is an element whose importance only ignorance or bad faith can deny.

9

COMMUNISM AND FREEMASONRY

IN his second work, *La Franc-Maçonnerie à l'Heure du Choix*, Mellor deals at length with the relations between Freemasonry and Communism. His conclusion is quite explicit: they are diametrically opposite to one another.

> "Today Communism has not yet reached the peak of its trajectory; accordingly, we do not have to formulate hypotheses about its immediate future, that is to say, we do not have to calculate where and when it will cease to progress and begin to decline. The only question of interest is what will happen when it comes up against the fact of Masonry. . . .
>
> "*How prodigious is the error of their common enemies in regarding them as allies, or as if Communism was a fruit fallen from the Masonic tree. This is what the Spanish Penal Code has done, by lumping them together under a single heading in Appendix III of the said Code.*
>
> "There is therefore direct opposition between Freemasonry and the Communist world, despite the obstinate error of those who professionally pursue error, the Catholic integralists, and despite also the illusions of certain elements in the Grand Orient of France.
>
> "Is not the existence of this opposition sufficient to indicate in what alternative direction Freemasonry, anxious to survive, cannot but help align itself?"
>
> (A. Mellor: *La Franc-Maçonnerie à l'Heure du Choix*, pp. 431, 447)

The Masonic writer G. Vinatrel goes still further; in the book which he has devoted to this question, one will find that he considers that Masonry is a barrier against Communism.

> "Communism is the fundamental enemy of Freemasonry.
>
> "All Freemasons are unanimous in considering that a man who is enslaved by dogma, who leaves it to others to do his thinking for him and to decide on his behalf, has no place in Freemasonry. This liberty of thought, which is the absolute right of the individual, is the accompaniment of individual liberty in society.

"Communists, on the contrary, take it for granted from the outset, that a small group of men forming a so-called 'Central Committee' has the right to control the thoughts of other men without consulting them.

"The fundamental opposition of Communist principles to those of Freemasonry implies the existence of an implacable hostility between them from the outset, at all times and in all places; for Communism has discovered that Freemasonry is one of the forces, perhaps even the only real force, which could one day knock it out of the ring.

"Whether or not the Freemason invokes the name of the Great Architect of the Universe, according to the rite which he obeys, it is always the case that he believes in man. The Communist believes only in his own party. That is the whole difference."

(G. Vinatrel: *Communisme et Franc-Maçonnerie*, pp. 81, 115)

But is it really a fact that this antinomy exists between Communism and Freemasonry, as these two writers ask us to believe? It is a complex problem, to which it is not easy to reply categorically "Yes" or "No". This doubt always arises when it is a question of anything to do with Freemasonry, in which everything is cloudy, fluid, unformulated and impossible to grasp. Let us try and clarify our perspective.

What is the view of the Vatican and the Catholic Hierarchy? The Popes are by no means in agreement with Mellor on this point. Leo XIII in 1884, Pius XI in 1937, the Association of the Bishops of the Argentine in 1959, to quote only the principal authorities, flatly state the opposite.

In the Encyclical *Humanum Genus*, Leo XIII analyses the problem in the following words:

"In the sphere of politics, the Naturalists lay down that all men have the same rights and that all are equal and alike in every respect; that everyone is by nature free and independent; that no one has the right to exercise authority over another; that it is an act of violence to demand of men obedience to any authority not emanating from themselves. All power is, therefore, in the free people. Those who exercise authority do so either by the mandate or by the permission of the people, so that, when the popular will changes, rulers of State may lawfully be deposed even against their will. The source of all rights and civic duties is held to reside either in the multitude or in the ruling power in the State, provided that it has been constituted according to the new principles. They hold also that the State should not acknowledge God and that, out of the various forms of religion, there is no reason why one should be preferred to another. According to them, all should be on the same level.

"Now, that these views are held by the Freemasons also, and that they want to set up States constituted according to this ideal, is too well known to be in need of proof. For a long time they have been openly striving with all their strength and with all the resources at their command to bring this about. They thus prepare the way for those numerous and more reckless spirits who, in their mad desire to arrive at equality and common ownership of goods, are ready to hurl society into an even worse condition, by the destruction of all distinctions of rank and property. . . .

"In this mad and wicked design, the implacable hatred and thirst for vengeance with which Satan is animated against Our Lord Jesus Christ becomes almost visible to our bodily eyes."

(ibid., pp. 13-14)

And further on in the same Encyclical, Leo XIII added:

"From the anti-social character of the errors we have mentioned, it is clear that the greatest dangers are to be feared for States. For once the fear of God and the reverence due to His laws have been taken away, the authority of rulers treated with contempt, free reign and approval given to sedition, popular passions recklessly fanned, and all restraining influences eliminated except the fear of punishment, then there will necessarily follow a revolutionary upheaval and a period of wholesale destruction of existing institutions.

"*A complete change and upheaval of this kind is being carefully prepared by numerous associations of Communists and Socialists, in fact, it is their openly avowed aim; and Freemasonry is not only not opposed to their plans, but looks upon them with the greatest favour, as its leading principles are identical with theirs.* If the Freemasons do not immediately and everywhere proceed to realise the ultimate conclusions contained in these principles, this is not because they are restrained by the discipline of the organization or by lack of determination, but partly on account of the power and virtue of that divine religion which cannot be crushed out of existence, and partly because the more balanced part of mankind are unwilling to sink into slavery under the domination of secret societies, and offer vigorous resistance to their insane endeavours."

(ibid., pp. 16-17)

On 23rd May, 1958, in an address to the 7th week of Pastoral Adaptation, Pius XII mentioned that the roots of modern apostasy lay in scientific atheism, dialectical materialism, rationalism, illuminism, laicism, and Freemasonry—which was the mother of them all.

On 20th February, 1959, the Plenary Assembly of the Cardinals, Archbishops and Bishops of the Argentine, under the presidency of Cardinal Caggiano, published a long collective declaration on Freemasonry, from which we have taken the following passages:

> "In the course of its plenary reunion, the Argentinian Hierarchy, confronted by various articles published in the Press by Freemasonry, felt obliged to make a public declaration to the faithful, following the recommendation of Leo XIII to 'first of all, tear away the mask from Freemasonry and let it be seen as it really is'. . . .
>
> "In 1958, the IVth Interamerican Conference of Freemasonry, which was held in Santiago, Chile, declared that 'the Order helps all its members to obtain important posts in the public life of the nations.' *After this came a dissertation on the theme of 'The Defence of Laicism', to be followed by directions as to the new tactics to be adopted by Freemasonry, which coincide with the latest instructions of the Communist International.* Freemasons are to work for the triumph of laicism in all walks of life, and Communists are to subvert social order in order to create a favourable terrain in which to achieve their ends. This is how the instruction is worded: 'Intensify the campaign of laicisation through the intermediary influence of the different political parties. Try and appease the alarm of the Catholic Church at Freemasonry by avoiding direct Masonic action. Intensify the action which will unsettle the unity of the working-class movements, so that they may the more easily be stifled afterwards. Freemasonry and Communism for the moment are pursuing the same objective in Latin America, which is why they must try and work together in the best possible way, without allowing the slightest sign of their alliance to become public. . . .'
>
> "Proof that this is no dream is The Second International Congress for Universal Fraternity.
>
> "World Freemasonry and Communism are preparing for a Congress which will be held at Montevideo, called 'The Second International Congress for Universal Fraternity'. It is a Masonic Congress of Communist inspiration which aims to subordinate the Masonic ideal of 'universal fraternity' to the expansion of the Soviet Communist International. The congress will take place in Holy Week, from 26th to 28th March, and its object is to prepare for the struggle for human confraternity and world peace'. . . .
>
> "To achieve its ends, Freemasonry uses high finance, high

politics and the world press; Marxism, on the other hand, uses the social and economic revolution against the country, the family, property, morality and religion.

"Freemasons achieve their ends by secretly subversive means, Communists by openly subversive movements. Freemasonry activates sectarian political minorities; Communism relies on mass political movements, exploiting their aspirations to social justice....

"Every Argentinian, and especially the young, should know that Catholicism and Freemasonry are completely contradictory and self-exclusive, like Christ and anti-Christ. Also they ought to know that Liberalism or laicism, under whatever form it may take, is the very embodiment of Masonic ideology.

"The Church of Christ presides over every level of the life of our country. It is present, vigilant and active in every important event in our history. Catholicism is the origin, the root and the essence of the people of Argentine. In other words, to make an attempt on Catholicism is to conspire against one's native country.

"We draw the attention of all who love their country to the two enemies of our traditions and our future greatness, Freemasonry and Communism, which are seeking the destruction of everything that is noble and sacred in our land.

"Given at the Villa San Ignacio, on 20th February in the Year of Our Saviour 1959, and signed by Cardinal Caggiano, president of the Plenary Assembly of the Argentinian Hierarchy, and by the Argentinian Archbishops and Bishops present at the reunion."

In 1961, Monseigneur Perraudin, Archbishop of Ruanda in Africa, on his return from Europe, addressed a letter to all the priests of his diocese, in which he said:

"It is impossible to give even a brief account in this letter of all the journeys and approaches that I have made in Europe. My visits and my contacts have shown me how completely they support us in Europe in these difficult times. I have encountered many most praiseworthy and generous gestures of help.

"*My dominant impression, however, is that insufficient account is taken in Europe of the amplitude of the struggle for which the whole of Africa is the prize; Communism and Freemasonry are playing a satanic gamble for it, and the older Christian countries do not sufficiently understand that it is the Church of which they are members, their own Church, which is in mortal danger in Africa.*

"The people in Europe are very little informed, indeed they are often badly misinformed, about the situation. . . ."

(Quoted in the Catholic review *Verbe*, July-August 1961, p. 66)

Let us now examine the facts in the light of modern history: the real history, the one which does not appear in official books.

Freemasons as a whole are not Communists; nevertheless, everywhere Freemasonry has prepared the ground for the coming and triumph of Communism, very often without the knowledge of its members, many of whom would probably have been terrified if they had seen clearly where the principles which they propagated with such ardour and unawareness were leading.

It was the same story in 1789; the majority of the Masons who had contributed to the unleashing of the French Revolution, themselves fell victims to it. It was the same in Russia in 1917 and in Spain in 1936, and indeed it was the same in almost all the modern revolutions.

Today, there are a number of Masons, such as the ex-prefect Baylot, who belongs to the small group of the Neuilly Lodge, which is recognised by the Grand Lodge of England, who have struggled openly and very courageously against Communism; but that is a far cry from accepting that Freemasonry is innocent of any collusion with Communism, and numerous facts can be brought in support of the assertion that there *is* collusion between the two.

Firstly, throughout the nineteenth century and up to the Second World War, the various Masonries of the Grand Orient have been violently anti-Christian as regards religion, and they have also been militantly active, as regards politics, on the side of Socialism, which has become more and more radical. A perusal of the reports of the Grand Orient will bring to light numerous examples of this fact. The Masonic historian, Gaston Martin, sums up the situation when he says, in his *Manuel d'Histoire de la Franc-Maçonnerie en France*, (p. 252):

> "All Freemasons of the three obediences which are on friendly relations with one another belong to what in politics is called 'the Left'. The shades of doctrine which divide them are not such as to hinder agreement among all their members."

There is therefore an affinity of concepts and interests in these two vital fields (that is to say, religon and politics); and Freemasonry lays down as its party line of action: "no enemies on the left".

Secondly, several times during this period between the two World Wars there was close political collusion between Freemasonry and Communism; striking examples are the Popular Fronts in France and Spain, which were alliances of left-wing parties, including Communists, under the aegis of Freemasonry.

And thirdly, the numerous revolutions which have disturbed modern Europe and led to bloodshed have generally been triggered off with the efficacious help of Freemasonry; since 1905 these revolutions have become more and more Socialist and Communist in tendency.

A particularly flagrant example is to be found in the European revolutions of 1917 and 1918.

The Russian Revolution of 1917 was fomented at the height of the First World War with the help of international Freemasonry, and the principal leaders of the Kerensky régime were Masons; this movement quickly degenerated into Bolshevism.

All the revolutions which overthrew the monarchist régimes of Central Europe in 1918 were inspired and directed by Masons, and it was Masons who were given posts in the new governments of Hungary, Germany, Austria and Czecho Slovakia. Almost all these revolutions rapidly degenerated into bloody convulsions with distinctly Communist tendencies, under Bela Kun, Liebnecht, Rosa Luxembourg, Kurt Eisner and others.

It would take too long to relate in detail the part played by Freemasonry in all these revolutions. We will only examine its action in Hungary—a very interesting country from this point of view, since after the Bolshevic revolution of Bela Kun, the government seized and published the Masonic archives, which reveal Masonry's blatant connection with the revolutionary movement.

On 29th April, 1918, the Grand Master of Hungarian Freemasonry, Dr. Arpad Bokay, delivered an extremely patriotic speech in Vienna, in the course of which he said:

> "The enemies of Hungary are also the enemies of Austria; those who are in league to destroy Austria wish to do the same to Hungary; it is the monarchy which, amid the tempest of the world war, has most effectively protected the peoples of Austria-Hungary. . . ."

In November of the same year the Imperial Government was overthrown, and on the first page of the first number of its Bulletin, which could now appear without hindrance, Viennese Masonry hailed the event with these words:

> "The new state of things came as a surprise. All at once we had become free republicans, masters of ourselves. We were no longer the slaves and martyrs of a bureaucratic government servilely cringing to absolutism and militarism."
>
> (*Wiener Freimaurer Zeitung*, No. 1/2, May 1919, p. 1)

For his part, Dr. Arpad Bokay made a significant speech on 2nd November, 1918, of which the following extracts have been taken from the *Wiener Freimaurer Zeitung*. It is important to bear in mind at this point that the revolutionary government of Karolyi had just been formed.

> "This masonic programme (which he had just described) is also the programme of the national Hungarian council and of the popular government which has just been formed.
>
> "Our way is thus made clear to us.
>
> "We are marching shoulder to shoulder with them, we are working with them and we are helping them in their great and weighty, but noble task so that the Hungary of old may unperturbed enter the blessed land of the new Hungary, which is the most ardent wish of every good patriot.
>
> "Our elder and highly esteemed brothers are working today in the first line, and that entirely reassures us, for we know them and we know that they will carry out in a Masonic spirit the work which they have undertaken."
>
> (*Wiener Freimaurer Zeitung*, No. 1/2, May 1919, p. 41)

The same article added in a footnote that six Freemasons belonged to the first Hungarian republican government in the capacity of ministers, secretaries of State, and under-Secretaries.

With the advent of Bela Kun, Freemasonry was confronted with certain difficulties, for by an ironical twist of fate, it was held to be too bourgeois and was distrusted.

After the collapse of Bolshevism, the Hungarian government dissolved the lodges and published their archives. In their distress the Hungarian Masons called upon their brethren throughout the world, and it was then that the Masonic newspaper, *Latomia*, of Leipzig, published the following interesting article:

> "We are able to give the following information concerning the sad fate of Freemasons in Hungary from information supplied by one of our Hungarian brothers resident in Nuremberg.
>
> "After the catastrophe the Freemasons, who had sent another address of welcome to the Emperor Franz-Joseph during the war, fervently embraced the socialist republican ideology out of the noble conviction that the time had come when the Masonic ideal would be accomplished. In their writings they made active propaganda in its favour and most of the leaders were Freemasons.
>
> "But next, when Hungary was overwhelmed by a wave of Bolshevism, the men in power soon began to oppress Masonry as a bourgeois institution.
>
> "The reaction which, thanks to foreign assistance, shortly afterwards set in and succeeded in regaining power, inspired by clerical

leadership, closed the lodges, occupied their premises, seized their funds and anything else they found there. . . .

"In their distress, our Hungarian brothers turned to the North American Grand Lodges. The result was that, as Hungary was then negotiating a loan in America, the reply came back that this loan could not be considered until lawful institutions were re-established in Hungary—a clear allusion to the prohibition of Freemasonry.

"Thereupon the Hungarian government was obliged to open negotiations with the ex-Grand Master. The free resumption of Masonic work was proposed to him, on condition that non-Masons should have the right of access to the sessions. This was naturally refused by the Grand Master and the loan miscarried."

(*Latomia* of Leipzig, No. 2/3, 1922, p. 31)

A number of conclusions of the utmost importance arise from this brief article; among others, that:

(1) From its own admission, Freemasonry played a directing part in the Hungarian Socialist revolution, which very rapidly degenerated into the horrors of Bolshevism;

(2) American Freemasonry came to the help of Hungarian Freemasonry when it was banned by law in Hungary. This proves the international liaison of universal Freemasonry, and shows that the divergences which separate Anglo-Saxon Freemasonry from the continental variety are effaced when vital interests are at stake;

(3) International Freemasonry intervenes in the internal politics of certain countries and wields enough power to cause international loans to fall through;

(4) Freemasonry considers that the secrecy of its proceedings is so vital to its activity and its power that it prefers to be dissolved rather than to allow a government to scrutinise its internal affairs.

Finally, it is important to remember that all these conditions flow from the avowal of a Masonic journal; they are therefore of indisputable authenticity.

To come nearer to our own times, let us consider the rôle of Freemasonry in the Spanish Revolution.

The revolution which overthrew the Spanish monarchy, and the civil war which was its outcome, are a tragic example of the destruction caused by Masonry.

Like most of the European revolutions since 1917, this one began under the slogan of liberalism and democracy. It soon brought about disorder, social conflicts, chaos, and finally left all the other left-wing parties in the grip of Communism. Yet, under the Popular

Front, the alliance of the Freemasons and the left-wing parties, including Communism, held fast throughout the revolution until it was finally obliterated by the Spanish Nationalist uprising.

We will now submit to the reader documents which will serve to enlighten our understanding of this subject, and which leave no doubt whatever as to the part played by Freemasonry in the Spanish Revolution.

"The Day after the Dictatorship" was the title of the following article by F. Coty, which was published in *Le Figaro* on 2nd March, 1931, one month before the triumph of the Spanish Revolution, and which, because of its singular importance, we reproduce here almost in its entirety.

> "We have said that the faults committed by the Spanish Dictatorship had ended at last by compromising the numerous and important favourable results which it had obtained at the beginning. We have enumerated some of these faults. But the most serious was certainly its entrance, ill-prepared and unorganised, into the struggle against Spanish Freemasonry. . . .
>
> (*Le Figaro*, 1st March, 1931)
>
> "For Primo de Rivera, who understood vaguely the evil work being done by the lodges, made the mistake of attacking Spanish Freemasonry, alarming it and scotching it, but in the end leaving it all its power to do harm.
>
> "In 1928, knowing that he was being secretly combated by the sect, which on the other side of the Pyrenees has a particularly uncompromising revolutionary spirit (we have but to recall the Masonic Anarchist, Ferrer, who was truly typical of the Spanish Mason), he ordered investigations to be made at the headquarters of the Grand Orient of Madrid and the Grand Symbolic Lodge of Barcelona. This would have been a reasonable move if it had been the opening of a resolute offensive. But it was anything but that.
>
> "A number of Masonic documents were seized and submitted to the examination of men whose loyalty to the Dictatorship was above suspicion, but whose competence, unfortunately, in such a specialised matter, was not equal to the task they had been set. For they were soon disconcerted by the strange 'jargon' or phraseology employed by the lodges and understood by only a few specialists outside Masonry. The enquiry dragged on interminably while the investigators strove to thread their way through a labyrinth of Masonic degrees and symbols. The real way in which the sect functioned and its revolutionary activity escaped them altogether. Thus the enquiry was inconclusive, and far from diminishing the noxiousness of the Spanish Lodges, rather provided them

with an opportunity, which they did not fail to seize, of appealing to the solidarity of International Freemasonry. Evidence of this solidarity was, as ever, immediately forthcoming in favour of the 'persecuted brethren'. Thus the Dictatorship, which at first had been regarded quite favourably in foreign countries, notably in the Anglo-Saxon world, where order and possessions are esteemed, now found ranged against it, almost overnight, a world-wide coalition of the Press and of Masonic influences.

"Systematic attacks on Primo de Rivera were the consequences of this challenge. Their special target was the exchange rate of the peseta, which the Dictator had left unstabilised because he hoped to restore the gold standard. The same politico-financial forces, which have so often attacked French credit, now worked against Spanish credit, and had no difficulty in compromising it. The peseta dropped by 33%. At last his opponents had got hold of a serious grievance against the Dictator, one which affected the material interests of the whole Spanish people. This they turned to pitiless account against him.

"We have pointed out the other errors committed by Primo de Rivera, errors which, taken together, sufficed to bring about his downfall. But the error of declaring open war on Spanish Freemasonry without striking a serious blow was the greatest of all his mistakes. It suddenly changed the international status of the Dictatorship and provoked a formidable coalition against it.

"Meanwhile, Spanish Freemasonry, recognising the threat to its existence, redoubled its intrigues in the Administration, the Army and the trade unions. The tension became so great that the King himself asked the man who had served him so faithfully to pacify the country, but this time by his withdrawal.

"That step, however, left out of account the agitators among the Masons, who finding the occasion favourable, remained under arms and continued their offensive while changing only their objective. Instead of condemning the Dictatorship they attacked the Monarchy itself. Instead of working for the downfall of Primo de Rivera they sought to dethrone the King, notwithstanding that they had assured him a few months previously that they did not want to involve him in the struggle. Their international accomplices all came out in support of the attack on Alfonso XIII and set to work to prepare public opinion for a Socialist-Republican revolution in Spain. Léon Blum's falsetto added its piercing note to the chorus, while Jean Longuet, a past master in the art of conspiracy, went to Madrid in April 1930 to give a last word of advice to the conspirators.

"In June violent agitation commenced with revolutionary strikes at Malaga, Granada and Cordova. Sedition raised its voice among the peasants of Andalusia. A campaign of meetings demanding the establishment of a Socialist Republic deeply disturbed the inhabitants of the big towns. Whipping up feeling, co-ordinating the activities of the various bodies opposed to the Government, inducing discontented monarchists to collaborate with bourgeois republicans, and trade union officials with declared revolutionaries, Spanish Freemasonry briskly led the attack. Soon blood flowed in tragic clashes.

"Then came military mutinies in Aragon, and at the aerodrome of Cuatro Vientos outside Madrid. A few defects in the preparation of the rising caused the failure of the movement as a whole, though conceived according to the best Masonic and Carbonarist traditions. The military lodge at Jaca marched too soon, and the Masonic captains Galan and Hernandez were shot before they could be succoured by their fellow-conspirators in other garrisons, but not before they had caused the death of many in the defence of order.

"In order to judge the part played by Spanish Freemasonry in these events, and what it expected to gain if the plot succeeded, it suffices to study the list of the members of the Provisional Government, which the conspirators of Jaca and of the Madrid aerodrome had agreed to proclaim in the event of their success:

"President: *Alcala Zamora.*[1] Members: *Indalecio Prieto*, Miguel Maura, *Alexander Lerroux*, *Fernando de los Rios*, *Manuel Azana*, Santiago Casaras, *Alvaro de Albornoz*, *Largo Caballero*, *Martinez Barrio* and Nicolau d'Olwer. All the names we have put in italics, eight out of eleven, are those of militant Freemasons. As Benois, former Chief of the French Judiciary Police, said recently concerning the Oustric scandal: 'These gentlemen had met in the lodges'.

"The only reason for the inclusion of three non-Masons in the Provisional Government drawn up by Spanish Freemasonry was to establish contact between the conspirators and the malcontents of the Right (Miguel Maura), the Navy (Santiago Casaras), and the Catalan element (Nicolau d'Olwer).

"After this attempt at revolution, which was nipped in the bud, Alfonso XIII, manifestly at a loss, accepted the principle of constitutional revision, and on this the efforts of his assailants were now to be brought to bear. For they hoped to obtain from this step what mutiny in the Army had not, as yet, been able to secure.

---

[1] It is not absolutely certain that Alcala Zamora was a Freemason. It is a point which has still to be cleared up. I myself have read a passage in a Masonic review which stated that he was not. It is true that in this respect one cannot rely blindly on Masonic assertions—Léon de Poncins.

The tenacity of the Masons is clearly shown in the doggedness of their efforts against a régime to which Spain is indebted for half a century of social peace and prosperity."

(*Le Figaro*, 2nd March, 1931)

This article was a veritable prophecy, as the course of events was soon to show. For the Spanish Socialist Republican Government was indeed constituted exactly as the above article foretold, and Freemasonry gloried in the rôle which it had played in the revolution and the places which its adepts took in the new government.

The following extracts are taken from the Argentinian Masonic review, *La Cadena de Union*, which is very well informed about Spanish affairs. We quote from some of its most typical passages in which the same ideas are found expressed in different form.

"We found the Monarchy an obstacle to the historical march of the country and we have got rid of it . . . but the Monarchy is not the only obstacle. . . .

"Our task now is to uproot the whole mediaeval structure with its two powerful supports, the Monarchy and the Vatican."

(Article by A. Labriola in *Cadena de Union*, July 1931)

"As the new Spanish Republic gains in political solidarity, both internally and externally, one can see clearly how with the collapse of the Monarchy, an out of date institution no longer in harmony with the liberal ideas of the century in which we live, the pernicious power of Roman Catholic clericalism is also in process of disappearing from Spain for ever—this power that has for so long sustained at intermittent intervals a succession of violent quarrels in the political life of the Iberian peninsula, perfidious casuistry and lying quibbles, which fill the greater part of history with their resounding scandals. . . .

". . . Soon the Constitutional Assembly will be convoked to proclaim the transformation of the Spanish Government and to decree the separation of Church and State, which will thus deprive Spanish clericalism of its innumerable privileges.

"The Spanish Republican Government also intends to secularize the schools and to introduce complete liberty of conscience, putting Catholicism on the same level as other religions. . . .

"The Spanish Monarchy could only survive because it had in clericalism a faithful ally that maintained the people in ignorance, superstition and fanaticism.[1]

---

[1] Note that primary and secondary education in Spain was begun and directed by religious establishments—a curious method of keeping people in a state of ignorance.

"To break and bring to nought the power and influence of this very clericalism will be the greatest and noblest task of the new Republic, and if this sublime endeavour is achieved the Spanish Republicans will have rendered an immense service not only to their country but to the whole of humanity, which will owe them a perpetual debt of gratitude for this conquest and emancipation."

(*Cadena de Union*, May 1931, article by Teodoro de Szigethy)

"Soviet Russia has shown to the whole world that it is no sacrilege to transform a church into a theatre or a Masonic temple.

(*Cadena de Union*, July 1931, article by M. Lucchini)

"The triumph of Republican-Liberalism in Spain, one of the last bastions of Jesuit clericalism, marks a great stride forward in the pursuit of the ideal of democracy and free thought. It will be a warning to all those who do not wish to or cannot understand that the spiritual progress of humanity can no longer tolerate the dominion of the oppression of ideas any more than religious fanaticism, the greatest and most terrible of the wounds that afflict humanity.

"It is to be hoped that the work of restoration and emancipation undertaken by the Spanish Republicans will be definitely consolidated and that thus Inquisitorial Catholicism, which has been the cause of every corruption in Spain, killing all liberty of thought, profaning the secrets of conscience and annihilating civic liberties, will disappear for ever, and with it all moral and spiritual oppression, thus opening the way for emancipation from outmoded atavisms, and for liberty of thought, for the moral and material well-being of the Spanish people, who after such a long period of suffering and oppression deserve a better fate.

"Times have changed. Progress has dealt the death blow to dictatorship and clerical obscurantism. The Spanish Republic bears witness to it.

(*Cadena de Union*, April 1931; article by T. Szigethy)

"*All praise to the distinguished architects of the redemptive evolution. All praise to our brother Masons who on the other side of the broad Atlantic in the vanguard of world opinion have succeeded in laying the foundations of the great work that the new Spain, the antithesis of the one which has just disappeared, is to accomplish: a happy era of peace, progress and respect.*"

(*Cadena de Union*, April 1931, article by M. Gualdi)

In the joy of their success, certain revelations were triumphantly displayed in favourably disposed secular papers. *El Liberal*, for instance, published an article which was reproduced in the *Boletin oficial del grand oriente espanol* (No. 61, 10th December, 1931), from which we have taken the following brief extract:

> "However, a considerable section of public opinion was frightened of Masonry and certain papers reflected that state of mind. One of them gave a list of the politicians who were Masons. At the head was Lerroux, followed by Fernando de Los Rios and Marcelino Domingo. It is indeed a brilliant list. It includes nearly all the men who had anything to do or say in Spain. . . .
>
> "The best, in this instance as anywhere else, who are not Masons, deserve to be.
>
> "It was as a Mason that the Minister for Public Instruction spoke in Morocco; it is as a Masonic creation that the Government directs us; as a Mason that Lerroux has led the State. After a Jesuit Monarchy it is only natural that a Masonic Republic should act as a liberator . . . (Catholicism) had been on the point of converting Spain into a vast trogolodyte cavern. Today the Masons are in power, and it was high time that they should be."

Masonry was disturbed by this awkward publicity for, as we know, it prefers to work in secret, and the *Boletin* of the Grand Orient from which the above passage was taken, continues:

> "The statements of our disinterested friends can cause Masonry more harm than all the united attacks of its adversaries.
>
> "It must not be published in the columns of important newspapers that Masonry does in fact rule. That is not certain. In its bosom Masonry shelters politicians whose personality emerges in their public life and it is possible that its principles may have exercised an influence on their inner formation, but Masonry as a body does not interfere in political struggles. . . .
>
> "It is clear that Masonry does not govern the country. But the Government is composed of men among whose numbers some can add to their merits the honour of belonging to the loveliest, the freest, the noblest and holiest institution, the august Masonic Order. . . ."

Naturally, Masonry does not govern. But all the men who govern are Freemasons. That recalls the famous distinction between the Soviet Government and the Third International.

Masonry, says the Freemason Lantoine (see Léon de Poncins: *La Franc-Maçonnerie d'après ses documents secrets*, 1936), must not openly take part in political struggles, so that no defeat can affect the Order, which remains cleverly concealed in its speculative rôle.

The Spanish Revolution provides clear proof of the fact that a well-organized minority can profit by a period of unrest to ensure the success of a *coup d'état*. It was in fact sufficient for a few Masonic intriguers who held key positions to get together in the lodges and devise a concerted plan of action, to succeed in bringing about the revolution and imposing a Masonic Government on a Catholic and Monarchist country, whose people however held themselves aloof from political struggles.

Once power has been attained it is easy to represent the whole movement as an expression of the people's will, and by remaining in power long enough the opinion of the masses can be moulded in the desired direction. This can be achieved by different means, of which the two principal are the school and the press, and it must be admitted that in work of this kind Freemasonry is supremely accomplished.

In December 1931 the left-wing weekly, *Vu*, published an important article on Spain by the well-known writer, P. Dominique, from which we have taken the following passage dealing with the Spanish Revolution.

> "Here we find Freemasonry active again. The people reacted against a spiritual domination which had weighed on them for centuries, but were they directed towards this reaction, and are they still being directed? There has been a lot of discussion about Masonry, particularly in regard to the Ferrer incident. It has been said that the whole opposition at the time was composed of Masons, and at the present time it seems that at least five members (there are surely others) of the Government are Masons: Largo Caballero, Indalecio Prieto, Marcelino Domingo, Alexander Lerroux and Fernando de Los Rios. These are evident signs of the activity of a counter-church. But how can one build up the State otherwise? The only people who seem logical to us are, on the one hand, Philip II and his successors, or the Basque-Navarre deputies who invoke 'Christ the King', and, on the other hand, the avowed anti-religionists who meet philosophy with philosophy, and Church with counter-Church. The foundation of every State that aims at universality and perpetuity rests on a spiritual basis —for in every state, in every human community, there is an empire which is sometimes unaware of its own existence.
>
> ". . . Spain, unlike France, was once profoundly theocratic. That gives us reason to think that she could become so once again, but in a sense quite contrary to Catholicism. When the Articles of the Constitution relative to the relations between Church and State were voted, Mr. Azana, who today is President of the Council, apparently declared: 'At last Spain is no longer Catholic'.

> "And without doubt the meaning of the future President's thought was: 'At last Catholicism is no longer the State religion'.
>
> "But what if Spain had need of a religion or a state philosophy? The Soviets gave their people one. But if Spain felt such a need, what religion, what philosophy—one for which one might die if necessary—would Mr. Azana give to his country?"
>
> (P. Dominique: *Vu*, 30th December, 1931)

Let us conclude this brief study of the rôle of Freemasonry in Spain with the report of the Extraordinary General Assembly of the Spanish Grand Orient, held at Madrid on 20th February, 1932, and succeeding days.

This document is of the utmost importance in that it affords us proof of the close surveillance which Masonry exercises over those of its members who hold political positions, and the strict obedience which it exacts of them, an obedience under oath to secret orders, and subject to Masonic penalties in case of transgression.

This is a fact which the Freemasons have denied and of which therefore this document brings us absolutely indisputable evidence. It was published in its entirety in the *Revue Internationale des Sociétés secrètes*, 15th December, 1933.

The following passages are taken from:

Official Bulletin of the Spanish Grand Orient, Madrid, 10th September, 1932, VIth year, No. 64.

> "Decisions taken at the extraordinary General Assembly of the Spanish Grand Orient, held at Madrid on 20th February, 1932, and succeeding days.
>
> "First Motion on the Agenda:
>
> "(2) All Freemasons of the Spanish Grand Orient will confirm their oath according to the rank they hold; those absent or impeded will do so in any suitable way, and those present, at the first meeting of the lodge. The Venerable Master will warn the Freemasons that they must renew their oath, verbally or in writing, to be always ready to appear before their respective judges in order to explain and justify the correctness of their Masonic conduct in every action of their Masonic or secular life.
>
> "(6) The Venerable Masters will see to it that those Brother Masons take the oath before the Altar with all solemnity at the Apprentice Lodge, which will in no way prevent the ceremony being repeated at the lodge corresponding to each Brother's degree, the aforesaid oath to be inscribed in the Acts and celebrated with a triple battery of rejoicing.

"(7) The Lodges and Triangles will file a report on each Freemason, on which will be recorded his actual work, the posts he holds or has held in the State or private enterprise, and the reasons for his leaving; as also a record of his meritorious services and Masonic achievements. This file must be specially complete and specific for those Masons holding a political post through popular vote or by Government nomination, such as councillors, deputies, etc. The said files will be sent to the Grand Lodge of the district concerned to be transmitted to the C.P. of the G.S.F.C.

"Second Motion on the Agenda:

"(11*a*) The Masonic authorities are bound to see to it that, as often as necessary, Freemasons holding public positions renew their oaths to explain and justify their conduct as Masons before their superiors.

"(*b*) Freemasons in public posts must be reminded of their duty of charity and fraternal tolerance, and care must be taken to see that this spirit of Masonic brotherhood remains above all differences of opinion which may separate them in political contests.

"(*c*) All this supervision, help and collaboration will depend on the lodge of the Degree concerned, and should be carried out in a spirit of absolute respect for the political views of Masonic brothers, without the slightest trace of partisan spirit but solely for the defence of the great principles of our August Order.

"(12) A vast activity of Masonic propaganda will be organised by means of pamphlets, personal contacts, publication of biographies of great Spanish Masons of the past, and lectures, etc., for the purpose of increasing—always, however, with due discrimination—the number of Masons and the lodges depending on the Spanish Grand Orient.

"(13) In order to be able to determine correctly the immediate or remote projects of Freemasonry, this Assembly should not limit its scope merely to drawing up rules regarding certain concrete facts, but it is its business especially to ratify, recall to mind and explain the fundamental principles which guide the whole movement.

"And this we must do in the religious, political and social spheres.

"It is the function of this Assembly to recall and explain the Masonic principles which, in these three spheres, should inspire the work of Spanish Masonry today and in the future.

"Work in the religious sphere is the most important thing. It is the foundation of all the others, since every political and social doctrine must be erected on an ethical foundation, which in turn is based on metaphysics, or an attempt to explain the order of the world—such an explanation constituting a religion in the widest and noblest sense of the word.[1]

"In the political domain, although there is less occasion for doubt and confusion, it will be a good thing for this Assembly to reassert our faith embodied in the motto: 'Liberty, Equality, Fraternity', a faith that is both liberal and democratic, and incompatible with any form of dictatorship, tyranny or despotism, no matter whence it springs.

"With regard to the social sphere, we think that Masonry should hold the same broad and elevated views as in politics. The motto: 'Liberty, Equality, Fraternity' binds socially as well as politically.

"Our ideal of Liberty, Equality and Fraternity cannot allow one man to be exploited by another, or certain people to live in luxury and idleness, while others are in misery and compelled to work hard. That is the problem which today divides the world into two opposing camps. Freemasonry cannot be indifferent to this problem if it is to survive and continue its work of building the ideal Temple. Freemasonry must draw up a statement of principles condemning the injustice of the economic system under which we live, and just as it has fought for the conquest of political liberties, it must fight for the establishment of a régime of true social justice."

Speaking of the relations between Freemasonry and Communism, Alec Mellor tells us in his second work, *La Franc-Maçonnerie à l'Heure du Choix*, that the Spanish Penal Code has made a prodigious error by lumping these two movements together under a single heading. (For full quotation, see p. 150 above.) But it is not the Spanish Code but Mellor who is making a tragic blunder, in wishing at all costs to acquit Freemasonry of all responsibility in the revolution. This means that he must be either writing in bad faith or else completely ignorant of all the Masonic actions behind the scenes which brought about the Spanish Revolution.

---

[1] We know what Masonic conceptions about religion mean, and with regard to the relationship of Freemasonry with religion, it is useful to quote here some sentences from the pen of Aulard, a well-known Freemason and Professor of Revolutionary History at the Sorbonne, which put the whole question in its true colours:

"It is absurd to continue to say: we are not aiming at destroying religion, since we are at once obliged to make the opposite assertion, that this destruction is indispensable for the rational foundation of the new political and social State. Let us, therefore, no longer proclaim that we do not want to destroy religion, but, on the contrary, that we do want to destroy religion, in order to set up the new State in its place."

We will conclude this chapter on the relationship between Freemasonry and Communism, with an exposé of documents on the agreements arrived at between the Allied leaders at Yalta which were to weigh so heavily on the future of the world.

These documents have been published before, but they have remained isolated and practically unknown; yet they stand out dramatically when they are assembled and related to one another. Once more we shall see Freemasonry, Judaism, and Communism secretly associated in an operation of revolutionary subversion to bring off a gamble which for some years was to place the American government at the service of the Kremlin and of Stalin's policy of world domination.

There is one man whose name is closely connected with the secret agreements concluded at Yalta, preceded and completed by those at Teheran and Potsdam: namely, President Benes of Czecho-Slovakia—a fact which is all too little known.

After he had deserted from the Austrian army in the 1914 war, Benes was welcomed, together with Masaryk, by the Western allies. With the help of Freemasonry, for which he was all his life a fanatical agent, Benes founded the Czecho-Slovak Government in exile at Versailles and continually benefited from the material and moral help afforded to him by the Western governments, principally the French and the American. As a militant Freemason and a democrat of very advanced ideas, Benes played a great part in international politics, through the Little Entente group of States of which he was the undisputed leader, and by the favour of certain high dignitaries of America. Now, Benes has always been a ferocious partisan and devoted ally of Soviet Russia; it was to cost him his country, his political career and finally his life. Here we shall describe only the little known but essential part which he played in the preparation and conclusion of the Yalta agreement.

The Saturday Evening Post, on 17th April, 1948, published an article by Demaree Bess on the Yalta drama; and almost simultaneously, W. Bullitt, a former ambassador of the United States at Paris, published in *Life* of 27th September, 1948, a long study on the same subject, under the significant title: "How we won the war and lost the peace". These two articles are of supreme importance; Demaree Bess and W. Bullitt knew intimately the principal figures in the drama, both were direct participants in the Yalta negotiations and both express themselves with great frankness. The facts they bring to light deserve to be studied with great care, for their accounts agree entirely with one another and they are of extreme gravity.

Let us first briefly summarise the essential facts, in so far as they have a direct connection with the Yalta agreement:

Early in 1945, the American general, Patton, succeeded in piercing the German front, and his armoured vehicles, spreading out at top speed, drove deep into Germany; he advanced so quickly that he lost contact with superior command and established his headquarters at Pilsen, about fifty miles from Prague.

What happened then was a mystery which remained incomprehensible until recently, for General Patton stopped dead in his forward thrust. He had plenty of petrol, provisions and fighting spirit. The road to Prague was wide open, yet, to the general amazement, he did not occupy that city. This is what happened: officers of Patton's army entered Prague in a jeep when it was still occupied by the Germans. A colonel of the American intelligence service was quickly brought into the presence of the German general commanding the city, who said to him point-blank: "I suppose you have come here to accept the surrender of my troops?" The American colonel concealed his surprise and the general then explained the situation: "This is the territory we are occupying (pointing on the map to several hundred square miles centred on Prague), it is completely under our control and we can hand it over to you without difficulty; the Russian troops of General Malinovsky are here (once more pointing on the map to Slovakia, which is a considerable distance from Prague). They are poorly supplied and we can easily hold them for as long as is necessary to complete the formalities of surrender. If you have any doubt about it, I will give you a staff car and you can verify the situation on the spot." The American colonel replied that he was not authorised to negotiate a surrender but that he would go at once to put the matter to General Patton. Then he went at top speed to Pilsen where he made his report to one of Patton's Chiefs of Staff. This officer threw up his hands in horror: "It is more than my life is worth to tell the Boss that. He will blow his top worse than ever. He has just had a rocket from Eisenhower for having outstepped his orders in coming this far."

In other words, the American troops could have occupied Prague and the whole sector offered them by the Germans but General Eisenhower acted in conformity with the Yalta agreement which was secret.

Some days later, the Czechs, who knew that the allied armies were close at hand, rose against the Germans who were still in occupation of the city, and they called to the Americans by radio for help. Patton received this appeal with impotent rage. The Czechs saved Prague from destruction by making an agreement with General Vlassoff whose troops were in the neighbourhood. Vlassoff, who had raised an anti-Communist army under German protection, accepted on condition that the Czechs would guarantee him a free passage for himself and his troops so that he could subsequently surrender to the Americans. The Czechs kept their promise but, a year later, the Americans handed Vlassoff over to the Soviet forces to be shot.

The German general was right when he said that the troops of General Malinovsky were poorly supplied, for they never got as far as Prague. It was finally General Koniev near Berlin who made the long march from there to Prague, entering the city in triumph as its "liberator". Czecho-Slovakia thus found itself helpless in Soviet hands.

What happened at Prague was repeated at Vienna and Berlin. The allies could have occupied these three cities without difficulty and the only reason why they did not do so was because the cities had been assigned to the Russians, at Yalta.

From the 5th to the 10th February, 1945, the famous meeting between Stalin, Roosevelt and Churchill took place at Yalta, in the Crimea, where certain agreements were concluded which put in pawn the future of the world. Almost all the discussions took place between Roosevelt and Stalin. It was Roosevelt who personally and in secret took the Yalta decisions. Without any mandate, without consulting anybody outside his two or three intimate counsellors who were present, without reference to anyone at all, Roosevelt signed agreements of extreme importance which committed the Western World as a whole.

In fact the clauses of the Yalta treaty remained secret for several years and it is only recently that they have come to be known; it is still not sure that they are known completely.

When Patton, as we have seen, learnt about the Yalta agreement while stationed before Prague, he was exceedingly angry, and the American Ambassador to Poland, A. Bliss Lane, was utterly astounded when he learnt that part of the truth which concerned Poland. It is worth quoting his account of it, as related in his memoirs:

> "Stettinius and some of his principle advisers . . . were at Yalta. Yet the first word regarding the Conference which reached the State Department in Washington was the report by J. Daniels, Administrative Assistant to the President given out for release on 12th February, 1945. A copy was immediately brought to me at my desk in the State Department. As I glanced over it, I could not believe my eyes. To me, almost every line spoke of a surrender to Stalin. . . . (p. 51)

> "By President Roosevelt's own admission, the Yalta agreement with respect to Poland was a compromise. To put it more brutally, it was a capitulation on the part of the United States and Great Britain to the views of the Soviet Union on the frontiers of Poland

and on the composition of the Polish Provisional Government of National Unity. Yet at the time the report as a whole was acclaimed by Members of Congress of both parties as an outstanding achievement. The American people hailed it as a definite milestone along the highway of international peace.

"'At the Yalta Conference the physically disabled President of the United States was outwitted, outmanoeuvred and outfoxed by Stalin', asserts Rozmarek, President of the Polish-American Congress, in a recent letter to me. Immediately after the announcement on 12th February, 1945 of the Yalta decisions, Mr. Rozmarek had stated publicly:

"'It is with sorrow, dismay and protest that we greet the decisions of the Big Three to give all land east of the so-called Curzon Line to Russia in direct contradiction to all sacred pledges of the Atlantic Charter. This tragic revelation is a staggering blow to the cause of freedom.' (p. 54)

"As for the Poles not subservient to the Kremlin, they had no hesitation in terming the Yalta decision the betrayal of Poland. To them it was the negation of their hopes for independence and for the restoration of the territory which their enemies had confiscated in 1939 in the face of non-aggression treaties. But this time it was not the enemies but the allies of Poland, co-members in the United Nations, who gave the *coup de grâce* to the aspirations of the Polish people for a restoration of their liberty and democracy."

(A. Bliss Lane: *I Saw Poland Betrayed*, p. 55)

We will now give a summary of the Yalta agreements.

At Yalta, Roosevelt handed over to the Russians:

1. The Baltic countries—Latvia, Esthonia, Lithuania;
2. All the eastern part of Poland, which the Russians had occupied in 1939, following the Molotov-Ribbentrop agreement;
3. All eastern and central Europe, including Berlin, Prague and Vienna.
4. Access to the Mediterranean through the recognition of Tito as ruler of Yugoslavia, and the abandonment of his rival, the monarchist Mihailovich;
5. Manchuria, ceded to Russia without the knowledge of Chiang Kai-shek, the Chinese republican leader, and in flat contradiction of the undertakings which had been given to the latter at Cairo;
6. Inner Mongolia, North Korea, the Kuril Islands, and the northern part of Sakhalin; in practice, Chiang Kai-shek was sacrificed to Russian ambitions and China was virtually put

within the grasp of the Communists, as subsequent developments were to show;

7. The rights of France in Indo-China were virtually sacrificed, and the origin of the bloody revolutionary war which has engulfed Indo-China can be said to date from these agreements.
8. In addition, on the debit side of Yalta, may be quoted certain clauses such as the following: the Allies engaged themselves to hand over to the Russians all nationals classed as "Soviet citizens", that is, all anti-Communist Russians who had sought refuge in the English, American and French zones, together with all refugees from satellite countries such as Hungary, Rumania, Bulgaria, etc. . . . This clause led to innumerable personal tragedies; for years afterwards, secret police agents of the N.K.V.D. tracked down Soviet or ex-Soviet nationals even in the heart of Paris.

In the French zone of occupied Germany they soon realised that Russians who were handed over under the clause were likely to suffer deportation or to be shot in the neck; they contrived to hand over as few as possible. The English took longer to understand the truth, but stopped it after a while. The Americans went on for a long while and stopped only after atrocious tragedies had occurred, when their relations with the Soviet had become very strained.

In conclusion, at Yalta, in exchange for definite advantages, Stalin gave only vague and theoretical engagements, which consisted in allowing democratic, free and independent governments to be established in the zone assigned to Russian domination.

Once the Yalta agreement was signed, the Russians demanded and obtained the fulfilment of all the clauses which were favourable to them, but did not observe any of those which they had undertaken to respect.

Bullitt was right when he wrote: "How we won the war and lost the peace". Yalta was a diplomatic disaster such as seldom has been known in history.

How is Roosevelt's attitude at Yalta to be explained?

Various explanations have been given, one as little convincing as another.

The inadequacy of Roosevelt as a negotiator has been attributed to the ignorance and political inexperience of American diplomacy.

It has been suggested that the Allies were scared of the prospect of a separate peace between the Russians and the Germans, of the same sort as the Ribbentrop-Molotov pact, and that they were ready to make any concession to avoid it. This argument does not hold water; too many millions of dead on either side lay between the

Russians and the Germans to allow any possibility of this taking place.

It has been said that, at Yalta, Roosevelt and Hopkins were two moribund figures, physically incapable of defending western interests. It is true that both were very ill when they arrived at Yalta and that they died a few weeks after their return; but the policy of Yalta had been followed by Roosevelt for a long time before the event. Since then a most remarkable document has been published which we shall discuss later: a secret letter from Roosevelt to Zabrousky, reproduced by Señor Doussinague in his memoirs, published while he was Spanish Ambassador to Chile. He was, at the time of Yalta, principal private secretary to Count Jordana, Foreign Minister of Spain. (See Sr. Doussinague: *España tenia razon*, Ed. Espada Calpe, Madrid 1949.) If, as it appears, this document is authentic, the theory of Roosevelt's illness is no explanation and becomes an argument without validity.

William Bullitt and Demaree Bess discuss the question of Roosevelt's responsibility at great length in the two articles already mentioned. The gist of what they have to say is summarised below:

In the course of his article, Bullitt says:

> "*We* had to *prove* our good faith to Stalin—who had ordered the murder of millions and had broken his word whenever it had suited him to break it . . . this was the topsy-turvy, world-turned-upside down, Alice Through the Looking-Glass attitude towards the Soviet Union which our government adopted in the latter part of 1941.
>
> "Winston Churchill, although he was delighted that our main war effort would be turned against Germany, constantly worried about the consequences of letting the Red Army into Eastern and Central Europe. From time to time he suggested that the British and ourselves should launch a secondary attack through the Balkans or Trieste, so that the Danube Valley might be in our hands and not in the hands of the Communists at the close of the war. Adoption of this project might have saved a large portion of Central and Eastern Europe for the free world. But General Marshall, on the grounds of military logistics, adamantly opposed such an expedition. President Roosevelt supported General Marshall.
>
> "Nevertheless, the President knew that he must find some solution to the problem of Soviet Imperialism—and under the influence of Harry Hopkins, who had become his chief adviser, he adopted a 'solution' which was a supreme example of wishful thinking. The President and Hopkins together evolved a plan to

convert Stalin, by appeasement, from Soviet Imperialism to democratic collaboration.

"The means by which the President hoped to accomplish the conversion of Stalin were four:

"(1) To give Stalin without stint or limit everything he asked for the prosecution of the war and to refrain from asking Stalin for anything in return.

"(2) To persuade Stalin to adhere to statements of general aims, like the Atlantic Charter.

"(3) To let Stalin know that the influence of the White House was being used to encourage American public opinion to take a favourable view of the Soviet government.

"(4) To meet Stalin face to face and to persuade him into an acceptance of Christian ways and democratic principles.

"*The President knew that he was gambling with the vital interests of the U.S. He personally approved publication of the statement: 'Mr. Roosevelt, gambling for stakes as enormous as any statesman ever played for, has been betting that the Soviet Union needs peace and is willing to pay for it by collaborating with the West.'*

"At the close of a three-hour discussion setting forth my objections to his course, which the President had asked me to prepare, he said: 'Bill, I don't dispute your facts. They are accurate. I don't dispute the logic of your reasoning. I just have a hunch that Stalin is not that kind of a man. Harry says he's not and that he doesn't want anything but security for his country, and I think that if I gave him everything that I possibly can and ask nothing from him in return, *noblesse oblige*, he won't try to annexe anything and will work with me for a world of democracy and peace.'

"I reminded the President that when he talked of *noblesse oblige* he was not speaking of the Duke of Norfolk but of a Caucasian bandit whose only thought when he got something for nothing was that the other fellow was an ass, and that Stalin believed in the Communist creed which calls for the conquest of the world for Communism.

"The President then said: ' . . . It's my responsibility, and not yours; and I'm going to play my hunch.'

"After President Roosevelt decided to gamble on his ability to appease Stalin and turn him from Soviet imperialism to democratic collaboration with us, he did everything in his power to please the Soviet dictator.

"The epic bravery of the Red Army and the Russian people had prepared the field for propaganda in favour of the Soviet Government. On this fertile ground the power of the White House was used to sow a crop of propaganda. Mr. Joseph E. Davies, who had been Ambassador to the Soviet Union from 16th November, 1936 to the spring of 1938, was encouraged to publish a volume entitled *Mission to Moscow* and to act as adviser to the producer of a motion picture with the same title. In his book and film Mr. Davies spread before the American people an alluring picture of the Soviet Union, and made many speeches throughout the U.S. in which his theme was, 'by the testimony of performance and in my opinion the word of honour of the Soviet government is as safe as the Bible.'

"The Department of State employed its influence with Washington correspondents and columnists to add rosy colours to the Soviet picture. All the agents of the Soviet government in America, all the Communists and fellow travellers, joined happily in bamboozling the people of the U.S. with regard to the nature and aims of the Soviet dictatorship.

"The President and Hopkins gradually began to be swept away by the waves of propaganda they had started. In spite of the President's statement of 10th February, 1940, that: 'The Soviet Union is run by a dictatorship as absolute as any other dictatorship in the world', they developed the theory that the Soviet Union was a 'peace-loving democracy' and bestowed favours on persons who subscribed to this perversion of the truth. Able and patriotic officers of the Department of State and the Foreign Service who knew the truth about the Soviet Union and refused to lie in favour of the Communist dictatorship were moved to unimportant posts. Clever young men who knew the truth but cared more about their careers than their country and were ready to testify that 'Stalin had changed', were promoted rapidly—and became contemptible profiteers of American disaster. The Department of State, the Treasury Department and many wartime agencies had Soviet partisans poured into them. The War Department began to admit fellow travellers and to allow known Communists to serve as officers with access to confidential information. A network of Soviet sympathisers was established in Washington, and apologists for Soviet policies were sent as American advisers to the Chinese Government and to Latin America. . . .

"It was by his concessions to Stalin's desires in the Far East that the President most gravely endangered the vital interests of the United States. On 30th October, 1943, in Moscow, Stalin had stated to Cordell Hull 'clearly and unequivocally that, when the Allies succeeded in defeating Germany, the Soviet Union would then join in defeating Japan'. In commenting on this statement the Secretary of State wrote, 'The Marshal's statement of his decision was forthright. He made it emphatically, it was entirely unsolicited, and he asked nothing in return. . . .'

"In November 1943, one month after this promise of Stalin, the President—on his way to Teheran—held a conference in Cairo with Churchill and the Chinese president, Generalissimo Chiang Kai-shek. The three signed and published the following declaration: '. . . that all the territories Japan has stolen from the Chinese, such as Manchuria, Formosa and the Pescadores, shall be restored to the Republic of China.'

"At Yalta on 11th February, 1945, President Roosevelt broke the pledge which he had made to the Chinese government at Cairo and—secretly, behind the back of China—signed with Churchill and Stalin an agreement by which . . . Roosevelt gave to the Soviet Union not only 'pre-eminent interests' in the great Manchurian port of Dairen and full control of the great naval base which protects it, Port Arthur, but also 'pre-eminent interests' in the railroads which lead from the Soviet Union to Dairen and split Manchuria from the northwest to the south.

"In view of Roosevelt's pledge that Manchuria would be restored to China this secret agreement was entirely dishonourable. It was also potentially disastrous not only to China but also to the United States, because it gave Stalin a deadly instrument for the domination of China and the eventual mobilization of her manpower and resources for war against us. . . .

"The actions of the Soviet government in Poland, Hungary, Austria, Roumania, Bulgaria, Eastern Germany, Iran, Manchuria and Korea during the remaining months of 1945 proved beyond a shadow of doubt that Stalin had remained faithful to Lenin's teaching: 'It is necessary . . . to use any ruse, cunning, unlawful method, evasion, concealment of truth.' *The President had lost his gamble for 'stakes as enormous as any statesman ever played for.' In truth there had never been a gamble. There was never the slightest possibility of converting Stalin from the creed which calls for the installation of Communist dictatorship in all countries of the world. . . . Roosevelt had not gambled. He had been gulled. . . .*

"In the autumn of 1945 General P. J. Hurley, our Ambassador to China, returned to Washington and resigned after stating publicly that his work had been hampered by Communists and fellow travellers in the Department of State and the Foreign Service. To quiet the national scandal which ensued, President Truman asked General Marshall, who had retired, to go to China as his personal representative . . . and to draft his own instructions. . . .

"There are few Americans today who do not understand what result is produced when a national government is forced to enter into a coalition with Communists. The story has been written in blood and slavery in Estonia, Latvia, Lithuania, Poland, Roumania, Bulgaria, Yugoslavia, Albania, Hungary and Czechoslovakia. But when General Marshall went to China in December, 1945, co-operation with Communists seemed to him and to President Truman quite a happy thought. . . . In his attempts to bend Generalissimo Chiang Kai-shek to his will, General Marshall used not only arguments but also a form of pressure that was potentially as damaging to the security of the U.S. as it was to the immediate security of China. He cut the military supplies of the Chinese government armies . . . and in the field of aviation, in September 1946, he deliberately broke the contract of the American government to deliver to the Chinese government planes, and spare parts, and ammunition, and materials needed for ground services to maintain 'eight and one-third air groups' for three years. In spite of the mortal peril in which General Marshall's action placed China, Generalissimo Chiang Kai-shek would not embrace the Communists. He knew what Communists were, and General Marshall did not. President Truman in his ignorance of the Far East blindly followed General Marshall's lead, and our Far Eastern policy became one of the blind leading the blind. This was acutely dangerous . . . since China is the key to the Far East. Communist control of China would lead rapidly to Communist victory in Indo-China . . . which would almost inevitably be followed by Communist subjugation of Thailand (Siam) and the Malay Peninsula.

"Where does that leave us today?

"The present 'peace' is an uneasy armistice which will last only so long as the Soviet Government wants it to last. As in the decade before the First World War, 'Peace is at the mercy of an incident'. And sooner or later the incident will occur.

"Unless something is done, the Continent of Europe and the Far East will fall into Stalin's hands. And the people of the United States will face assault by overwhelming masses of Communist-driven slaves. Once more, as in August 1940 it is necessary to use the tragic words: 'America is in danger. Unless we act now, decisively, to meet the threat we shall be too late. It is clear as anything on this earth that the United States will not go to war, but it is equally clear that *war is coming* towards the Americas.'

"We face today a struggle not for security but for survival."

(Article "How we won the War and lost the Peace", by W. Bullitt, former American Ambassador to Moscow, in *Life*, international edition, 27th September, 1948, pp. 44-52)

The article by Demaree Bess, which appeared in *The Saturday*

Evening Post, on 17th April, 1948, is perhaps even more important than Bullitt's, for it brought to light hitherto unpublished material on the rôle of Doctor Benes in influencing Roosevelt in his disastrous policy:

"The following account of how President Roosevelt and Doctor Benes worked together in formulating wartime Russian policies was told to me by Doctor Benes himself, in several conversations which I had with him during and since the war. . . .

"The story begins in the spring of 1939, several months before the outbreak of war. The Czech statesman first sought refuge in London, but after a few months he visited the United States . . . and a secret meeting was arranged one week-end at the Roosevelt's Hyde Park home. The two statesmen talked without an interpreter for several hours. Their discussion covered a wide range, but the subject to which the President returned again and again was Soviet Russia, and particularly the personality and character of Josef Stalin. Mr. Roosevelt knew that Doctor Benes was a close student of Russian affairs, and that he was personally acquainted with Stalin. President Roosevelt explained that his own advisers completely disagreed among themselves about Russia and Stalin, and that it was a difficult problem to decide which side was right. The President listened carefully while Doctor Benes outlined his own impressions of the Soviet system. . . .

"Mr. Roosevelt then continued seriously, 'The chief question in my mind is how to get an agreement with the Russians which will stick. Some of my advisers say that is impossible. They insist that the Russians cannot be trusted to keep any agreement if they see an advantage to themselves in breaking it. What do you think about this?'

"The Czech leader replied confidently, 'I have given long and careful thought to that matter. I have studied and restudied the actions of the Soviet Government ever since it was founded, and particularly since Stalin rose to power. And it is my considered opinion that if Stalin himself pledges his personal word, then he can be trusted completely.'

"The President sat for some moments in silence after hearing this answer. It seemed to make a deep impression upon him. Today, as we piece together the record of the eventful wartime years, it appears that Mr. Roosevelt was wholly convinced by Doctor Benes' conclusion, and that henceforth the President's policy towards Russia was to be based upon his confidence in Stalin's personal word. This explains his intense desire to meet Stalin face to face, first at Teheran and later at Yalta. It may also explain why, the week before his death, he told Mrs. Anne O'Hare McCormick of *The New York Times*, that many Russian actions were disturbing him, but that he still believed in Stalin's good intentions.

"Doctor Benes returned to England when the war broke out, and I had a long talk with him . . . during the first Russo-Finnish war. President Roosevelt had just made a public statement in which he declared, 'The Soviet Union, as everybody who has the courage to face the fact knows, is run by a dictatorship as absolute as any other dictatorship in the world. It has allied itself with another dictatorship, and it has invaded a neighbour (Finland) so infinitesimally small that it could do no conceivable possible harm to the Soviet Union'. . . .

"Doctor Benes admitted to me that this statement distressed him. The Hitler-Stalin pact was then still in force, but Doctor Benes told me he had sent word to the President, through an American intermediary, urging him not to lose faith in Stalin.

"When the break between Hitler and Stalin did come, in the summer of 1941, Doctor Benes was naturally pleased, as were all Allied statesmen. The big question everybody was asking then was, 'How well can the Russians fight?' Mr. Roosevelt sent a personal envoy to get Doctor Benes' opinion. The Czech leader expressed the confident belief that the Russians would never surrender to Hitler, and would remain in the war until the end. He said, 'We must now make our postwar plans upon that assumption.'

"This astute estimate of Russian fortitude, reaching the President at a time when many American military observers were predicting a swift Russian collapse, must have impressed Mr. Roosevelt. Probably he remembered this two years later in the winter of 1943, when Doctor Benes sought our President's support for a projected visit to Moscow to confer with Marshal Stalin. . . .

"President Roosevelt, disregarding Churchill's objections, made it possible for Doctor Benes to visit Moscow. The Czech leader had two long talks with Stalin himself. The result was a treaty of alliance, signed on 12th December. The two countries agreed to combine against any possible future German aggression. Doctor Benes pledged that he would suppress all organized anti-Russian groups in Czechoslovakia after the liberation of that country. Stalin in turn personally guaranteed that Russia would not interfere in Czechoslovakia's postwar development. When the pact was announced in a joint conference, Doctor Benes faced the Russian leader directly and said, 'Mr. Stalin, I have complete confidence in you. We have signed an agreement for non-interference in domestic affairs, and I know you will keep it. . . .'

"Of course, President Roosevelt received full reports of these Czech negotiations in Moscow. They seemed to confirm Doctor Benes' confidence that it was possible to do business with Stalin personally, and they probably re-inforced the President's faith in his own personal understanding with Stalin, reached only a fortnight before at Teheran.

"But Doctor Benes, when I talked with him in Prague after the war, admitted to me that several Czech ministers in London had been gravely disturbed by the Moscow agreement. They said to him, 'You have put yourself at Stalin's mercy'." (And they were proved absolutely right, for Stalin subsequently completely disregarded the agreement of Moscow, and himself brutally dismissed Benes in favour of Gottwald, later seizing the country without striking a blow. Benes died not long afterwards, virtually a prisoner of the Russians, in a residence that was kept under observation—Léon de Poncins.)

However that may be,

"Once the Czecho-Russian treaty was signed, Winston Churchill raised no further objections. Whatever his private doubts, the British statesman had no desire to quarrel with President Roosevelt about the future of Czechoslovakia. He accepted without protest the Czech proposals for the postwar expulsion of their German racial minority, 3,000,000 people. More important still, he concurred in Stalin's suggestion, at the Yalta Conference of the Big Three in February, 1945, that the liberation of Prague should be left to the Red Army."

(Article "Roosevelt's Secret Deal Doomed Czechoslovakia" by Demaree Bess, in *The Saturday Evening Post*, 17th April, 1948)

From all this it appears that, for various reasons, Roosevelt put a personal and blind trust in Stalin. It is indisputable that this trust existed, or at least that Roosevelt consistently acted as if he believed Stalin whole heartedly. The reasons for this confidence are obscure; in as much as Bullitt says that on some occasions Roosevelt did realise Stalin's bad faith. It is sufficient in this context to state the facts and to stress the mysterious nature of the problem without seeking the answer to it.

However, there is another document which sheds further light on the revelations of Bullitt and Demaree Bess, and completes the picture.

In March 1943 the Spanish Government became aware of an extremely important document which boded a grim future for a great number of European countries. It concerned the following secret letter addressed by President Roosevelt on 20th February, 1943 to

Zabrousky, who was Jewish, and who was then acting as a liaison officer between President Roosevelt and Stalin.

The White House, Washington

Dear Mr. Zabrousky, 20.2.43

As I have already had the pleasure of telling you, together with Mr. Weiss, *I am deeply moved to hear that the National Council of Young Israel has been so extremely kind as to propose me as mediator with our common friend Stalin in these difficult moments,* when any menace of friction among the United Nations—in spite of the many self-denying declarations which have been obtained—would have fatal consequences for all, but principally for the U.S.S.R. itself.

It is therefore in your interest and ours to round off the corners—which becomes difficult to bring about with Litvinoff, to whom I have had, very regretfully, to point out that 'those who sought a quarrel with Uncle Sam would get something to complain about', with regard to internal as well as external affairs. For, having regard to Communist activities in the States of the American Union, his claims are absolutely intolerable.

Timoshenko proved more reasonable in his brief but fruitful visit, and indicated that a new interview with Marshal Stalin might constitute a rapid means of arriving at a direct exchange of views. I reckon that this is more and more urgent, particularly when one remembers all the good which has resulted from Churchill's talk with Stalin.

The United States and Great Britain are ready, without any reservations, to give the U.S.S.R. absolute parity and voting rights in the future reorganisation of the post-war world. She will therefore take part (as the English Prime Minister let him know when sending him the first draft from Aden) in the directing group in the heart of the Councils of Europe and of Asia; she has a right to this, not only through her vast intercontinental situation, but above all because of her magnificent struggle against Nazism which will win the praise of History and Civilisation.

It is our intention—I speak on behalf of our great country and of the mighty British Empire—that these continental councils be constituted by the whole of the independent States in each case, with equitable proportional representation.

And you can, my dear Mr. Zabrousky, assure Stalin that the U.S.S.R. will find herself on a footing of complete equality, having an equal voice with the United States and England in the Direction of the said Councils (of Europe and Asia). Equally with England and the United States, she will be a member of the High Tribunal which will be created to resolve differences between the nations, and she will take part similarly and identically in the selection, preparation, armament and command of the international forces which, under the orders of the Continental Council, will keep watch within each State to see that peace is maintained in the spirit worthy of the League of Nations. Thus these inter-State entities and their associated armies will be able to impose their decisions and to make themselves obeyed.

This being the case, a position so elevated in the Tetrarchy of the Universe ought to give Stalin enough satisfaction not to renew claims which are capable of creating insoluble problems for us. In this way, the American continent will remain outside all Soviet influence and within the exclusive concern of the United States, as we have promised the countries of our continent it shall.

In Europe, France will gravitate into the British orbit. We have reserved for France a secretariat with a consultative voice but without voting rights, as a reward for her present resistance and as a penalty for her former weakness.

Portugal, Spain, Italy and Greece will develop under the protection of England towards a modern civilisation which will lift them out of their historical decline.

We will grant the U.S.S.R. an access to the Mediterranean; we will accede to her wishes concerning Finland and the Baltic and we shall require Poland to show a judicious attitude of comprehension and compromise; Stalin will still have a wide field for expansion in the little, unenlightened countries of Eastern Europe—always taking into account the rights which are due to the fidelity of Yugoslavia and Czecho-Slovakia—and he will completely recover the territories which have been temporarily snatched from Great Russia.

Most important of all: after the partition of the Third Reich and the incorporation of its fragments with other territories to form new nationalities which will have no link with the past, the German threat will conclusively disappear in so far as being any danger to the U.S.S.R., to Europe and to the entire world.

Turkey—but it will serve no useful purpose to discuss that question further, it needs full understanding and Churchill has given the necessary assurances to President Inonu, in the name of us both. The access to the Mediterranean contrived for Stalin ought to content him.

Asia—we are in agreement with his demands, except for any complications which may arise later. As for Africa—again what need for discussion? We must give something back to France and even compensate her for her losses in Asia. It will also be necessary to give Egypt something, as has already been promised to the Wafdist government. As regards Spain and Portugal, they will have to be recompensed for the renunciations necessary to achieve better universal balance. The United States will also share in the distribution by right of conquest and they will be obliged to claim some points which are vital for their zone of influence; that is only fair. Brazil, too, must be given the small colonial expansion which has been offered to her.

In view of the rapid annihilation of the Reich, convince Stalin—my dear Mr. Zabrousky—that he ought to give way, for the good of all, in the matter of the colonies in Africa, and to abandon all propaganda and intervention in the industrial centres of America. Assure him also of my complete understanding and of my entire sympathy and desire to facilitate these solutions, which makes more timely than ever the personal discussion which I propose—the above is only a general outline of a plan which is intended for further study.

This is the issue and the whole issue.

As I told you at the time, I was very pleased at the gracious terms of the letter informing me of your decision and of the desire you expressed to offer me in the name of the National Council a copy of the greatest treasure of Israel, the scroll of the Torah. This letter will convey the confirmation of my acceptance; to those who are frank with me, I respond with the greatest confidence. Be so good, I beg of you, to transmit my gratitude to the distinguished body over which you preside, recalling the happy occasion of the banquet on its 31st anniversary.

I wish you every success in your work as interpreter.

Very sincerely yours,
(signed) Franklin Roosevelt.

This letter (which has been translated from a French version) is reproduced in Señor Doussinague's book, written when he was Spanish Ambassador, entitled *España Tenia Razon* (pp. 198-199). In it, he explains Spain's attitude to Soviet Communism, to the Axis powers and to the Allies during the various stages of the war. During this period, Señor Doussinague was the assistant of Count Jordana, Foreign Minister of Spain. He was therefore directly concerned with the events whose history he describes, and of which his book is first-hand evidence. He makes the following comments on the Roosevelt letter:

"So, by the benevolent resolve of Mr. Roosevelt, who was then preparing for the Teheran conference in full agreement with Stalin, Central Europe, with the exception of Turkey and Greece—

though the latter was to be deprived of Thrace in order to give the U.S.S.R. free access to the Mediterranean—the Baltic countries, and certain countries of Western Europe such as Holland, Belgium and Switzerland, were to come under Soviet domination; Germany was to be dismembered; while the Asiatic continent, including the French colonies, would also enter the Soviet sphere. In Africa certain promises were made to Stalin. As the counter part to this, in Western Europe, Italy, France, Spain and Portugal were to pass under the protection of England. America would remain entirely outside the influence and propaganda of the Soviets.

"But what is more, the U.S.S.R. would take a hand in the choice and preparation of international forces which were to be active within all European States, including those of the West; and the Asian States, constituted as the Council of Asia, and the European States, constituted as the Council of Europe, were to be directed by a group comprising the United States, the U.S.S.R., England and China, on a footing of complete equality, in complete disregard of the right to independence possessed by each of the countries so disposed of, and also of all that was representative of Christian civilisation in the Continent of Europe.

"Spain, together with all the other European countries, would be subject to this directory body of which her worst enemy would be a member—the same enemy which had led the fight against us throughout the Civil War, and which could never forgive Spain for the defeat that had been inflicted on it under the guidance of General Franco.

"*A mere glance at this letter is enough to explain the amazement, the agitation and the fear we felt when we became aware of it.* Our ardent desire to see peace come with all speed, before President Roosevelt's plans could be realised, can easily be imagined. Knowledge of this letter was the key to all the actions and gestures of Spain and served as a basis for the political discussions of its rulers. Thanks to this letter we knew what to expect of the post-war period . . . an immense catastrophe threatened to descend on Europe and on all its old civilisation."

It seems an extraordinary thing that this document, reproduced in a book of an official character, written by a diplomat who had been the secretary of Count Jordana, and placed publicly on sale in Madrid, it seems—I say—extraordinary that this document should have remained practically unknown outside Spain.

The Spanish government has not divulged its source, nor in its place, would any other government have done so. All we know is that it was a feminine personality in the immediate circle around

Roosevelt, who secretly communicated this document to the Spanish Government.

The Spanish government was absolutely certain of its authenticity, since their policy and the speeches of their rulers have been profoundly influenced by it; furthermore, it is an undeniable fact that the agreements reached at Teheran and Yalta were in conformity with the lines indicated in this famous letter.

I have personally questioned the author of the book, Señor Doussinague, who granted me an interview when he was Ambassador at Rome. Naturally he did not reveal any diplomatic secrets, but he made the following very judicious remarks:

> "*The authenticity of the document is apparent merely from its context. Carry yourself back to the time with which it deals; who was there among us—unless it were some prophet, who would have been accused of being out of his mind—who could have imagined in advance that Roosevelt, acting in his personal capacity, was about to hand over half of Europe and Asia to the Soviets, secretly and without gaining anything in return?*"

The reader must form his own opinion, but we would observe that a number of conclusions may be drawn from this document:

1. There have been attempts to excuse Roosevelt on the score that at Yalta he was a dying man unable to defend himself in the conduct of the negotiations. The letter to Zabrousky, on the contrary, proves that the Yalta agreement had been prepared far in advance by a secret understanding between Roosevelt and Stalin.
2. There were certain Jews, such as Zabrousky, and Freemasons, such as Benes, who served as intermediaries between Roosevelt and Stalin; this confirms the enormous influence which the Jewish and Masonic advisers of his immediate circle exerted over Roosevelt, and their Communist tendencies.
3. Jewish circles therefore bear a heavy responsibility for the disastrous treaty of Yalta and for the seizures made by the Soviet in Europe and Asia.
4. This does not relieve Roosevelt in any way of his personal responsibility. His lack of awareness of what he was doing and his failure to comprehend Stalin's Communism remain utterly amazing. There are only two possible explanations for his attitude: either he was truly ignorant, to an astonishing degree for a politician normally so astute: or he was a conscious agent of subversion, entirely dominated by the Jewish influences around him.

10

TWENTIETH-CENTURY FREEMASONRY

THE victory of the Allies in 1918 was also a triumph for Freemasonry, for it had prepared the bases of the treaty of Versailles and presided over the creation of the League of Nations in the course of a secret congress of the Masonic members of allied and neutral nations held at the Grand Orient of Paris on 28th, 29th and 30th June, 1917 (see Chapter 3). Freemasonry inspired and dominated most of the democratic Governments of the new Europe which had succeeded the monarchies overthrown by the defeat of the Central Powers.

Benes, who was the sectarian and activating soul of Freemasonry in Central Europe, solidly supported by the U.S.A. held unopposed sway over the Little Entente (Czechoslovakia, Yugoslavia and Rumania) and lost no opportunity of showing his sympathies for Soviet Russia. Freemasonry was the reigning power in France from 1918 to 1939.

The Order promised the world an era of peace, happiness and prosperity but after the war there rapidly supervened disorder and financial breakdown, revolution and universal chaos.

In Germany, Hungary and Italy, Bolshevism was eventually strangled at the cost of great efforts and much blood-shed.

In Austria, Socialism brought about the ruin of the country. Everywhere Masonic democracy, which as we have seen, is an admirable instrument for the disruption of order, showed that when in power it was incapable of governing and maintaining order itself. As a more or less general reaction, authoritarian régimes sprang up by popular consent, for example those of Admiral Horthy in Hungary, Mussolini and Fascism in Italy, Chancellor Dollfuss in Austria, Hitler and National Socialism in Germany. Traditional monarchies had been suppressed in favour of democratic régimes; but everywhere dictators more despotic than former sovereigns came into power. Freemasonry, thinking herself mistress of the future, found that she had fallen on difficult times.

In France three great events which marked a turning point in the history of the Third Republic, had profound repercussions on the politics of the country: the Cartel des Gauches in 1924, the Stavisky affair in 1934 and the Popular Front in 1936. Parallel to this chain of events in the outside world came Hitler's rise to power in Germany, the Spanish civil war, and finally the Second World War.

Let us first turn to the affair of the Cartel des Gauches in 1924. The 1924 elections brought into power a coalition of left-wing elements which, under the leadership of Herriot, pushed through a long string of Socialist laws of Masonic inspiration and Marxist tendencies. A complete account of their elaboration and origin is to be found in Chapter 3. As to their effect, suffice it to say that in 1925, Poincaré was recalled to power and achieved a spectacular restoration of the currency: the first attempt at a Masonic Socialist government had proved an ignominious failure.

But a new crisis arose over the Stavisky affair of such dimensions that the democratic republican régime was profoundly shaken by it. Let us briefly summarise the facts:

Alexander Stavisky, of Russian Jewish origin, had swindled an official State organisation out of several hundred millions of francs. Important political personalities were directly involved; quite incredible details were soon brought to light; Stavisky, it appeared, was a friend of radical Socialist politicians and gave huge sums of money to the Party and even to some of its members; he had partly financed the election of the Radical party in 1932; in exchange he enjoyed the protection of high government circles, which assured him of impunity. Publicly indicted, he was found guilty and condemned nineteen times, and nineteen times he was let off again through the intervention of his illustrious protectors.

There was an explosion of indignation in Paris. As the government was obviously trying to stifle the affair in order to protect the politicians who were implicated, outbursts of protest took place in the streets. These were violently suppressed by the police, which had the effect of pouring fuel on the flames. Parliament was unable to sit without the protection of an enormous deployment of police forces.

In the midst of all this a new bombshell exploded. Stavisky, who had disappeared as soon as the affair became a scandal, had just been found by the police at Chamonix; his house was surrounded and he committed suicide just as he was about to be arrested. There were no witnesses except the police and a man named Voix, an informer, known to the police and friend of Stavisky.

There were stormy scenes in the Chamber and certain deputies, Ybarnégaray among others publicly accused the police of having executed Stavisky to stop him talking.

Violent riots took place in the evening of 28th January, and in the face of the strong popular reaction, the government felt obliged to resign. A new team of young ministers took office but ran into more and more violent opposition. The national organisations and ex-soldiers' associations organised a mass meeting for the evening of 6th February, a date which will remain forever historic. All the police forces, gendarmes and mounted police available had been mobilised. There was a veritable night of civil war, in the course of which the police fired point blank on a dense crowd; thirty people were killed and two thousand wounded; all the Paris hospitals were full. The crisis was so serious that the President of the Municipal Council and the President of the Republic telephoned the former President, Doumergue, then in retirement on his estate in the Midi, and asked him to form a cabinet of National Union, including ministers belonging to all the principal parties. The régime was saved by the skin of its teeth, but the affair did not end there and was to have far reaching consequences.

Trotsky, who at that time had secretly taken refuge in France, pronounced the following judgment, which the future was to bear out. The agony of democracy in France, he said, may well endure longer than the Bruning-Papen Schleicher pre-Fascist period in Germany, but for all that it would not cease to be an agony. Democracy would be swept away, and the question was simply who was to wield the broom.

The Socialist and Communist papers then openly proclaimed that it was a race between them and Fascism, and the appearance, on 12th February of a huge Communist Manifesto in the Paris district revealed the collusion between Socialism and Freemasonry.

The Stavisky affair brought home to everyone the power and the danger which a secret association like Freemasonry represented in French politics. It let loose a vast Press campaign against the Masons which did not let up until the war and finally led to the banning of the sect under Marshal Pétain's government.

The *Revue des Deux Mondes*, a very staid organ of moderate opinion which certainly could not be accused of political extremism, voiced popular sentiment very fairly in an article from which we have taken the following passages:

> "Stavisky seems to have been the head of a gang, a Mafia, as the Minister of the Interior Albert Sarraut described it . . . which was not only practising swindling on a grand scale, but also espionage and corruption. At the bottom of the affair we shall find an undertaking aiming at the breakdown of French power.
>
> "But this gang was protected by powerful politicians and, through their intervention, profited from the indulgent tolerance of senior judges whose duty it was to punish their crimes."

On 21st February, the body of one of these judges, M. Prince, was found on the railway line at Dijon. It had been cut to pieces by a train. The autopsy revealed that he had been anaesthetized and tied to the rails while still alive and that his body had been shattered by an express train.

He was the man who knew most about the Stavisky affair, and the very next day he was due to hand in his report to M. Lescouvé, the first President of the Court of Appeal. The assassins were never discovered.

> "This audacious crime", the *Revue des Deux Mondes* went on, "was cleverly premeditated and organised, and has sent a shudder of horror and consternation throughout France; public opinion, on the side of justice, clamours for light on the matter which the government hopes to be able to bring it.
>
> "If the assassination is the deed of the Stavisky gang, who can tell what power and organisation it must possess? And what crimes as yet unknown has it to conceal? If it is a political or a Masonic crime, what high ranking personalities can be glimpsed behind it? Is the collusion between politics and brigandage, so rife in America, about to be acclimatised in our own contaminated country? So long as the truth remains unknown and the guilty go unpunished, a frightful nightmare will continue to weigh down the conscience of France.
>
> "*More and more we are receiving the impression that what we are witnessing is only the dance of puppets whose guiding strings remain hidden. Are attempts being made to form a new Ministry following the dictates of some hidden power?*
>
> "We, however, have to take what comes to us, being only powerless and bewildered spectators.
>
> "This impression of mystery which hangs over us, this feeling of shady goings on and tortuous connections lurking in the shadow, is what makes the atmosphere at present so heavy and painful. It is to be hoped that the Ministry of National Union and its spirit of devotion to the country will free us from it. Like the ancient historian at the threshold of an era of reform, we shall breathe a sigh of deliverance. *Tum demum respirare coepimus*—then only shall we begin to breath."
>
> (*Revue des Deux Mondes*, 15th March, 1934)

Finally, under the threat of the rise to power of Right wing elements, the three great Left wing parties, the Communists, the Socialists and the Radical-Socialists, united in a common front, known as Le Front Populaire. This alliance was made under the aegis of Freemasonry. The League for the Rights of Man, under the leadership of Victor Basch and Emile Kahn, played a preponderant part in this union of Left wing parties.

In June 1936, Léon Blum formed a cabinet to combat the Fascists. This included a number of Jewish officials and a dozen ministers and under secretaries who were Masons, Camille Chautemps, Maurice Viollette, Marc Rucart, Roger Salengro, Jean Zay, Paul Bastid, Georges Monnet, Raoul Aubaud, F. Blanch, P. Ramadier, etc. . . . Immediately Blum initiated a vast complex of Socialist laws, thus provoking a series of extremely grave social troubles, with the inevitable repercussion of a new and spectacular failure of the franc, which seriously weakened the government.

On the eve of war, European Freemasonry was in complete confusion. In 1918 it thought it was on the eve of universal triumph; and now it suddenly felt the soil giving way under its feet in every direction at once—whether political, social, economic or religious.

> ". . . So long as democracy remained confined in the lodges, so long as it was only a talking point, it could cast a deceptive spell. The mystical Masons believed that they could construct a viable régime. . . . But Masonry was put to the test. It wielded power, and what was the result?
>
> *"It held sway in Russia with Kerensky, and in Italy under Giolitti and Nitti; it had a hand in the Labour Government of Henderson and Ramsay MacDonald in England; it had a short lived triumph in Germany under the Social Democratic Party with the complicity of Brüning; it is now ruling in Spain with Largo Caballero, Indalecio Prieto, Rodolpho Llopis and Alexandre Leroux; it still rules France. . . .*
>
> *"But everywhere without exception the test of the power it has wielded has proved a baneful experience. . . .*
>
> "Masonry is beginning to realise that its democratic ideology leaves it bankrupt and that it will not provide it with the least guidance on how to resolve the political conflicts that confront it. It knows this and admits it."
>
> (Text of the speech by P. Loyer at a public conference in Paris)

The most clear-sighted of the Masons were able to recognise that there was disorder, but, prisoners of their own ideology, they were unable to grasp the cause of their failure, least of all to find the remedy to the situation, and so they clung in desperation to their out-dated concepts.

> "The unrest is universal in time and space", wrote the Freemason Paul Bezault, in the *Bulletin* of the Grand Lodge of France on 1st August, 1932.

"Amidst the slaughter of the political, social and religious forms of a conservative way of life, the modern Frenchman is still seeking a way out.

"He wants to find a direction, to put an end to his aimless existence. . . .

"The metaphysical absolute is once more gnawing at the French soul. . . .

"The need for an absolute, the need to know with certainty whether the metaphysical ideal exists outside us, or within, as an immanent value of the world, the need to know about things beyond the tomb, all this is yet another aspect of the unrest of contemporary France. . . .

"This need for an absolute is in reality only the undertow of religious sentimentality, which returns periodically in every disturbed epoch and at moments of intellectual and moral strife to shake the ship of faith in which timid consciences take refuge, since they are never masters of themselves; it is their subscription against the contingent risks of the beyond, their insurance policy for immortal happiness.

"How can this need for an absolute be cured? It is an artificial need, which has influence only in proportion to our intellectual and moral weakness, and to our metaphysical desire to shore up by science what can never be proved.

"Masonry, together with other independent minds, replies by exerting itself to lead individual and social morality back to its natural sources . . . but the ascendancy of religious sentimentality remains, and it has even increased since the (First) war.

"*As against this sentimentality*, which it would be vain to underestimate in its activity, and dangerous to clash with until it has been taught to come down from the turbulent regions in which it persists in soaring, as against this *there stands the whole work of Masonry, not in political antithesis, and still less as a method of combat, but as a constructive theory designed to reorganise the human conscience.*

"*To secularize the constitution of a people is but a small thing, but to secularize the soul of that people is better. . . .*

"The recasting of a better kind of humanity, more sure of itself and its aim, and better endowed with a sense of responsibility and truth, calls for all the efforts of complete and integral secularism, whose principles, scattered on the dissolving waves of political struggles, have not yet found the synthetic formula which will weld them into a doctrine capable of achieving true renovation—a secularism whose apostles, ceasing at least to appear as the demolishers of the past, will restore the values of an objective

> philosophy and morality, without which the most ethereal system of metaphysics cannot exist, except by throwing men and societies into the indescribable chaos over which we have been called to brood."

What does Freemasonry propose as a remedy for the spiritual chaos in which the world is struggling? Nothing less than the complete and integral reign of secularism! What a sterile and wretched solution. How dessicating and negative. As if one can cure the effects of a poison by administering a massive dose of the same venom.

Comes the ominous years 1939-40, which saw the outbreak of war, the defeat of France, first Europe and then the world set alight, the collapse of the republican régime in France, the German occupation and the government of Marshal Pétain.

In his works Mellor describes the abominations perpetrated against the Freemasons during the occupation in France. This is in fact what happened.

On 13th August, 1940, the Minister of Justice, Raphael Alibert, and the Minister of the Interior, Adrien Marquet, delivered the following report to Marshal Pétain:

> "Monsieur le Maréchal,
>
> "There are in existence in France organisations of an occult character which have been founded or developed either as formal associations or as mere groups which happen to have come into being.
>
> "No government can allow the existence of groups pursuing a clandestine or secret activity, least of all in present-day circumstances.
>
> "*It is totally inadmissible that the enterprise which has been undertaken with a view to national reform should be opposed by organisations which are all the more dangerous because they remain concealed, because they recruit a great number of their members amongst the Civil Service, and because their activities too often tend to disrupt the machinery of the State and paralyse the actions of the Government.*
>
> "Thus it would appear to be necessary, on the one hand, to dissolve all groups and associations which are secret in character and to prohibit their reconstitution; and on the other hand to require from all those who exercise a public function, an honourable undertaking that they do not belong and will never belong to such an organisation.
>
> "This is the object of the law which we have the honour to submit for your distinguished approval."

On the same day, the Marshal promulgated a law decreeing the dissolution of Freemasonry, the first three articles of which are set out below:

"We, Marshal of France, Head of State; having taken counsel from our ministers,

"Decree:

"*Article I*

"Dating from the promulgation of the present law, the bodies mentioned below are dissolved without exception:

"(1) Every association and group in existence whose activities are carried on even partially in a secret or clandestine manner;

"(2) Every association and group in existence whose members impose on themselves the obligation to conceal from public authority, even partially, the nature of their activity;

"(3) Every association and group in existence which refuses or neglects to make known to public authority, after being required to do so, its statutes and regulations, its interior organisation, its hierarchy, the list of its members with the positions which they occupy, the object of its meetings, or which intentionally provides false or incomplete information on these subjects.

"*Article II*

"The nullity of groups or associations falling under the scope of the preceding article is to be established by decree.

"*Article III*

"The movable and immovable property of associations and groups dissolved in virtue of the preceding article will, at the request of the public ministry, be confiscated by order of the president of the civil tribunal of the place where they are situated.

"Steps will be taken to liquidate them under the authority of the president of the civil tribunal and under supervision of the public ministry.

"The sums produced by the liquidation will be handed over, in Paris, to the general administration of public assistance, and in other localities to the welfare office of the commune concerned."

Article V decreed:

"No one can become a civil servant or an agent of the State, or of the local Departments or public establishments, colonies, protectorates or territories under French mandate; no one can be employed by a concessionary of the public service or in an enterprise financially assisted by the State or by one of the public bodies afore-mentioned:

"(1) If he does not declare, on his honour, that he has never belonged to one of the organisations defined in Article I, or that he has broken all connections with it.

"(2) If he does not pledge himself, on his honour, never to adhere to such an organisation, in case it should ever be reconstituted.

"The declaration and pledge mentioned in the present article are to be certified by written documents.

"Whoever shall have made a false declaration shall be dismissed from his office and punished with the penalties mentioned in Article IV."

(Published at the time in *Le Journal Officiel*, and reproduced in "La République du Grand Orient", a special issue of *Lectures Françaises*, 5th January, 1964)

In practice the anti-Masonic measures were applied with very great leniency. Civil servants who said that they had been Freemasons were not disturbed and continued to occupy their positions in complete tranquillity; those who were convicted of false declarations were theoretically compelled to resign but in fact very few measures of that kind were taken by Vichy.

Besides, the government did not possess official lists of Masons, since membership of Masonry was kept secret; the only means of drawing up lists was to study systematically the documents seized in the lodges. But this task was only slowly and tardily organised. The sites of the lodges had been confiscated, but that was as far as things went. Before any action happened, there was an announcement that anti-Masonic measures were going to be taken, which gave the sect time to put its most essential archives into hiding. It had not waited for the defeat of France to do so and some weeks before the Armistice important documents had been sent to Bordeaux.

Eventually, a study and research group was set up under the direction of Bernard Fay, Professor of the College of France and a historian of Masonry in the eighteenth century, the naval Captain Labat, Colonel de Verchères and several anti-Masonic workers of the pre-war period, such as Robert Valéry-Radot, Henri Coston, J. Marquès-Rivière, an ex-Mason, Georges Olivier, an assistant on Mgr. Jouin's *Revue Internationale des Sociétés Secrètes*, etc. This team was installed in the premises of the Grand Orient and the Grand Lodge at Paris, it made a systematic study of the documents which had been seized, and published the results of its researches in a review entitled *Les Documents Maçonniques*.

But when Laval came to power there was a radical change in the government's attitude: Laval set himself up as the protector of Freemasonry and rapidly put an end to all the measures directed against the secret societies, in spite of the tenacious opposition of Admiral Platon, a firm Protestant animated by a lively sense of national duty and the only member of the government to take the Masonic question seriously. He was to pay with his life for that attitude.

In a recently published and well documented book, *La République du Grand Orient*, Henri Coston (who spent several years in prison after the Liberation) gives us a very clear account of what happened during the occupation. Speaking of Laval, he says:

> "Nothing could have been more significant than to watch him step by step bringing to naught the anti-Masonic legislation. He was careful not to destroy it, for that would have caused too much noise. He steadily and surely whittled it away. From 19th August, 1942, he attached the services of the secret societies to the Sûreté Nationale, the state intelligence service."
>
> (H. Coston: *La République du Grand Orient*, p. 219)

He took a series of measures in this direction.

> "Platon was not put in the picture; he complained vehemently, and Laval soon afterwards got rid of him. . . . A circular directed the ministries to reopen in a sympathetic vein the dossiers of officials who had been put out of office. '19 out of 20 of the officials who had been dismissed were reinstated', Maurice Reclus declares. 'No one who had made a false declaration was prosecuted'.
>
> "Laval was so little anti-Masonic that he had until January 1941 a secretary, Roger Stora, who was a Mason, whom he afterwards appointed as special Receiver of Taxes at Grasse. . . . He arranged for a friend of the latter, the high official Moatti, who fell under the provisions of the law on secret societies, to continue to draw his salary although he had had to give up his position in the Central Administration. He also retained as long as he could, the Masonic Prefects whom the Marshal's cabinet had indicated as undesirables. On the other hand, he displaced prefects and sub-prefects considered to be too favourably disposed to the 'national revolution', and he came down vigorously on 'national revolutionaries' who were convinced anti-Masons and who objected too openly against his policy.
>
> "It was also Pierre Laval who had the secret societies police suppressed by René Bousquet, secretary general of the Ministry of the Interior (now director of the Bank of Indo China) and a protégé of Sarraut, whom the president had made a deputy minister of the French State.
>
> (H. Coston, ibid., pp. 220-221)

"At last to put an end to Platon's opposition (Mallet and

Bousquet in their evidence made him out to be a rabid anti-Mason, which the cold and austere Platon certainly was not) Pierre Laval had the Admiral placed under house arrest in his estate at Pujol-en-Dordogne. But if the guard was sufficient to prevent Platon from leaving his house, it was clearly insufficient to keep out the Dordogne *maquis*. The former minister was carried off by the F.F.O. tortured and killed.

"But it was at the German Embassy in Paris that the Masons, however little they called themselves 'Europeans', found the best and most efficacious protection. . . .

"Those who lived in political circles in Paris during 1940-44 will know that the Embassy was the worst enemy of the Pétainists and the 'national revolutionaries'. . . .

"On the other hand one remembers that the Communist newspaper *Humanité* only just failed to reappear in 1940. For the Communists had obtained the necessary authority from the Germans, and it was the French police service which intervened—on the authority of the laws and decrees of the Daladier government—and stifled that attempt before it was hatched. . . .

"The tolerance enjoyed by former Masons in the occupied zone, who were pursued by the Marshal's cabinet, however small was the political rôle they appeared to be playing, is largely explained by the tendency to favour left wing influence which was displayed by the German Embassy in Paris. (H. Coston, ibid., pp. 222-224)

"But it must also be recognised that the charm shown by the Germans accounted for much in rallying many Freemasons in support of the policy of Franco-German collaboration, as Weil-Curiel had admitted.

"For certain men of the left, Abetz, the German ambassador, was a proven Francophile and a sincere partisan of the reconciliation of the two peoples. They were seduced by this man, who never spoke to them about National-Socialism, but only of European Socialism, and who showed himself so favourable to the French Republic. Numerous Masons were active in collaborating with the Germans but it should be recognised that some of them were definitely anti-Communist.

"The tendencies of ambassador Abetz and also, doubtless, the anti-clerical sentiments of the occupying authorities, who were not displeased at stirring up an opposition to the 'Vichy reactionaries' —accordingly allowed certain Masons to indulge in important political activities. For the most part they remained faithful to their Masonic ideal and this explains their intervention.

"It is also a fact, little known but true, that the Germans were never whole-hearted opponents of Freemasonry, for as Dr. Helmut Knochen, Chief of Staff of the S.S. at Paris during the occupation, declared: 'Berlin hardly insisted on anything concerning the Masonic question'. He remarks elsewhere that 'on the German side, there was no special commissioner (for the secret societies) as there was for the Jewish question, the latter being in receipt of continual directives from Berlin'. (H. Coston, ibid., p. 227)

"In actual fact, there was an Obersturm-führer named Stubert, under Knochen's orders, whose duty was to carry out research into Masonic documents in so far as they were directly of interest to Germany, and to control the police service dependent on the Prefecture, which was installed at Rapp square, in the building belonging to the Theosophical Society, under the direction of Inspector Moerschel. . . .

"The German occupation authorities—whether Ambassador Abetz, counsellor Achenbach, or Knochen—were not then hostile to Freemasons; far from it, in fact. But were the leading National Socialists in Germany any more so? . . ."

(H. Coston, ibid., p. 227)

From the time of his arrival to power in Algeria, General de Gaulle, who governed then with Communist support, re-established the Masonic organisations with all their prerogatives and gave back to the Jews the same positions they had held before the war. As an example of his use of Communist support, when the de Gaulle government installed itself in Paris, Maurice Thorez, Secretary General of the Communist Party, who deserted in 1939 and took refuge in Russia, was appointed Minister of State, while General Weygand, who had been liberated from a deportation camp, was incarcerated in a Parisian prison.

The Liberation of France was followed by the *épuration*, or purge of the French "collaborators". Few people outside France know how murderous this was: more than 100,000 Frenchmen were assassinated without trial, and this figure was admitted by the former Minister of the Interior, Adrien Texier, in a conversation in February 1945 with Colonel Passy, the head of General de Gaulle's D.G.E.R., or secret service. Robert Aron, in his history of the purge, estimates that some 40,000 people fell victim to the summary executions of the maquis.

The repression was particularly severe towards writers and anti-Masons. Here, as far as the latter are concerned, is a brief resumé of what Henri Coston says in his book from which we have just quoted:

"Henri Béraud was condemned to death for the articles he wrote in *Gringoire*. The prosecutor, the future President Raymond Lindon, who demanded the capital sentence against the great writer, may not have been a Mason, but the presiding judge of the Court of Justice, who sentenced Béraud, certainly was. Happily he was not executed, but five years later he came out of prison in a wheeled chair.

"Bernard Fay and his collaborators and friends were tried on three different counts. The professor was condemned to hard labour for life, as were two other anti-Masons, another was condemned to twenty years, two to fifteen years, several to ten and five years, and many were sentenced to national degradation.

"The detective in charge of the inquiry, Superintendent Paul Sertillange, was a member of the Socialist Workers Lodge, and the judge who drew up their dossier, Alexis Zousmann, was one of the most brilliant and ruthless of the magistrates involved in the *épuration*—a recently liberated prisoner-of-war who had been a member of the Francisco Ferrer lodge before the war. He it was who had drafted the charges against the journalists P. A. Cousteau and Lucien Rebatet, who had been condemned to death some months previously.

(Alexis Zousmann, a Jewish emigré from Russia who became a naturalised Frenchman before the last war, today occupies an important position on the Magistrates' Bench, and presides over the Masonic group, Condorcet-Brossellette. Recently he was responsible for repressing the Algerian O.A.S.—Léon de Poncins.)

"Three of the men who served in the secret societies service died in prison: Commander Labat was killed by a warder, Colonel de Verchères died in a forced-labour camp, and Paul Lafitte died at the hospital of Fresnes. A fourth, H. Babize, who remained four years in prison, died several years afterwards from an intestinal disease contracted during his detention. The former Freemason Paul Riche, against whom so much hatred had accumulated, was condemned to death and shot. Another ex-Mason, Albert Vigneau, who had left the Order in 1934 after the Stavisky affair, and who had written several books against the lodges, died in prison. Jean Boissel, an anti-Mason who had been severely disabled in the war, met with the same fate." (H. Coston, ibid., p. 239)

Meanwhile, Philippe Poirson, who was the head of the anti-Masonic service established at the rue Cadet during the occupation, had been arrested by the Germans and died during deportation.

Robert Vallèry-Radot and Jean Marquès-Rivière disappeared at the time of the Liberation. The latter has not been heard of since, and

Vallèry-Radot apparently died recently after taking Holy Orders. Having dropped out of circulation, he had escaped a judicial pursuit.

> "Those who were at last liberated after a long detention were left without resources on being released from prison, without a position in life, without employment, often without a home; and their health, sapped by years in gaol, was never completely restored. *Too many people are unaware that the* épuration *which took place in 1944 struck down 400,000 of Pétain's supporters.*"
>
> (H. Coston, ibid., p. 239)

We come now to the conclusion of this study, in which we have attempted to show, by reference to documents of unimpeachable authority, that Freemasonry as a system is fundamentally hostile to the whole civilisation, culture and way of life of Western Europe, which was created by and founded upon Christianity, and which, until recently, was deeply impregnated with Christian history, traditions and morality. We have traced the development and the various forms and expressions of Freemasonry up to the present day, and it now remains to ask where Freemasonry stands in Europe today.

Following the upheavals which, as we have seen, began in the First World War and preceded and followed the Second, Freemasonry has lost much of its prestige and preponderance in Europe.

The check to its domination after 1918 has left a profound mark upon it. It has been unmasked and has lost a great deal of its prestige. It has been banned and so remains in many countries under various political régimes. Its adversaries have discovered its subversive techniques, its methods of infiltration and political penetration, and they have learned how to combat them.

Its recruitment has dried up for some years and on the whole it is not supported by the younger generation. It is not finding it easy to build up its ranks.

It has lost its position as the intellectual leader of left-wing parties to the Communists, synarchist technocrats (a French secret society of leading engineers, industrialists and business men) and progressive Christians.

On the other hand, its methods of insidious penetration have enabled it to infiltrate into the Church, where it finds powerful support in progressive circles. Being essentially chameleon-like and infinitely variable in form, it is reconstituting itself on new foundations to become an international force once more, adapted to the new political environment. The subversive movements today consider that burrowing inwardly is more efficacious than open, bloody revolution.

APPENDIX

PAX AND POLAND

WHILE not directly related to the subject of this book, the Report on *Pax* prepared by Cardinal Wyszynski is of such vital interest and seems to be so little known in the English-speaking world that this Appendix, describing the background of the movement and quoting in full the text of the Cardinal's Report on *Pax*, was drawn up by the translator with the agreement of the author. Moreover it will become clear to the reader that this document is not unrelated to the subject of the book as a whole, since it exposes a very determined attempt by the Soviet secret police to destroy the Church in Poland by seeking to penetrate and subvert it from within, frontal coercion and force having been completely defeated by the faith of the people. We have seen in earlier chapters in the present work how Freemasonry failed to impose itself on the nations by force and how, in consequence, and especially since the Second World War, it has resorted to subversion from within. The interest of the document we are about to lay before the reader is that it presents a particularly clear and recent instance of Communism's like failure to eradicate faith by force, and of its resorting to similar tactics to achieve its ends.

Before we quote the text of the Cardinal's letter, it will be useful to give the reader the background to this organisation which was set up in Poland by the Soviet political police, to infiltrate the Church with Communist cells and impregnate it with Marxism. Originally a Polish party, *Pax* spread throughout the countries of Western Europe and took root principally in France. The following information is taken from Lucjan Blit: *The Eastern Pretender*, a biography of Boleslaw Piasecki, the founder of *Pax*, and one of the most remarkable men behind the Iron Curtain.

In 1946 Piasecki and a number of progressive Catholics set themselves up as a group which published a weekly *Today and Tomorrow* and talked vaguely about marching with the times and being realistic, by which they meant that any political régime in Poland would have to be acceptable to Moscow. The majority of Catholics viewed these moves with suspicion, and it came as no great surprise when in March 1947 the Polish Primate, the late Cardinal Hlond, stated that Piasecki's daily *Universal Voice* could not be considered representative of the Catholic community.

Shortly after his installation as Primate of Poland, Cardinal Wyszynski, in a pastoral letter, warned all believers of the activities and aims of Piasecki's *Pax* and the progressive Catholics whom he described as "traitors to the Catholic Church". On 12th February, 1950, the Cardinal said that they were lacking in Catholic sense and learning, and yet they wanted to teach the bishops; furthermore, he rejected their claim to publish genuine Catholic works while at the same time attacking the Holy See, and he explicitly condemned them for assisting the Communist régime in the destruction of Catholic organisations.

> "As soon as the party and state went over to an open attack on the hierarchy *Pax* gave full support to all the actions, political, moral and even of a police nature, which the régime adopted against the Church. Not once during the whole period of brutal repressions between 1948 and October 1956 did *Pax*, or the progressive Catholics, or Piasecki himself, as much as whisper any criticism. They were not even neutral. Whole-heartedly they supported the actions of the Stalinist Politbureau against people who they claimed were their co-religionists in the same Church."
>
> (L. Blit: *The Eastern Pretender*, p. 168)

The trial of Bishop Kaczmarek, one of some 2,000 priests interned by the secret police purely for exercising their functions as priests, is an example of the way the *Pax* movement assisted in the persecution of the hierarchy of the Church to which they claimed to belong. Far from protesting at the trial, some members of *Pax* made public speeches in which they attacked the accused and the hard-pressed Episcopate, who were unable to answer their accusations, which were repeated day after day in the Communist Press and propaganda apparatus. Other, bolder spirits, actually appeared at the trial itself as prosecution witnesses, and condemned the hierarchy in accordance with the line the régime had taken.

Among their other activities, in November 1952 Piasecki and a number of his more prominent followers announced that they had joined the international Communist peace movement, and *Pax* sent a delegation to North Vietnam to persuade the large Catholic community there to give the Communist rulers of the country their unreserved collaboration.

At the height of the anti-clerical campaign Piasecki published his own *Essential Problems*, the main theme of which was described in the following terms:

> "Religion, instead of being the most noble and sublime means for the achievement of salvation, was to become for Piasecki a means of securing for the Church a temporal existence in the revolutionary world. Consequently all Catholics, including bishops and priests, were required to use Catholicism as a source of inspira-

tion for the building of Socialism and to devote most of their time and energy to the realisation of social and economic goals, determined by the atheistic leaders of the state."

(*Survey*, December 1961, quoted by L. Blit.)

This book was placed on the Vatican Index, and thus is a prohibited book for Catholics throughout the world, and on 8th June, 1955, the Congregation of the Holy Office condemned the propagation of ideas which urged Catholics to help Communism to victory, as voiced especially in Piasecki's weekly *Today and Tomorrow*.

"In its commentary to the decree of the Holy Office the official Vatican daily, the *Osservatore Romano*, explained that Piasecki's theory, developed in his *Essential Problems*, that Communism continues the works of creation and that Communists even while combating religion and the Church are by their work paying homage to God, must be considered blasphemous by any Christian and is certainly in complete contradiction to the basic dogma of the Catholic Church." (L. Blit: *The Eastern Pretender*, p. 180)

Following this step by the Vatican, the next day the Polish government banned the circulation in Poland of the *Osservatore Romano* and the *Acta Apostolicae Sedis*. Although *Pax* adopted an attitude of defiance, Piasecki was forced to give in, and his book was withdrawn and the weekly was stopped suddenly in 1956. However, this did not deter Piasecki from starting a new weekly, *Kierunki* (*Directions*) in May of the same year, in which he openly demanded recognition from the party for himself and *Pax* not just as "auxiliaries" but as direct allies of the party who were "entitled to co-govern the country". The Vatican's reply to this move came in the summer of the following year, when the Congregation of the Holy Office forbade members of religious orders and priests to have their books published by *Pax* or to write in any of Piasecki's periodicals or to assist their distribution among the faithful.

Piasecki's rise to power since the end of the war was little short of meteoric. Successfully riding out every kind of political weather, he consistently defended the rôle of Soviet Russia as the leader of the Communist world, notwithstanding accusations from the *Osservatore Romano* of accepting funds from Soviet and Polish government sources, and aimed to secure the recognition of the Communist party as their natural ally as the first step towards his ultimate goal of ruling Poland. In this way, within ten years he had become master of a vast economic empire, a unique and perhaps the most astonishing spectacle which has ever been seen behind the Iron Curtain.

On the face of it, this is an impossibility. The existence of a huge capitalist enterprise within the bosom of the Iron Curtain seems to defy all the most sacred canons of Communist philosophy. What is the explanation of this paradox?

> "The decisive reasons for the enormous profits which the *Pax* enterprises made, and which gave Piasecki an independence which no other organisation outside the Communist party could dream of enjoying, were that the *Pax* organisation, contrary to all laws in Communist Poland and the publicly expressed intention of its economic leaders, was given privileges which not only no other organisation of a similar character had but which even the enterprises of the Communist state did not enjoy. All state enterprises pay income tax and transfer their profits to the state. Not so the *Pax* publishing firm." (L. Blit: *The Eastern Pretender*, p. 155)

Apart from this advantage, Piasecki enjoyed generous supplies of newsprint and machine space, which had been strictly rationed by the party after the war, and had a virtual monopoly in publishing the works of many authors not necessarily sympathetic to the party. This, and the assurance of protection and even material support from the security organs of the Polish and Soviet Russian states, as well as the Soviet secret police, which controlled every tolerated form of Polish public life and political or social activity after the war, enabled Piasecki to turn *Pax* into the second largest publishing firm in Poland.

Piasecki's alliance with the political police was openly described in a sensational article by Leopold Tyrmand, which was published on 18th November, 1956 by the popular Warsaw weekly, *Swiat* (Issue No. 47—the censor's number is given on page 23 as B-34), whose chief editor, Stafan Arski, was a member of the central party organs.

> "It took the *Pax* people a full year to come out with a statement in which they rejected the accusation. By then the censorship was back to its old form. The opponents of *Pax* could not pursue the matter publicly any further."
>
> (L. Blit: *The Eastern Pretender*, p. 147)

Nevertheless, some public scrutiny was permitted, for in July 1957 a detailed, well-documented and highly sensational article by Grzegorz Pisarski, a member of the Communist party and a prominent Polish economist, appeared in the Warsaw weekly *Zycie Gospodarcze* (*Economic Life*). *Pax* was shown to pursue its political and propaganda activities with financial lavishness. They were mostly concerned with Poland, but Pisarski quotes the sum of one hundred and ten thousand roubles allotted for use in *Pax's* activities in the U.S.A., England, Italy, France and other countries in the West.

All the evidence we have produced above would seem to confirm that the real reason for the apparent phenomenon of *Pax's* survival and existence is the explanation given to the author of Piasecki's biography by high officials of the Communist party in Warsaw. They told him:

"*Pax* is of use to us. It may be of less value in times when we have a moment of real truce with the Church hierarchy. But we are a Marxist state. We are atheists and want the future Polish generations to consider materialism as the only philosophical explanation of the rules governing the universe and the fate of humanity. Piasecki may be a Catholic, but he is certainly against the Militant Church and against the Polish Episcopate interfering with the activities of the party and state, even in the question of educating the young. We will use him because, willingly or unwillingly, he makes our task easier."

(L. Blit: *The Eastern Pretender*, p. 208)

It is against this background of events that the Secretariat of the French Episcopate received a letter on 6th June, 1963 from His Grace the Apostolic Nuncio in which he stated that the Cardinal Secretary of State at the Vatican had asked him to draw the attention of the Episcopate and the Major Religious Superiors in France to the enclosed report on the activities of *Pax*, drawn up by Cardinal Wyszynski, who had summed it up in the following words:

"Firstly, *Pax* is not an organisation with a cultural objective. It is purely a medium for the dissemination of propaganda in disguise in order to denigrate the work of the Church in Poland by spreading false information.

"Secondly, this movement receives its orders and directives from the Communist party, the secret police, and the office for religious affairs.

"Thirdly, in return for its submission, *Pax* enjoys certain facilities and support, as for example, in its publications and commercial undertakings."

There now follows below the complete text of the report prepared by Cardinal Wyszynski, as forwarded to the Bishops and Major Religious Superiors in France:

For some time, but especially since the beginning of the Council, the *Pax* group, which claims to be the "movement of progressive Catholics in Poland", has been intensifying its propaganda activities in the West, and particularly in France, disseminating false or ambiguous reports which are damaging to the Church.

Pax exploits the ignorance of certain Catholic circles in the West in respect of what has come to be called "the Polish experiment in co-existence" as well as the enforced silence of Polish bishops, priests and laymen who refuse to give any information concerning "the realities of the Polish situation", knowing full well that on their return every word they said would be subject to the scrutiny of the police and that the least indiscretion on their part could lead to severe reprisals.

Under these conditions, which favour the proliferation of erroneous opinions to the great detriment of the Church in Poland, a word of warning is timely.

1. Outside Poland *Pax* represents itself as a "movement" of progressive Polish Catholics. As a result it tends to be compared to Western progressive movements, which, living under democratic forms of government, are completely free to proclaim their opinions and sympathies for the programmes and leanings of the political Left of their respective countries.

In reality, *Pax* is not a "movement" but a closely-connected organ of the police machine, directly responsible to the Minister of the Interior, and blindly obedient to the directives of the secret police, the U.B.

This fact is well known in Poland, but people realise that it is dangerous to talk about it. Once only, under cover of the "thaw" in October 1956, Communists and Catholics joined in denouncing and stigmatising publicly the character and activities of this secret, Stalinist agency of the U.B. It was an outburst of long pent-up resentment against notorious and feared double agents whose activities sickened not only Catholics but also honest Communists. Let us emphasise that at this time the Communist Press was particularly savage in its attacks on *Pax*. It even went so far as to publish its balance sheets in an economic review in order to show the very special favours it enjoyed from the government, including, among others, exemption from all income tax, lucrative concessions and a monopoly in certain reserved fields of production (religious publications and sacred art), which had turned *Pax* into a veritable capitalist trust under a Communist régime.

The freedom of expression due to the "thaw" of 1956 was quickly throttled, but the Polish people had made full use of the interval to find out truths which had been so long withheld from them, and *never*, since then, has *Pax* been able to exercise the slightest effective influence over the masses, the labourers and peasants, from whom it has become completely cut off.

The justification of its existence on the political chess-board of the Communist party is thus reduced to its efficacity abroad where its collaboration is proving to be most valuable. France, notably, was confided in a quite exceptional manner to the services of *Pax*, discreetly supported by Polish diplomatic circles.

2. In order to understand fully the activities of *Pax*, it is as well to go back to its beginnings. Its founder, Piasecki, condemned to death by the Soviet authorities for resistance activities, *saved his life at the price of an explicit undertaking to penetrate and enslave the Church for the benefit of the Communist revolution.*

From the beginning, therefore, Pax *has borne the character of a strictly controlled secret agency.* All its members are salaried officials (the forms of payment vary) appointed to carry out and report on definite projects.

Their orders emanate from the central office of the Communist party. Mr. Piasecki is *directly* subject to the "Security Office" (U.B.), and to the Office for Religious Affairs, which has absolute, and in fact total power over everything concerning the Catholic Church in Poland.[1]

Piasecki's rôle has not always been easy. He has had to steer between the reefs of the "Party" and the "Anti-Party". Disgraced after the thaw of 1956, he has been able to re-establish his position bit by bit, owing to the valuable services he is rendering abroad, particularly in France.

In Poland, *Pax* is completely cut off from the masses of peasants and labourers, who are more independent and have greater freedom to demonstrate their distrust. The intellectuals, especially the writers, are clearly more vulnerable due to the fact that *Pax* owns a prosperous publishing business, which pays well. In a country in which even the government admits that salaries seldom reach the minimum subsistence level, the temptation to collaborate with *Pax* is obviously great and a refusal to collaborate in any way presupposes an unusual strength of character. Some recognised writers have allowed themselves to be enlisted for the material advantages offered. No one is unaware of the influence *Pax* has over certain intellectuals due to these material advantages, nor that, stripped of its funds, it would lose overnight the only power of attraction it possesses in Poland.

Above this starveling mob of unwilling profiteers and traffickers

[1] When required to deal with questions which concern the Church, even if only indirectly, the Polish Ministries immediately declare that they are "incompetent" (as the Ministry of Defence did, for example, when seminarists were called up for military service as a reprisal for the "over-stubborn" attitude of the Bishops) and refer them automatically to the Office for Religious Affairs, the head of which, Mr. Zabinski, a former Stalinist sent into retirement in 1956 and since rehabilitated, disposes of practically unlimited powers for dealing with all matters concerning the Church. This Office and its director are commonly called "the Tribunal of the Communist Inquisition" and its Grand Inquisitor.

in progressivism, there is a limited circle of "initiates", who form a closed, and impermeable caste bound by pledges, and even by precise and binding oaths. Piasecki is the undisputed head of *Pax* at all levels.

In 1955 Piasecki revealed his capacities with the publication (at the height of the Stalinist terror and during the imprisonment of Cardinal Wyszynski and other Polish bishops) of his book, *Essential Problems*, which has since been condemned by the Holy Office. This condemnation obliged Piasecki to revise his position. Western Catholics loudly publicised his submission without suspecting that it was only as one who had "submitted", and who thus was not outside but inside the Church, that he was of the slightest value to the Communist party. Leaving aside therefore, the possible merits of the withdrawal of his book and the new orientation of his review, let us not forget that once exposed, *Pax* had no alternative but to submit. It is significant that since then, and until very recently, *Pax* has shown a great concern for orthodoxy in its publications.

4. In fact only the tactics have changed. The strategic plan has not been altered in any way. For some months, *Pax* has been busy reviving and disseminating the far-fetched ideas of *Essential Problems*.

It is noteworthy that the years of Cardinal Wyszynski's imprisonment mark the apogee of Piasecki's power. It was at this time that, on the orders of its mighty masters, *Pax* took over all the Catholic publications that had up to then been independent. Under de-Stalinisation it suffered an eclipse and for a time barely ticked over. It is only quite recently that Piasecki's star has begun to shine once more, thanks to the task entrusted to him in connection with the Ecumenical Council.

5. Before considering in detail the character of his mission to the Council, let us recall briefly the principles which have never ceased to guide Piasecki's activities, and which, moreover, have always dovetailed faultlessly into the Communist party plan.[1]

"To put an end to religion", said Lenin, "it is much more important to introduce class war into the bosom of the Church than to attack religion directly."

---

[1] This identity of outlook and even of expression strikes every reader of the Polish Press. The *Pax* publications are a servile reproduction, even down to their very use of expressions, of the official Press. There seems to be an invisible conductor whose task it is to score in the minutest details. Thus quite recently the servile conformity in the opinions of the entire Polish Press on the Council leapt to the eye. We do not know of one single instance in which *Pax* has given proof of independence by siding with the Church and against its paymasters.

The technique is to act as a solvent and form cells of disunity among the faithful, but especially in the ranks of the priests and religious; split the bishops into two blocs, the "integralists" and the "progressives"; use a thousand pretexts to align the priests against their bishops; drive a subtle wedge into the masses by cleverly contrived distinctions between "reactionaries" and "progressives"; never attack the Church directly, but, "only for her own good" attack "her antiquated structure" and "the abuses which disfigure her." If necessary appear to be more Catholic than the Pope; skilfully undermine the Church by attracting into ecclesiastical circles groups of "discontented" Catholics, so as to lure the former bit by bit "into the fertile climate of class struggle"; slowly and patiently work for this "adaptation" by introducing new forms into traditional ideas. The ambiguity of certain terms, such as "progressivism" and "integralism", "open" and "closed" attitudes, democracy and socialism, and so on, which have entirely different meanings in France and in Poland, help to create misunderstanding.

In short, it is not a question of "liquidating" the Church, but of putting the Church in step by enlisting her in the service of the Communist revolution.

"We are working to facilitate an inevitable historical process which will compel the Church to reconsider her position", wrote Piasecki in an editorial on 11th November, 1955.

At the same time, Piasecki strives to exploit the messianic ideas which flatter national *amour propre*: might not Poland be called by Providence to serve as the model for co-existence between the Catholic Church and the Communist state?

"Obviously", he writes, "in order that Poland may serve as a model, it is essential that Polish Catholicism becomes progressive as quickly as possible and collaborates increasingly actively in the construction of a socialist economy. That is the daily task of our progressive movement." (Whitsun, 1956)

6. In order to achieve these objectives, it was absolutely necessary for "intelligent Catholics, both priests and laymen, to pluck up the requisite courage and valid arguments in order to make the bishops hear reason and win them over to a true appreciation of temporal politico-social reality."

When these attempts by *Pax* failed, "in the autumn of 1953 a fresh, very determined effort had to be made in order to assure a normal development in the relations between the Church and state . . . by the decision of the government forbidding Cardinal Wyszynski all activities."

(Piasecki: *Essential Problems*, pp. 184-185)

This "decision" seemed to open before Piasecki an unlimited

field of action. Drunk with success, he then openly took the part of the government against the prisoner bishops.

The brutal frankness of his announcements revealed his true character to the people. During the years of Cardinal Wyszynski's imprisonment, Piasecki, sure of himself and of his masters, no longer hid his hand. Cynically, he only assigned a "functional rôle" to the Church in the socialist camp, that of a "productive function verifiable throughout history."

(Piasecki: *Essential Problems*, ibid.)

The release of Cardinal Wyszynski in the autumn of 1956 was a grave personal set-back to Piasecki, and the resentment born of it explains the rancour which he pours into his campaigns of denigration, insinuation, nay calumny of which Cardinal Wyszynski more than any other Polish bishop bears the brunt. Though ineffective in Poland, this campaign is not without influence on foreigners who do not know the facts of the situation.

Here, by way of example, are some of the main charges insidiously put about through Piasecki's agencies:

The Polish bishops are said to be "Great Lords" in the feudal manner, well-furnished with the goods of this world, and keeping the priests and faithful at their distance.

The laity are supposedly "kept down" by bishops who deny them all initiative under an out-of-date form of clericalism.

The truth is that in Poland today, no bishop has a bank account, for the simple reason that it would be immediately confiscated by the Treasury. The façade of "Great Lords", therefore, conceals a genuine poverty, which no one in Poland likes advertising (especially before foreigners), and which entails living from day to day on such means as Providence may provide. But there is something more. The Polish bishops guard their poverty jealously because through it they are brought into close contact with the masses. When, during the "thaw" in 1956, Gomulka's government offered to restore confiscated Church property to the Episcopate, the bishops, meeting in plenary session on 14th December, 1956, unanimously declined the offer "in order to remain close to the heart of the masses". A Polish bishop spends his life in pastoral visitations and feels perfectly at ease and "at home" among the peasants or labourers. This is a social phenomenon which is unknown in those countries where the masses have become dechristianised.

As for the laity, every bishop and every parish priest has his diocesan or parish "council", which renders invaluable service and forms a veritable bastion against repressive measures by the Office for Religious Affairs. When such measures are implemented despite their opposition, the laity protest silently by attending church in their thousands. What bishop, having received some cruel blow the night before, has not seen the crowds of silent men gather at his Mass, old and young, their bearing grave and resolute? These laymen, denied the means for apostolate accorded in Western countries, by their character and numbers represent a force which the government fears, and which explains, at least in part, the exceptional position of the Church in Poland under a Communist government. Let us stress that no member of *Pax* is nor could become a member of the diocesan or parish councils.

Foreign visitors sponsored by *Pax* and shown only what their *Pax* guides want them to see, obviously know nothing of the true relationship between the laity and their pastor.

7. With the calling of the Ecumenical Council, Piasecki was entrusted with a mission which has restored weight to both his political prestige and his finances.

One hundred million zlotys as an annual grant (instead of fifty million), one hundred regions as his sphere of operations, instead of thirty: such is the price, paid in advance, for securing Piasecki's active participation in the exploitation of the Council for the benefit of the "socialist camp".

It is a significant fact that it is Polish Communists who are disgusted by Piasecki's activities and who regard him as a "notorious double agent", who keep the bishops informed and on their guard. "We want a straightforward ideological struggle", they say, "not a system of oppression which uses the police machinery and administrative measures to achieve its ends".

It is interesting to note that some Polish atheist bodies occasionally invite the bishops to secret discussions on questions in which they are deeply interested, whereas they refuse to debate with *Pax*, which they distrust.

8. It is abroad, therefore, that the only available field of action remains open to *Pax*. Having failed to disrupt the unity of the Polish Episcopate, *Pax* is now endeavouring to represent it as being in opposition both to John XXIII, who is acclaimed as "the Pope of co-existence", and to the "open" and "progressive" French Episcopate.

Since the beginning of 1963 this thesis, which had been ceaselessly hammered out for some time, suddenly acquired a new depth and particular over-tones. The style of the *Pax* press becomes increasingly virulent and aggressive.

The Encyclical *Pacem in Terris* was hailed noisily and "with deep satisfaction" as the "official consecration" and "coronation of the efforts" which Piasecki and his group had made for so long.

"The head of the Church has agreed with those who have pledged themselves to an ideology of co-existence and co-operation with those professing different ideologies, and that is precisely the essence of the programme of our political Left."

(*Slowo Powszechne*, 2nd May, 1963)

According to *Pax*, thanks to Pope John XXIII, the "tridentine era" in the history of the Church seems definitely over and a new epoch is beginning, "more open and more tolerant, ready for compromises".

Of course, "John XXIII's line . . . calls on the Polish Episcopate to reconsider its out-of-date position and its attachment to the integralism of Pope Pius XII". The *Pax* press insinuates that Cardinal Wyszynski and the Polish bishops are very disturbed by this "revolutionary" change of position by John XXIII and that with the help of "conservative elements" in the Vatican they are doing everything within their power to minimize the scope of this "historic" encyclical.

9. It goes without saying that *Pax* refuses to see in *Pacem in Terris* anything which is contrary to its ideological professions, and the censor's refusal for the publication of the Polish translation of *Mater et Magistra* is passed over in silence.

On the other hand the duties of the Polish bishops which apparently derive from this great charter for co-existence, as *Pax* calls *Pacem in Terris*, are minutely described:

"The ground-work for the normalisation of relations between the Church and State, which is so keenly awaited, involves the formal recognition by the Polish Episcopate of the permanency of the socialist order with all that this implies".

(*Slowo Powszechne*, 25th April, 1963)

This statement of Jankowski's, editor of *Slowo Powszechne*, the *Pax* daily paper, leaves no doubt as to the conditions required by the Warsaw government for the "so keenly awaited" normalisation of relations between the Church and State. It is a question, in short, of the acceptance in full of the notorious principle "Politics First", by the total subordination of the Church to the advancement of the Communist revolution.

In order that there may be no doubt on this point, Jankowski insists:

"The chief lesson to be drawn from the dialogue between the Catholic Left and the socialist world is above all the acknowledgement of the inescapable need to enrich the content of Socialism through Christians allying themselves to the party of the working class." (*Slowo Powszechne*, ibid.)

Jankowski instructs the bishops in this vein: the Pope "having formally recognised the primacy of the principle of peaceful co-existence", the Polish Episcopate should draw from it the consequences "consistent with the needs of Poland by publishing a special declaration which would be the starting point for the normalisation of relations between the Church and State."

(*Slowo Powszechne*, ibid.)

In other words, this "normalisation" can only take place at the price of a formal commital of the Church in Poland to the service of a particular party.

Now the representatives of *Pax* "feel that Pope John has given them a mandate for action".

Consequently, the *Pax* press lavishes advice and even thinly veiled threats on the Polish bishops, which recall in a striking manner the psychological campaigns of the Stalin era.

Thus the protests by Cardinal Wyszynski and the Polish Episcopate against the intrusion of the State into religious education, which may only be carried out within a Church, has met with the official displeasure of *Pax*.

In an editorial in *Slowo Powszechne* on 11th April, 1963 headed "Responsibility for a long term view" we read the following:

"Peaceful co-existence is not helped by carrying over into the realm of politics obvious philosophical contradictions. It is necessary to state with profound disquiet that, unhappily, some sermons of the Primate of Poland are not free from this tendency. Thus the Cardinal judged it opportune, in a sermon to the Religious Orders, to return to the question, which has already been settled and is in full operation, of religious teaching outside the schools, and this in a way which, unfortunately, does not help towards the solution of the difficult and complicated problems besetting the relations between the Church and State".

However, three weeks before this article appeared, a pastoral letter dated 21st March, 1963 had been circulated by the Polish Episcopate, giving the faithful a short review of the question which was supposedly "settled and in full operation".

(a). Since the beginning of 1963 there has been a constant increase in the number of enactments aimed at religious teaching.

(b). The Office for Religious Affairs forbade priests belonging to religious orders, even if they were parish priests or curates, and nuns and even many lay catechists to teach catechism.

(c). Religious instruction is forbidden in private houses, parish halls, chapels and even in certain churches.

(d). Some Inspectors of Public Education demand from parish priests detailed reports on the religious instruction given in their churches, and they are increasing the number of their inspections.

(e). The parish priests who refuse to draw up these reports are punished with crippling fines of up to ten thousand zlotys or more. Those who are unable to pay these exorbitant sums are threatened with, and often suffer, imprisonment or distraints.

(f). All manner of intimidation and even threats are used to hinder children attending catechism. Parents who refuse to submit are heavily punished. Certain social groups (civil servants, agents of the U.B., etc.), are officially forbidden to send their children to catechism under pain of dismissal.

(g). Every year thousands of children gather at the holiday centres, and a thousand and one pretexts are advanced to prevent them attending Mass on Sundays. In some cases they are kept behind barbed-wire enclosures for the duration of the parish Masses.

(h). No priest has any right whatever to enter the boundaries of these holiday centres or camps.

(i). The children who do succeed in escaping to Mass on Sundays are punished.

(j). Young people who go out on excursions with a priest are followed by the police, often in helicopters, in order to check whether they are attending Mass in the shelter of the forest or the mountains. Caught in the act, students are often refused the right to continue their studies.

All this pettifogging vexation is in direct contradiction not only to the Constitution of the People's Republic of Poland and the agreement of 1950, but also to the international laws and charters, guaranteeing liberty of conscience and freedom of religious instruction, which are officially recognised by the Polish government.

Alerted by the Office for Religious Affairs, agents of the secret police visited every parish priest in Poland and forbade them to read this pastoral letter from their pulpits, since it would jeopardize the régime. Faced with their resistance, they resorted to threats and told the priests to expect serious consequences.

"Nothing could be worse than it is!", replied Mgr. Choromanski, the secretary of the Polish Episcopate.

10. The attitude of *Pax*, in the light of the pastoral letter of the Polish Episcopate, is most instructive. Far from associating itself with the protest of the bishops, who were faced with an agonising situation, which arouses furious indignation in every honest man, even among unbelievers, *Pax* claimed that the question of religious instruction in Poland, which was more open to discussion than ever, "had been settled and was in full operation". In so doing, it obeyed the Party to the detriment of the Church.

No one is deceived by these tactics in Poland. It is well known in advance that every Communist slogan published in the official press is taken up and minted anew by *Pax*. But it is not the same abroad, especially in France, where *Pax's* propaganda continues to grow in intensity, skilfully exploiting the sympathies and leanings of the French progressives and profiting from their support. The greatest secrecy is maintained about everything concerning *Pax's* direct subordination to the secret police in Poland.

On the other hand, the agents of *Pax* entrusted with assignments in France loudly proclaim the "persecutions" they allege they have suffered at the hands of the "retrograde" and "integralist" Polish Episcopate. This campaign of denigration is particularly aimed at Cardinal Wyszynski.

11. Having at its disposal considerable funds, *Pax* has been busy for some time building up its contacts and propaganda through the distribution, in French, of a *Review of the Catholic Press in Poland*, which serves its ends.

Pax also helps to arrange tours in Poland for Catholic priests and laymen, whom it sponsors, and who return to France with a very partial, one-sided, and indeed erroneous view of the real situation in Poland. The French priests shown round by *Pax* only meet "patriotic priests" in Poland. The Polish bishops decline to meet them, fearing indiscretions. They return to France to spread reports about Poland, often over the wireless, as in the case of Father Molin, which, although perhaps they are made in all good faith, bear little relation to the truth.

In France the agents of *Pax* are in permanent contact with certain groups of Catholic progressives who rally to their defence whenever they believe them threatened. *Pax* has managed, in the main, to implant in certain French Catholic circles the belief that it is persecuted by Cardinal Wyszynski and the Polish Episcopate on account of its progressive tendencies.

This attitude was most distinctly revealed when a series of articles on the position of the Church in Poland appeared in *La Croix* in February 1962. The Reverend Father Wenger, editor of the paper, was immediately taken to task by priests and laymen who vehemently denied the contents of these articles taking advantage of the fact that they had travelled and toured in Poland.

For the most part they were friends of *Pax* and belonged to the *Informations Catholiques Internationales*.

When he was told that Cardinal Wyszynski had confirmed the accuracy of the facts reported in *La Croix* articles, not daring to attack him openly, de Broucker, editor of *Informations Catholiques Internationales*, revealed his thoughts in one of his "Letters to the friends of I.C.I.", distributed only to the inner circle of his followers, in which he gave it to be understood that at the Council

Cardinal Wyszynski ought to render an account of himself to the Cardinals of the Roman Church, "his judges and his peers".

When the *La Croix* articles were about to appear as a book, the Ecclesiastical Censor for Paris informed the author that "not having found any doctrinal errors in the text, he was unable to refuse the *imprimatur, but that he hoped that the author would have the courage* (to use his very own words) *to suppress the chapter dealing with Pax*".

Once published, Pierre Lenert's book, *The Catholic Church in Poland*, became the object of a fierce campaign on the part of *Pax* and its French friends. Curiously, in its bulletin *Pax* expressed its surprise that the *imprimatur* could have been granted to this work.

Not one single fact in the book is denied. *Pax* admits that Lenert's book had been "circulated" during the first session of the Council, but omits to say that when the Polish bishops were consulted about it, they unanimously acknowledged the accuracy of the facts it contains. It is obvious that *Pax* is afraid of being exposed in France.

For its very existence is at stake. If it were recognised by Western Catholics that it is simply the agency of a police network entrusted with the penetration and subjection of the Church, it would lose its following in their ranks, and in so doing, it would lose its justification in the eyes of its paymasters.

"It is not the Communists whom we fear", said a Polish bishop. "What fills us with anguish is the spectacle of false brethren."

(Cardinal Wyszynski's Report on *Pax*, sent to the French Episcopate by the Cardinal Secretary of State at the Vatican in June 1963)

After the manner of Communism, Freemasonry no longer sets itself up as the declared adversary of the Church. Instead of openly attacking her, it is seeking to infiltrate and penetrate her in order to impose its own humanitarian, naturalistic and anti-traditional conceptions.

The success of the general penetration of the forces of subversion was made possible by the support, which at times attained a fanatical pitch, of progressive elements in the Church, and the last Council revealed to the whole world the strength and extent of their ascendancy. We are confronted here with a new and absolutely unprecedented situation in the history of Christianity, which would now appear to be in a state of permanent civil war. Subversion has entered the very heart of the Church, and all her traditional doctrines are being questioned. This is a state of affairs the gravity of which cannot be concealed.

BIBLIOGRAPHY

of principal works quoted

* denotes foreign works available in the British Museum

BATAULT, G. *Le Problème Juif*, 1921.

BENAMOZEGH, E. *Israel et l'Humanité*, 1961*.

BLIT, L. *The Eastern Pretender*, 1965.

BORD, G. *La Franc-Maçonnerie en France des origines à 1815*, 1908*.

CLEMENT XII. *In Eminenti*, 1738*.

CORBIN, R. *Symboles Initiatiques et Mystères Chrètiens*, 1929.

CORNELOUP, C. *Universalisme et Franc-Maçonnerie*, 1963.

DESCHAMPS, N., S.J. *Les Sociétés secrètes et la Société*, 2nd edition, 1880*.

DOUSSINAGUE, Sr. *España Tenia Razon*, 1949 (Calpe, Madrid).

FEJTÖ, F. *Dieu et son Juif*, 1960*.

HANNAH, W. *Darkness Visible*, 1966.

HUNT, P. *The Menace of Freemasonry to the Christian Faith*, 1929.

HUTIN, S. *Les Gnostiques*, 1906.

LANE, A. BLISS. *I saw Poland Betrayed*, 1948.

LEBEY, A. *Dans l'Atelier Maçonnique*.

LEO XIII. *Humanum Genus*, Encyclical Letter on Freemasonry, 1884, tr. by Rev. D. Fahey, 1953.

MARTIN, G. *La Franc-Maçonnerie Française et la Révolution*, 1926*. *Manuel d'Histoire de la Franc-Maçonnerie en France*, 1932*.

MELLOR, A. *La Franc-Maçonnerie à l'Heure du Choix*, 1963. *Our Separated Brethren*, 1964.

MICHEL, A. G. *La Dictature de la Franc-Maçonnerie sur la France*, 1924*.

PIKE, A. *Morals and Dogma*, 1927 (original edition 1832).

RIVIÈRE, J. MARQUÈS. *La Trahison Spirituelle de la Franc-Maçonnerie*, 1931.

SPIRE, A. *Quelques Juifs*, 1928*.

STEWART, T. M. *Symbolic Teachings—or Masonry and its Message*, 1917.

TEDER, *L'Irregularité du Grand Orient de France*, 1909.

VINATREL, G. *Communisme et Franc-Maçonnerie*, 1961.

WEBSTER, N. H. *Secret Societies and Subversive Movements*, 1964.

WIRTH, O. *Le Livre du Compagnon; Le Livre de l'Apprenti* (both of which were published in separate parts in *La Franc-Maçonnerie rendue intelligible à ses adeptes*, 1927), *L'Idéal Initiatique*, 1927.

WYSZYNSKI, CARDINAL. *Report on Pax*.

INDEX